The Ratings Game

Andrew Fight

JOHN WILEY & SONS, LTD
Chichester • New York • Weinheim • Brisbane • Singapore • Toronto

Copyright © 2001 by John Wiley & Sons Ltd,
Baffins Lane, Chichester,
West Sussex PO19 1UD, England

National   01243 779777
International   (+44) 1243 779777
e-mail (for orders and customer service enquiries): cs-books@wiley.co.uk
Visit our Home Page on http://www.wiley.co.uk
or http://www.wiley.com

Other Wiley Editorial Offices

John Wiley & Sons, Inc., 605 Third Avenue,
New York, NY 10158-0012, USA

WILEY-VCH Verlag GmbH, Pappelallee 3,
D-69469 Weinheim, Germany

Jacaranda Wiley Ltd, 33 Park Road, Milton,
Queensland 4064, Australia

John Wiley & Sons (Asia) Pte Ltd, 2 Clementi Loop #02-01,
Jin Xing Distripark, Singapore 129809

John Wiley & Sons (Canada) Ltd, 22 Worcester Road,
Rexdale, Ontario M9W 1L1, Canada

Library of Congress Cataloging-in-Publication Data

Fight, Andrew.
JK   The ratings game / Andrew Fight.
       p. cm.
       Includes bibliographical references and index.
       ISBN 0-471-49134-9 (cloth : alk. paper)
       1. Credit ratings.   I. Title.

HG3751.5 .F53 2000
332.7—dc21
                              00–043349

British Library Cataloguing in Publication Data

A catalogue record for this book is available from the British Library

ISBN 0-471-49134-9

Typeset in 10/12pt Garamond by Dorwyn Ltd, Rowlands Castle, Hants
Printed and bound in Great Britain by Biddles Ltd, Guildford and King's Lynn
This book is printed on acid-free paper responsibly manufactured from sustainable forestation, for which at least two trees are planted for each one used for paper production.

for
AJF
12 X 1917–23 III 1999

Contents

Preface

This book aims to situate the subject of rating agencies within the context of the economy at large; it is therefore not an exhaustive reference work on the various minutiae and arcane aspects of the business analysed to the nth significant decimal point. My goal was to identify the various players in the game, and examine their modi operandi, dynamics, motivations, and conflicts of interest.

It was primarily researched and written using information in the public domain. As a sign of the times, most of the research was conducted over the internet, using e-mail to communicate with various parties located throughout the globe, various search engines to locate information on servers in places such as the USA, Brazil, UK, France, Germany, Poland, Russia, Pakistan, India, Indonesia, and Japan, and web retrieval software enabling the storage of entire web sites on a local hard drive for off-line consultation. The rating agencies obviously post their promotional literature on the web. Other sources of information included the web site of the Federal Reserve Bank of New York and EDGAR, a searchable database on the web site of the Securities and Exchange Commission. These sources were gold mines of information and included data only rarely mentioned in the generalist financial press or rating agency literature.

I gratefully acknowledge the kind cooperation, assistance, and advice received from Mr Joseph Cantwell of Cantwell & Company, Mr Kenichiro Watanabe of Japan Center for International Finance, and Dr Oliver Everling of Everling Advisory Services in Germany. The market surveys produced by Messrs Cantwell and Watanabe form the bulk of Chapter 4 and provide invaluable insight into how the rating agencies are perceived by the issuer community. Dr Oliver Everling provided useful insight vis-à-vis certain issues about the rating agencies in Germany and continental Europe. Thanks must also go to Mr Craig S. Tyle, General Counsel of the Investment Company Institute in the USA, for providing insight into the investor viewpoint on the role and performance of, and granting of NRSRO status to, the rating agencies.

The book greatly benefited from the invaluable help, encouragement and assistance of these gentlemen. I readily concede that I would have been unable to marshal the time or resources required to conduct these market surveys, and that these data provide an invaluable counterweight to the policies articulated by the rating agencies and their parent organisations.

Valuable technical advice, comments, and assistance were received from the following experts on financial analysis and bank credit risk training: Mr Kenneth I'Anson (Director at DC Gardner/Euromoney Training, London), Mr François-Xavier Noir (Directeur Europe, Centre de Formation de la Profession Bancaire, Paris), Mr Klaus Pesch (Director TACIS Programme for Bank Training in the Russian Federation), and Mr Philip Blake (Commissioning Editor, Chartered Institute of Bankers, London).

In the interests of editorial independence no input into the content of the book was solicited or received from the ratings agencies. All material used from the ratings agencies is from publicly available material selected by the author for illustrative purposes only and is reproduced with the permission of the agencies concerned.

Although rating agencies rate a wide variety of entities as well as financial instruments, structured finance transactions, and special-purpose vehicles (SPVs), I have limited my coverage of methodologies to sovereigns, banks, and corporates since these are actual entities with a legal existence, management structure, and employees. Hence they are players in an arena rather than an abstraction designed to exploit a particular legal or financial situation.

The scope of the *The Ratings Game* unfolded as I made my own voyage of discovery through the various aspects of the ratings world. I only hope that by uniting hitherto disparate elements, the reader finds the book interesting and informative; perhaps it will stimulate thought as to the ultimate significance of these quasi-official arbiters and their position in the economic landscape.

Finally, I would like to thank Ms Sally Smith, commissioning editor at John Wiley & Sons for believing in this project, bearing with me throughout the long gestation period, and offering invaluable criticism, suggestions, and patience. Any errors of course are the sole responsibility of the author.

Andrew Fight
Vétraz-Monthoux
Savoie, France
March 2000

1 The world of ratings

The reality is that wealth can be translated into information power, and that the apathy of the people is allowing private wealth to control public information. We are very, very close to private tyranny.

Robert David Steele, President of Open Source Solutions (http://www.oss.net) in March 1993. Interestingly enough, John A. Bohn, chairman of the board of OSS Inc., previously served (1989–96) as president and CEO of that well-known privately controlled source of public information, Moody's Investors Service.

Introduction

The influence of credit rating companies in financial and capital markets has been growing rapidly. Their characteristics, modi operandi, market behaviour, and alleged abusive practices, however, have courted debate and lawsuits in the USA, and controversy in international markets such as Japan, the EU, and India.

Due to the status they have been granted by the USA's Securities and Exchange Commission (SEC) as arbiters fulfilling a quasi-official regulatory role (yet subordinated to the profit motive), they have grown in a protected market to become extremely powerful and profitable actors on the economic stage. They can literally make or break a company, exert influence on governments that circumvents the democratic process, and act in ways which have been compared to a classic Mafia protection racket and in some cases ultimately holding the taxpayer indirectly to ransom.

To situate the ratings landscape, I briefly introduce some of these controversial points then return to them in more detail later on.

Ambiguous status

The rating agencies' raison d'être is defined by the SEC's granting nationally recognised statistical rating organisation (NRSRO) status. The selection criteria and regulatory mechanisms used by the SEC in conferring NRSRO status are inconsistent and ambiguous, and are fostering hitherto unforeseen and undesirable developments, mainly related to issues of accountability, disclosure, regulation, and market abuse.

Perceived abuses

There have been allegations from various parties and sources that rating agencies occupy a dominant market oligopoly (the Moody's–Standard & Poor's duopoly) and that this power and lack of accountability has led them to act in a predatory and abusive manner. The high entry barriers, opaqueness of their methodologies, unclear rating criteria, selection criteria for companies getting an unsolicited rating, and fee pricing policy have all led to controversy, with which we shall soon become familiar.

Unsolicited ratings

Rating agencies have been accused of running an operation akin to a classic protection racket in summarily issuing unsolicited ratings to various entities that are perceived as vulnerable to paying rating fees. Their arguments justifying this activity can most charitably be described as simplistic and opportunistic. The unspoken implication is that better ratings can result if a fee payment is forthcoming.

International expansion

Rating agencies have been accused of exporting US models with no concern for the economic structures and realities prevailing in foreign countries. This effort to homogenise the planet according to their Weltanschauungen is obviously not currying favour with politico-business elites in various countries, and can result in misunderstandings as well as damaging and counterproductive ramifications for a number of different parties such as creditors, issuers, and governments.

International credibility

Credit rating traces its history back for nearly a century in the USA, and is well established as a source of information for investment decisions. This is because the accumulation of rating results over a long period of time has enabled correlations between ratings and default ratios to be established, with the result that investors use ratings as investment intelligence premised upon this relationship.

But the history of rating is short in markets outside of the USA, and it cannot yet be said to have found acceptance and credibility. This lack of credibility is based on two elements:

- How to strike a balance between the uniformity of global rating criteria and factors unique to individual countries whose corporate systems differ from those of the USA.
- How rating companies have responded to the new type of sovereign crisis in emerging markets that has been manifested in the Asian currency crisis. The Asian currency crisis has dealt a major blow to the credibility of rating agencies, as we shall see.

In countries outside the USA, the differences between the US rating companies and local rating companies are frequent subjects of debate. In the USA, an advanced country in the field of credit ratings, there is also vigorous controversy about the desirable form of the credit rating industry in both the public and private sectors. In addition, numerous surveys of individual rating companies are being made public and are being utilised as reference materials for the choice of rating companies by investors and issuers of bonds.

What is a credit rating?

What is a credit rating? Let's consider the definition provided by Moody's, one of the leading rating agencies in the business:

> A rating simply helps investors determine the relative likelihood that they might lose money on a given fixed income investment. More technically, it is an opinion of the future ability, legal obligation, and willingness of a bond issuer or other obligor to make full and timely payments on principal and interest due to investors.

But opinions can have varying effects and the impact should have a commensurate link with responsibility. The impact of a self-proclaimed messiah on a soapbox at Speakers' Corner may differ from the impact of a newspaper that prejudges a suspect as being guilty in a murder case. However, this definition only shows us the tip of the iceberg, and it certainly warrants further consideration.

Because the initial definition ignores the entire underlying scenario of the ratings industry, this begs a host of questions. All these questions will be treated in the book.

- Why are rating agencies so keen to issue ratings and export them internationally?
- How do they issue credit ratings?
- How do they define the fee structures they charge their issuers?
- Are they in the business of providing investor service or chasing fees?
- How do they select companies to be granted an unsolicited rating?

- How do they lobby the SEC to obtain NRSRO status?
- Are they accountable for their actions?
- Do they really depict their activities as fulfilling a socially and econom-
  ically redeeming role wholly separate from the profit motive?

What ratings do not measure

A credit rating is *not* an audit or control of the company's financial statements; it is an overall opinion or assessment delivered to investors pursuant
to an internal process known as the ratings process. Rating agencies do not
prepare or audit financial statements. A rating analyst may coincidentally be
an auditor or certified public accountant (CPA) but this is not necessarily the
case. Similarly, an auditor or a CPA is not a rating analyst. Rating analysts use
financial statements as part of their information pool but they are not necessarily auditors, CPAs, or financial analysts. No formal training, educational
certificate, or professional qualification is required to become a rating analyst. Yet rating analysts are endowed with unique skills which can best be
described as hybrid. And their pronouncements have legal ramifications.

Unlike CPAs, who certify (and assume a legal responsibility on) the financial statements they have audited and stated to be in conformance with good
accounting practice, rating analysts do not have any formal qualifications,
they do not sign off on statements, and they do not have a legal responsibility
to stand behind the opinions they proffer.

Rating analysts are individuals with a broad and eclectic range of skills:
analysing financial statements, assessing management acumen, writing and
communicating to the public, understanding of economic criteria, business
sectors, and regulatory issues. They work for companies that put out opinions
with disclaimers denying all responsibility for the accuracy contained within.
Ratings are intended only to measure the risk of credit loss. They are not
intended to measure other risks in fixed-income investment, such as market
risk (the risk of loss in the market value of a security.) As opinions of long-term
credit strength, they are not intended to rise with the business cycle or a
company's latest earnings report. Also, unlike stock ratings, credit ratings are
not intended to measure a security's potential for price appreciation.

Why get a rating?

Why do governments, corporates, and banks pay rating agencies lucrative rating
fees for a rating? There are several reasons, which we summarise as follows.

Access the markets

Any entity wanting to access the capital markets and issue debt in the USA needs to obtain a rating. This is a de facto prerequisite. Once this principle is accepted, one can understand that certain issuers obtain several (multiple) ratings in order to reassure the market further.

Build up market reputation

New companies or countries striving to establish a track record in the international financial markets (e.g. newly independent states such as Kazakhstan or Ukraine) may obtain ratings in order to build up their market reputation so they can demonstrate their credentials as enthusiastic converts to the cause and more easily integrate into the global financial system.

Lower cost of funding

A relatively unknown entity can perhaps lower its costs of borrowing (even on the debt as opposed to equity markets) if it obtains a favourable rating. An unknown entity becomes legitimised via the granting of a rating. But this process can backfire, as demonstrated by two lawsuits in Chapter 5, lawsuits taken out against rating agencies by Orange County and the Denver Public School System.

Prepare groundwork for share flotation or privatisation

An entity may be considering a share flotation or privatisation and may therefore obtain a rating as a method of preparing the groundwork. This will prepare the public and investor community with the reality of the new entity or flotation. Such a groundwork-setting exercise is demonstrated by the case study on CADES (Chapter 7), a special-purpose vehicle in France designed to plug a hole in the country's social security deficit, with no preceding track record, accessing the financial markets for the first time.

Distinguish oneself from the competition

In a sector with few competitors, such as banking or the car industry, a rating can be a means of distinguishing oneself from the competition. A car manufacturer such as the UK-based Rover Group may build fine cars, yet its dubious financial condition can set it at a disadvantage to a carmaker with less exciting products but a guaranteed long-term existence, as demonstrated by a solid credit rating.

A quick history of the ratings industry

Here is a cursory overview of how the ratings industry has developed; more detailed histories of the individual ratings agencies are given in Chapter 2.

Origins of the ratings industry in the USA, 1890–1980

The history of the ratings industry begins in the USA in the late nineteenth century with the building of the country's railway system. The debt instruments issued by the various railways were a tempting target for risk classification for investors. Standard & Poor's (S&P) traces its history back to 1860 when Henry Varnum Poor established a publishing house to produce manuals of railway companies. Moody's ratings business began when John Moody (1868–1958) published *Moody's Manual of Industrial and Corporation Securities.* He used the Aaa through C symbols that have since become oft-emulated, to rate some 1500 individual securities of over 200 US railroads.

The activity was mainly a US phenomenon during the 1920s, 30s, and 40s, with several other challenger organisations being bought out or merged, and new players taking their place, as we shall see in the histories of the individual agencies. Despite movements and shake-outs, Moody's and Standard & Poor's continued to publish and monitor ratings during the Great Depression. The agencies continued to remain a primarily US phenomenon with the exception of the odd sovereign rating.

International activities only really started to take off in the 1960s and 1970s. This international growth was stimulated by two main factors: the omission of the interest equalisation tax (1974) and attractiveness of the US markets for foreign borrowers, and the emergence of the euromarkets resulting in euro-issuers non-domiciled in the USA. Aside from the Moody's–S&P duopoly which took the first steps to expand overseas, most agencies remained primarily US focused during the 1960s, due to the relative weakness of the post-war European economies and preponderance and advanced nature of the US economy during this period.

As the US economy evolved and increasingly complex financial instruments were developed, the rating agencies branched out into the rating of new financial products. Ratings were extended to the commercial paper market and to bank deposits. Also in the 1970s, the major rating agencies began the practice of charging issuers as well as investors for rating services. In the USA, rating agencies kept pace with the evolving economy, broadening their offerings and market size. A major event, however, occurred in the early 1970s when Penn Central Railway went bankrupt leaving many investors holding worthless Penn Central commercial paper that had been rated as investment grade.

The repercussions of this fiasco led to the Securities and Exchange Commission (SEC) implementing certain reforms in the US securities market and implementing the concept of the nationally recognised statistical rating organisation (NRSRO); this began by conferring NRSRO status on a few select agencies and it has since evolved into a quasi-official regulatory function. Issues rated by an NRSRO would be eligible for more favourable capital deduction exercises known as 'haircuts'. This coveted NRSRO status was only conferred upon a select few agencies, and the admissions criteria have never been clearly defined.

It is increasingly alleged that the ambiguities surrounding the NRSRO approval procedure have resulted in the propagation of numerous problems, including lack of regulation, abusive pricing, lack of accountability, and lack of competition in the market; subsequent chapters treat them in more detail. The obtaining of a rating has effectively become a de facto prerequisite for any company seeking to access the US financial markets.

The rating agencies' business has since skyrocketed in scope and profitability due to the combination of the captive franchise they hold as NRSROs, the increasing growth in the globalised economy, the shift away from state pensions towards private pensions, the securitisation of debt, preference for equity modes of financing (as opposed to debt modes of financing), and the exporting of the rating agencies' methodologies to international markets in the wake of the EU single market, increasing cross-border flows, and development of various markets requiring ratings in countries such as Japan, Indonesia, India, Brazil, and Eastern Europe.

This trend means that the rating industry is expected to continue to grow, as markets in the USA, the EU, and Japan become increasingly mature and saturated (despite the extra wind offered by the trend of obtaining multiple ratings). Growth is expected to occur in international and developing markets. This in turn is fostering a wholesale move towards the establishment and takeover of 'home-grown' agencies in various international markets.

Formation of the US duopoly, 1970–1999

The development of the ratings industry and NRSRO status means there are relatively few players in the USA, and even less when one looks at the trend towards mergers and industry consolidation. The fact of the matter is that the industry is dominated by Moody's and Standard & Poor's. There are a few other players active in selected market niches in the USA but they are not viable 'across the board' full-service competitors. The market is hence an effective duopoly, a duopoly which has expanded into Europe and Japan, and exported its model or Weltanschauungen to developing markets in areas such as Eastern Europe, India, Indonesia, Thailand, and Brazil.

The duopoly does not foster competition since there is a tendency for issuers to obtain multiple ratings, e.g. ratings from both Moody's and S&P. Accordingly, a competitive situation cannot be said to exist since the choice is not 'get a rating from one or the other' but 'let's get rated by both in order to reassure our creditors'. The two agencies in the duopoly are therefore sharing a monopoly and have no risk of losing market share to their competitor (each other). This powerful position is leading to market abuses, lawsuits, and charges of anticompetition being levelled by various special interest groups and companies or governments which have suffered at the hands of the agencies. The full ramifications of the duopoly and its practices are discussed in further detail in Chapter 4.

Expansion into Europe and Japan, 1975

The development of Europe and the euromarkets provided the bridgehead for the US rating agencies (the duopoly mainly) to export their wares and modi operandi outside of the USA. This internationalised the ratings business, providing the duopoly with the experience and knowledge to embark on the second wave of expansion into the Japanese markets and developing markets. S&P rated its first eurobond in 1972; two years later the first structured financing was analysed, a business field which today is of significant importance to S&P. S&P began rating eurocommercial paper (ECP) in 1984. Only after the establishment of Japanese rating agencies did S&P begin, in 1986, to rate Japanese domestic market issues.

In 1984 S&P was the first US rating agency to open an office outside of the USA, in London. Further offices were created in Melbourne, Tokyo, Paris— where Moody's acquired the French Agence d'Evaluation Financière (ADEF) rating agency—and Brussels. In March 1990 the London-based Insurance Solvency International Agency Ltd, as well as the Melbourne-based Australian Ratings Pty Ltd, both specialising in ratings in the insurance sector for insurance, were taken over. Both of these agencies had connections with the London-based IBCA rating agency and these connections were severed following the acquisitions. S&P's international revenue has grown substantially, in line with the growth and development of the global capital markets. Its network continues to expand with office openings in São Paulo, Brazil, and Moscow.

Moody's similarly began rating commercial paper and eurobonds in the 1970s and expanded during the 1980s to cover insurance, bank deposits, and structured financing. Moody's international expansion in the 1980s began with the establishment of a Tokyo office (1985), followed by London (1986), Paris (1987), and Sydney (1987). The development of the activity lagged in Europe for several reasons: the need to catch up with the US economy in the post-war years, the different capitalist culture resulting in less public disclosure of information, different modes of financing favouring 'discreet' low equity percentages and high debt structures avoiding the possibility of hostile takeovers; cosy cross-shareholding structures between banks and industrial conglomerates

This substantially different business culture and culture of disclosure means that the ratings industry found Europe to be a quite different market. Impetus for growth would come from other developments: the creation of the unified market necessitating tools enabling cross-border comparisons of risk in order to favour cross-border financial flows within the confines of the EU. The need for benchmarks and intra-European expansion has served to stimulate the growth in ratings activities in Europe. This growth, however, has obliged the US agencies to partially adapt their homogenised exports to local market conditions. The clashes in culture and modus operandi have led to acrimonious debate and vociferous criticism of some of the rating agencies' practices in the Old Continent as well as Japan

Globalisation and emerging markets growth 1980–

With the increasing maturity of markets in the USA, the EU, and Japan, growth primarily occurs by broadening offerings such as 'educational services' and other ancillary offerings. These marketing strategies are examined individually in Chapter 2. As with any mature market, growth is primarily at the expense of other players; the market has accordingly been subject to acquisitions and mergers. In the USA, the Franco-British Fimalac-Euronotation-IBCA entity has acquired the Fitch rating agency and more recently Duff & Phelps, thereby reducing the number of players by two, leaving only Fimalac-Euronotation-IBCA-Fitch-Duff & Phelps to compete with the duopoly.

Hopes for expansion are therefore being pinned on overseas expansion in developing markets. An overview of the duopoly's 10-K filings with the SEC confirms they are pinning their expansion hopes on the extension of rating services into new financial instruments, and into new developing markets either directly or via the fostering of parent–tutor relationships with various 'home-grown' agencies earmarked for future acquisition when they have been sufficiently fattened.

The duopoly's international expansion can therefore be summarised in the following targets:

- Internationalisation of the global economy and cross-border investment funds, privatisation, growth in private pensions, dismantling of state-owned economies, etc.
- Increasing complexity of capital market instruments.
- Liberalisation spurred by EC legislation (e.g. stimulus of private pension schemes).
- Developing markets as regional economies develop (e.g. Capital Intelligence, Indonesia).
- 'Home-grown' agencies that usually get taken over by the majors when ripe.

The size of the world capital markets is increasing because, in general, the global political and economic climate has promoted economic deregulation. Moody's believes that the outlook is generally favourable for the continued growth of the world capital markets, particularly in Europe as a consequence of financial market integration under European Monetary Union (EMU).

Lower-cost information technology makes information about investment alternatives available throughout the world. This availability of information promotes globalisation and integration of financial markets. A number of new 'emerging' capital markets have been created. There is investor and intermediary interest in domestic currency debt obligations from such markets that are now being sold cross-border.

The complexity of capital market instruments is also growing. Consequently, assessing the credit risk of such instruments is a challenge for financial intermediaries and asset managers. In the credit markets, third-party ratings represent an increasingly viable alternative to traditional in-house research as the geographic scope and complexity of market instruments grow.

Multiple ratings: managing the ratings process

Various market studies and data show that the trend today is towards multiple ratings. In order to place bonds on the international financial markets on the best possible terms, companies are making increasing use of rating by a number of recognised agencies. This is underlined by a survey launched in 1997 and completed recently by Cantwell & Company. In Cantwell's survey, over 90% of respondents had long-term ratings from at least two agencies, and around 25% had three long-term ratings. Where issuers had multiple ratings, both market leaders were almost always represented.

The competition for ratings generated by additional rating agencies is reflected in the market leaders' changed approach. Compared with earlier surveys, the proportion of issuers given an unsolicited rating by Standard & Poor's in the USA was higher. This time, around 9% of issuers said that they had been given an unsolicited rating by Standard & Poor's.

The large number of companies which have only had at least one rating from a recognised agency for a relatively short time can be explained statistically by the sharp growth in the ratings market. For example, ratings have only been given for the first time in many countries during the past ten years. Reliable estimates put the annual market growth rate outside the USA at around 25%. Whereas in the past most issuers first obtained only a short-term rating in order to 'test' it, more and more issuers now appear to be switching to a policy of applying for a short-term rating and a long-term rating at the same time.

Issuers are often accused of 'rating shopping' if they go to agencies other than Moody's or Standard & Poor's to obtain a recognised rating. The purpose of rating shopping is to get the best possible rating from a rating agency. This suggests that the rating agencies are by no means rivals trying to squeeze each other out of the market. They in fact make clear that the agencies complement each other. If an issuer is already being rated by an agency, rating by another agency helps to make them happier with the first rating. Further ratings thus remove doubts, not only from the investor's perspective.

2 The rating agencies

The secret to success is to own nothing, but control everything.

Nelson Rockefeller

Introduction

Having taken a tour d'horizon of rating agencies, the most logical point to begin our examination is straight from the horse's mouth. More specifically, before seeking to understand the workings and dynamics of the business, and how these specificities impact the investor-creditor community and beyond, it would be useful to familiarise ourselves with some of the players in this arena, their tools, and modi operandi.

The world of rating agencies is somewhat wider than the press might have us believe. To the reader of the generalist press, there are the players known to all: Moody's and Standard & Poor's. To a finance or bank professional, one can perhaps add Thomson Bank Watch, or Duff & Phelps, who have a more specific focus. To players closely involved in the business or dealing with international banking and finance, one could add names such as Japan Credit Rating Agency, the Thai Rating and Information Service, or the Investment Information and Credit Rating Agency (ICRA) of India. Finally come the highly specific agencies such as Capital Intelligence, which specialises in analysing banks in emerging markets, and Skate, covering the debt markets in Russia.

Each of these agencies has a specific raison d'être and caters to a specific audience, and each has its own modus operandi. In other words, each credit rating agency strives to cultivate a unique image. And, if one listens to the carefully crafted messages they disseminate to the investor-creditor community and to the public at large, they each have a specific selling point making them unique market leaders: the largest agency to rate privatisation issues in emerging markets, the largest agency specialising in bank rating, the largest agency in rating structured finance, the oldest agency rating banks and corporates, the first (or largest, or only international) agency to rate banks in Eastern Europe, *EuroBank* magazine's top agency in the former USSR, etc., etc.

What is striking, however, is that once one gets past the largest this and the oldest that, there are many similarities in their modi operandi and their cross-poaching of analysts—lager beer branded 36 ways so to speak. Their rating methodologies are similar, the argumentative techniques are similar, the relatively qualitative nature of their arguments are similar, the arguments of self-justification and self-promotion, and posturing as providers of a much needed 'public information service' (as if immune from the dictates of market pressures) are similar. Their adoption of the internet to disseminate their wares is another similarity. Their disclaimers regarding the accuracy of their research, and the offloading of any repercussions their various pronouncements may have on unrelated entities are also similar.

Where they do vary is in less publicised areas. These areas are not immediately apparent to the average consumer of such services (who typically only wants an opinion to pin an investment decision on and really does not care about the various nuances existing among the agencies), but they do exist and can be revelatory to the interested party. Revelatory not only in better knowing the agencies, but revelatory in how the ratings business is driven and run. For, not surprisingly, these agencies are not in the information-providing business but in the money-making business.

These variations can encompass elements such as development and history, shareholding structure, parent ownership, driving mission statements, management changes, analyst recruitment policies, analyst qualifications, composition of revenue streams, what constitutes acceptable practice, the marketing of services and publications, who buys the services and publications and in what proportions.

Whilst mergers in the business are inevitably justified on the grounds of pooling skills and presented as 'providing better services to the end user', these moves have their own rationales and hidden agendas. They also lead to thorny issues which, by preference, are glossed over. Mergers, for example, may lead to the question of integrating what might be disparate rating scales and methodologies, leading to inconsistencies in ratings and rating scales. Mergers and acquisitions are also driven by the core turf the agencies are defending or hoping to penetrate; these doings can reveal how the agencies perceive their strengths and weaknesses, and how they view their core turf as a springboard to further expansion which, in a mature market, can only be at the expense of other players.

One could list some 50 or 60 agencies present in the ratings business (a table of URLs is given at the end of the chapter): market leaders, laggards, niche players, regional players, players flying the flag of national preference, and players in emerging markets whose raison d'être is simply to generate a client base sufficient to warrant the subsequent sale of the agency to a major player at a mark-up.

This chapter is not a directory of all agencies present in the business. However, to help examine the workings of the agencies later on, it does group a selection of the major players plus some of the more specialised entities active in the business; this aims to provide a representative overview of the business and some of the specialised approaches which can be adopted by the players. The selection has to be relatively limited but it does identify the major players and the major approaches to specialisation.

Today's two main disciples of the ratings business, Standard & Poor's Corporation and Moody's Investors Service, can trace their development history back to a common thread. Other agencies can be the result of haphazard and opportunistic moves leading to a patchwork structure such as the Fimalac-Euronotation-IBCA-Fitch-Duff & Phelps quilt. Others still can be the result of a nationalistic counterthrust to perceived outside (US) influences. And even others can be the result of a speculative venture such as fattening a calf prior to the season's auction to one of the larger agencies.

What should be borne in mind, however, is that ultimately these players are actors on a stage, but a unique stage where they have the capacity to act as quasi-official arbiters in the private sector. Their pronouncements can have effects such as downgrading a local government, which may result in higher financing costs borne by the taxpayer, or not seeing the risk in a foreign economy leading to huge losses by institutional investors. The players' responsibilities, however, are only limited to their credibility—any damage control arising from the inaccuracy or non-timeliness of their acts is ultimately of no concern to them.

The agencies meanwhile, as in the case of the Asian meltdown, may exhibit embarrassment akin to that of spilling wine at a banquet table, and rationalise their actions as merely constituting 'opinions' guaranteed by the US Constitution's provisions for 'free speech', but their modi operandi and motives nevertheless remain constant. And most importantly, they are often mandated by governments to perform the role they do.

Standard & Poor's

Background

Standard & Poor's (S&P) is a credit rating agency whose story begins in 1860 when Henry Varnum Poor established a publishing house to produce manuals of railway companies. The merger of the first establishments of Poor's and Moody's in 1919 resulted in the establishment of Poor's Publishing Company. Poor's Publishing obtained rights over certain publications using the name Moody's. Meanwhile James L. L. Blake created the Standard Statistics Office in 1906. Moody again recreated a publishing house in 1908, which became known as Moody's Investors Service in 1914. Only by 1924 did Moody's have sufficient financial power to buy back the rights of the name Moody's from Poor's Publishing, thereby preventing further confusion.

While Moody's was publishing its first ratings by 1909, Standard Statistics only began publishing ratings by 1923, and limited those to loans of industrial enterprises. Poor's Publishing meanwhile was experiencing repeated financial difficulties, which in 1941 led to its merger with Standard Statistics, forming the S&P Corporation. In 1960 S&P took over a portion of the New York–based Fitch Investors Service rating agency's operations, as well as the rating symbols introduced by Fitch, which are now in worldwide use. In 1966 McGraw-Hill, the US publishing house (owners of *Business Week* and *Aviation Week & Space Technology* among other titles), bought out S&P. This intertwined historical thread linking S&P, Moody's, and Fitch in part explains the similarities of the rating systems, scales, and methodologies in use by them.

Marketing orientation

Although S&P's rating of sovereign states' issues dates back to the 1920s, S&P's international activities only really started to take off in the 1970s. This international growth was stimulated by two main factors: the omission of the interest equalisation tax (1974) and attractiveness of the US markets for foreign borrowers, and the emergence of the euromarkets resulting in euro-issuers non-domiciled in the USA. In the USA, S&P rates almost all issues which come on the market.

The first eurobond was rated in 1972; two years later the first structured financing was analysed, a business field which today is of significant import-ance to S&P. S&P began rating eurocommercial paper (ECP) in 1984. Only after the establishment of Japanese rating agencies did S&P begin, in 1986, to rate Japanese domestic market issues. In 1984 S&P was the first US rating agency to open an office outside of the USA, in London. Further offices were created in Melbourne, Tokyo, Paris—where Moody's acquired the French Agence d'Evaluation Financière (ADEF) rating agency—and Brussels. In March 1990 the London-based Insurance Solvency International Agency Ltd, as well as the Melbourne-based Australian Ratings Pty Ltd, both specialising in ratings in the insurance sector for insurance, were taken over. Both of these agencies had connections with the London-based IBCA rating agency and these connections were severed following the acquisitions.

S&P's international revenue has grown substantially, in line with the growth and development of the global capital markets. S&P's network con-tinues to expand with office openings in São Paulo, Brazil, and Moscow. This focus on global expansion also includes a 50% joint venture in Taiwan Ratings Corporation, a 10% equity interest in CRISIL, India's leading rating service, and the signing of affiliation agreements with Fundacao Getuliuo Vargas in Brazil and CA Ratings in South Africa. As a result of deregulation, liberalisation, and privatisation of capital traffic, S&P is pinning its hopes on growth in national capital markets outside of the USA. S&P intends to sell its rating activities in the following three sectors:

- Europe contributes almost half of S&P's international revenues. S&P expects that EMU will provide further stimulus to its activities. For example, European companies that once financed their growth mainly by borrowing from banks in the syndicated loans market are shifting to the issuance of corporate bonds. The shift towards private pensions in Europe is also expected to stimulate the ratings business in Europe.
- In Asia, economic problems have slowed growth but have not seriously affected S&P's long-term outlook. A need for ratings in the Asian economies is not expected to significantly diminish over time.
- Latin America continues to be an area of interest despite the area's experience of economic problems.

S&P often relies on third parties for diffusion of its product offerings but hopes to use the internet to cut out such traditional intermediaries and further increase its profitability.

Competition

S&P obviously competes with other credit rating agencies, Moody's, owned by Dun and Bradstreet, being the most direct. Other competitors are Duff & Phelps and Fitch-IBCA. Other agencies are partial competitors such as Thomson Bank Watch, an agency that specialises in rating banks. Although Moody's and S&P are larger than Duff & Phelps and Fitch-IBCA, these two rating agencies are expected to provide increased competition as they seek to diversify.

Over the last decade, other rating agencies have been established, primarily in emerging markets, and as a result of local capital market regulation. The result of such regulatory activity has been the creation of a number of primarily national ratings agencies in various countries around the world. These agencies will most likely find the barriers to international credibility and expansion difficult to surmount and will most likely be bought out by one of the major agencies. Indeed, the establishment of such regional agencies can be seen as the nurturing of a start-up venture for future profitable sale to the highest bidder.

Ratings process, criteria, and post-review adjustments

S&P's rating process is typically initiated by the issuer. After being commissioned, S&P typically assigns two or more analysts to the account, usually a local analyst in a junior capacity to do the grunt work and a US-trained overseer with a reporting link to head office. The analysts conduct basic research on the company and industry background using publicly available information prior to initiating discussions with the issuer's management. In some cases, analyses may be recycled since S&P may have undertaken 'industry sector' research as part of another rating, and may have analysed competitors for comparative purposes without necessarily issuing a rating.

The preparations are then followed by meetings with the issuer's management. Usually lasting from one to two days, these meetings clarify certain key questions which may have arisen in the analysis such as the state of the business or the company's financing policy. The results of these discussions and analyses are then summarised in a rating report submitted to the rating committee; the committee then makes a provisional decision on a recommended rating. At this point, the issuer typically receives an opportunity to participate in the evaluation process, if necessary, by supplying additional documents, which may result in a reassessment of the provisional rating. If the issuer agrees, or if the supplementary information does not lead to a modification of the provisional rating, the rating is confirmed, released to the press, and incorporated into S&P's various publications. After publication of the rating, the issuer is monitored by S&P; if important industry sector data or the company's situation changes, a review procedure reassessing the rating is initiated.

Different groups or industrial sectors have necessitated the development of different ratings criteria, typically they are lengthy checklists depicting an ideal procedure for conducting the ratings process. Issuers in different groups (e.g. public sector, banks, mortgage banks, insurance companies, corporates, sovereigns, special-purpose vehicles) are rated according to different yardsticks whose criteria can most favourably be described as opaque. Similarly, issuers in these varying sectors are subject to varying required levels of presentation and disclosure. S&P differentiates in particular between these sectors. The rating criteria are shown in the sublists.

- Sovereign states
  - political and social stability
  - demographic characteristics
  - economic structure
  - economic balance
- State-supported entities (or sovereign-supported entities)
  - government's willingness to support the issuer
  - government's ability to support the issuer
  - letters of comfort that confirm government support

- Municipalities
  - population structure
  - economic infrastructure
  - financial position
  - general economic position
- Banks
- Industrial enterprises

An assessment of the issuer's legal situation is also undertaken; typically, this comprises an overview of the basic legal conditions prevailing in the issuer's home country relating to the business and political structures. In the case of banks, the assessment considers the quality of the assets held, particularly the quality of the loan portfolio, the nature and structure of the security or guarantees provided, the ability to access refinancing facilities, and aspects typically measured by financial ratios such as liquidity, profitability, and capital resources. In assessing corporates, the variety of businesses and economic sectors often leads to the analysis being enlarged to include broader aspects such as the position of the enterprise in various markets, its cost structure (referring to peer group analyses), and available financial flexibility (liquidity, cash flow, committed but undrawn facilities, etc.).

S&P notes that it only rates specific financial instruments and their likelihood of repayment, hence the rating does not reflect a general opinion on the solvency of an issuer. The ratings are assigned for commercial paper, medium-term notes, or loans, whose configuration has already been determined or specified—in the case of a planned issue—by the issuer. These instruments are also assessed in light of other factors surrounding the issue such as the specific terms and conditions of the facility, the background of the loan, as well as any other warranties, endorsements, or other guarantees or collateral pledged in favour of the facility.

Since S&P's reactions have often been late in issuing downgraded ratings, the company strove to defuse this situation in 1981 by introducing the concept of Credit Watch, an idea which has also been picked up by other agencies under other names (Ratings Watch, Bank Watch, etc.). Credit Watch is a special list with the names of the issuers who are currently being monitored and whose rating may be changed, if necessary.

Besides ratings, S&P provides several other services in the financial information sector:

- Ratings services for issuers (financial institutions, corporates, sovereigns, and structured finance transactions)
- Equity market yardsticks such as the S&P 500 index
- Financial databases and PC-based software for financial analysis

- Real-time analytical data feeds in the global money, bond, foreign exchange, and equity markets

S&P's publications

Credit Watch is a component of S&P's *Credit Week* publication, as well as the monthly *Credit Week International* publication, which contains ratings reports in addition to S&P's ratings, and *International Ratings Guide*. Credit Watch highlights the potential direction of short- or long-term ratings. These may include mergers, recapitalisations, voter referendums, regulatory action, or anticipated operating developments.

Ratings appear on Credit Watch when an event or a deviation from an expected trend occurs and additional information is necessary to evaluate the current rating. A listing, however, does not mean a rating change is inevitable; likewise, rating changes may occur without the ratings having first appeared on Credit Watch. The 'positive' designation means that a rating may be raised; 'negative' means a rating may be lowered; and 'developing' means that a rating may be raised, lowered, or affirmed.

Credit Week International represents a modest form of self-promotion. Along with other information, it is sent free of charge to 'important institutional investors' as a form of advertisement and self-promotion, and as a catalyst for new issuers to avail themselves of S&P's services. S&P also has other publications in its stable; for example, *Bond Guide*, a monthly statement specialising in ratings of approximately 7000 US bonds; *Commercial Paper Ratings Guide*, another monthly offering; or *Bank and S&L CD Rating Service*, to name a few.

As regards S&P's rating criteria, procedures, and evaluation principles, these are diffused to the public in other publications such as *Credit Overview Inform International* and *Debt Ratings Criteria*, which provide summary explanations of the company's analytical techniques and operating methods without delving too specifically into quantifiable details or methodologies.

S&P financial information services

S&P Financial Information Services expands by creating new offerings such as new indexes for the European market or for Canada, and following this up with indexes in other areas such as Latin America and the UK. S&P also seeks to diversify in new areas such as web-based data, commentary, and analytical services.

S&P rating evaluation service

Standard & Poor's has recently introduced its rating evaluation service which is designed to provide corporate issuers a definitive evaluation of the potential impact on their ratings of any proposed transaction. S&P's announcement stated:

> In response to market demand, Standard & Poor's is launching a new service that provides corporate issuers with a preliminary, confidential indication of how strategic plans would affect their credit quality and ratings. The service will also provide a framework for evaluating a company's capital structure. The service is available both to companies with current Standard & Poor's ratings and to new issuers. To date, no rating agency, investment banking firm or consulting company has been able to provide with certainty an independent credit evaluation to proposed corporate strategies.

Moody's has also established a similar version of S&P's rating evaluation service. Why would a rating agency want to get involved with quasi-consulting services? Naturally, it is a plausible extension of S&P's existing rating services. S&P has always tried to portray itself as 'issuer friendly' compared to Moody's unsolicited ratings practice, for example. This consulting activity could be a nice source of incremental profit since, in most cases, the fundamental analysis of the issuer will already have taken place (and the rating fees collected). In other words, twice the bang for the buck. However, it is debatable whether this 'independent rating evaluation service' necessarily benefits corporate issuers. As Cantwell & Company aptly point out:

> At the end of the day, rating agencies represent investors, not issuers. This is simply seeking advice from the wrong source. As an aside, S&P has recently joined Moody's in issuing unsolicited ratings, although S&P's 'public information' based ratings are clearly identified. An issuer might frighten a rating agency and seriously compromise the 'outlook' on its rating merely by presenting a series of aggressive potential transactions which are never consummated.

The traditional advisors on such matters, such as investment banks and consultants (like Cantwell & Company), routinely provide very specific estimates of the rating impact of potential corporate activities. The 'certainty' which a rating agency can give to a rating is, in S&P's own words, 'contingent on the issuer's ultimate action being consistent with what was presented'. There is a strong case therefore to look upon such offers circumspectly and perhaps consider more independent providers of such services.

S&P's revenue streams

S&P ratings group forms an organisational unit within the agency and is divided into four subgroups:

- Corporate finance
- Structured finance
- Financial institutions/LOC
- Municipal finance

Insurance rating services are represented by analysts in New York and London, as well as the London-based ISS subsidiary. International finance covers these areas:

- Australian ratings
- S&P ADEF
- S&P Tokyo
- S&P London
- Nordisk
- Corporates
- Structured finance
- Sovereigns, municipals and supranationals
- Banking and finance
- Business development, Europe
- International finance
- Publishing services
- Information management
- Seminars

Nordisk was a 1988 venture with the Stockholm School of Economics. Publishing services covers electronic news, printed media, and marketing; information management covers system planning, etc.

While S&P's rating service earns some revenues and notoriety from the diffusion of its various publications, it would be a mistake to assume the company is in the business of diffusing information or earning profits from the sale of research (this is borne out later in the book by entities specialised in the assessment of rating agencies and corporate polls as well as by breakdown figures of rating agencies' revenue streams). The bulk of the company's revenues are in fact derived from issuers paying rating fees in order to obtain ratings, which are required by the SEC for any entity accessing the US markets. The diffusion of information is an ancillary activity which serves to augment the company's visibility in the investor-creditor community.

Whilst we do not have a precise breakdown of the rating fees charged to issuers, we can make the following observations. Fees for a commercial paper (CP) rating are typically negotiable, depending upon the size of the issue. Initial euro-CP ratings may fetch a negotiable fee per annum, while further CP programmes may require a smaller fee for each issue. Sovereign entities may also pay a specific fee for a loan issue. For structured financings, fees may be defined in terms of basis points to the transaction volume. Financial establishments may pay a fee ranging in USD (US dollar) terms; with issuers who frequently tap the capital markets, rating fees can be subject to negotiation.

S&P rating scales and definitions

S&P essentially uses two rating scales: the commercial paper rating and the long-term rating, although numerous variations are in use for specialised sectors.

- Commercial paper (or short-term) ratings are denoted by the symbols A-1+ (highest category), A-1, A-2, A-3, B, C and D, and are assigned for issues with maturities of up to one year. Only A category CP issues are considered investment grade; the remaining issues are categorised as speculative grade.
- Long-term ratings apply to issues with maturities of more than one year. These ratings are assigned in accordance with a scale divided into two parts: investment quality is awarded to loans in the highest four categories (AAA, AA, A, BBB), and speculative grade includes the BB, B, CCC, CC, C as well as D classifications; D indicates loans of insolvent issuers or junk bonds.

The relative position of an issue within its category can be further refined by the modifiers + or − if necessary, according to whether the issue is considered as over or under the average of its class. The modifier 'p' is added when the issue is in an industrial sector classification whereby the issue's reimbursement is determined substantially by the successful completion of a certain project (e.g. project finance).

Fundamental and structural factors as opposed to liquidity factors are the main criteria in the evaluation process leading up to the issue of a long-term or short-term rating (Tables 2.1 and 2.2). While long-term ratings rely on factors such as industry structure and market positioning, short-term ratings focus primarily on various aspects of liquidity, as measured by various liquidity ratios. Finally the two scales stand out also in the relative size of the individual categories. Short-term ratings are assessed within a broader spectrum of issues when compared to long-term ratings.

An S&P issuer credit rating is a current opinion of an obligor's overall financial capacity (its creditworthiness) to pay its financial obligations. This opinion focuses on the obligor's capacity and willingness to meet its financial commitments as they come due. It does not apply to any specific financial obligation, as it does not take into account the nature and provisions of the obligation, its standing in bankruptcy or liquidation, statutory preferences, or

Table 2.1 S&P long-term issuer credit ratings

AAA	An obligor rated AAA has extremely strong capacity to meet its financial commitments. AAA is the highest issuer credit rating assigned by S&P
AA	An obligor rated AA has very strong capacity to meet its financial commitments. It differs from the highest-rated obligors only in small degree
A	An obligor rated A has strong capacity to meet its financial commitments but is somewhat more susceptible to the adverse effects of changes in circumstances and economic conditions than obligors in higher-rated categories
BBB	An obligor rated BBB has adequate capacity to meet its financial commitments. However, adverse economic conditions or changing circumstances are more likely to lead to a weakened capacity of the obligor to meet its financial commitments
	Obligors rated BB, B, CCC, and CC are regarded as having significant speculative characteristics. BB indicates the least degree of speculation and CC the highest. While such obligors will likely have some quality and protective characteristics, these may be outweighed by large uncertainties or major exposures to adverse conditions
BB	An obligor rated BB is less vulnerable in the near term than other lower-rated obligors. However, it faces major ongoing uncertainties and exposure to adverse business, financial, or economic conditions which could lead to the obligor's inadequate capacity to meet its financial commitments
B	An obligor rated B is more vulnerable than the obligors rated BB, but the obligor currently has the capacity to meet its financial commitments. Adverse business, financial, or economic conditions will likely impair the obligor's capacity or willingness to meet its financial commitments
CCC	An obligor rated CCC is currently vulnerable, and is dependent upon favourable business, financial, and economic conditions to meet its financial commitments
CC	An obligor rated CC is currently highly vulnerable
	Plus (+) or minus (–): Ratings from AA to CCC may be modified by the addition of a plus or minus sign to show relative standing within the major rating categories
R	An obligor rated R is under regulatory supervision owing to its financial condition. During the pendency of the regulatory supervision the regulators may have the power to favour one class of obligations over others or pay some obligations and not others. Please see S&P issue credit ratings for a more detailed description of the effects of regulatory supervision on specific issues or classes of obligations
SD and D	An obligor rated SD (selective default) or D has failed to pay one or more of its financial obligations (rated or unrated) when it came due. A D rating is assigned when S&P believes that the default will be a general default and that the obligor will fail to pay all or substantially all of its obligations as they come due. An SD rating is assigned when S&P believes that the obligor has selectively defaulted on a specific issue or class of obligations but it will continue to meet its payment obligations on other issues or classes of obligations in a timely manner. Please see S&P issue credit ratings for a more detailed description of the effects of a default on specific issues or classes of obligations
NR	An issuer designated NR is not rated

Source: Standard & Poor's, 2000

Table 2.2   S&P short-term issuer credit ratings

A-1	An obligor rated A-1 has strong capacity to meet its financial commitments. It is rated in the highest category by S&P. Within this category, certain obligors are designated with a plus sign (+). This indicates that the obligor's capacity to meet its financial commitments is extremely strong
A-2	An obligor rated A-2 has satisfactory capacity to meet its financial commitments. However, it is somewhat more susceptible to the adverse effects of changes in circumstances and economic conditions than obligors in the highest rating category
A-3	An obligor rated A-3 has adequate capacity to meet its financial obligations. However, adverse economic conditions or changing circumstances are more likely to lead to a weakened capacity of the obligor to meet its financial commitments
B	An obligor rated B is regarded as vulnerable and has significant speculative characteristics. The obligor currently has the capacity to meet its financial commitments; however, it faces major ongoing uncertainties which could lead to the obligor's inadequate capacity to meet its financial commitments
C	An obligor rated C is currently vulnerable to non-payment and is dependent upon favourable business, financial, and economic conditions for it to meet its financial commitments

Source: Standard & Poor's, 2000

the legality and enforceability of the obligation. In addition, it does not take into account the creditworthiness of the guarantors, insurers, or other forms of credit enhancement on the obligation.

S&P's credit ratings are based on information furnished by obligors or obtained by S&P from other sources it considers reliable. Note that the rating is not an audit, and typically relies on unaudited financial information such as management accounts.

Public information ratings

Ratings with a 'pi' subscript are based on an analysis of an issuer's published financial information, as well as additional information in the public domain. They do not, however, reflect in-depth meetings with an issuer's management and are therefore based on less comprehensive information than ratings without a 'pi' subscript. Ratings with a 'pi' subscript are reviewed annually based on a new year's financial statements, but may be reviewed on an interim basis if a major event that may affect an issuer's credit quality occurs. Ratings with a 'pi' subscript are not modified with + or – designations. Outlooks are not provided for ratings with a 'pi' subscript, nor are they subject to potential Credit Watch listings.

Local currency and foreign currency risks

Country risk considerations and currency of repayment can be key factors in the analysis. For example, an obligor's capacity to repay foreign currency obligations may be lower than its capacity to repay obligations in its local currency due to the sovereign government's own relatively lower capacity to repay external versus domestic debt. These sovereign risk considerations are accordingly incorporated in the debt ratings assigned to specific issues.

S&P unsolicited ratings

S&P also issues unsolicited ratings under the more palatable name, 'public information ratings'. The vast majority of S&P's unsolicited ratings are in the insurance sector. Unsolicited ratings appear with a 'pi' subscript and they are based on an analysis of publicly available information sources such as a company's published annual report. They do not benefit from in-depth meetings with an issuer's management and are therefore based on relatively more cursory information than those of classic ratings. S&P does not provide outlooks on unsolicited ratings or include them in Credit Watch listings.

Issue credit rating definitions

S&P issue credit ratings express an opinion about the creditworthiness of an obligor with respect to a specific financial obligation, a specific class of financial obligations, or a specific financial programme (including medium-term note and commercial paper programmes). It takes into consideration the creditworthiness of guarantors, insurers, or other forms of credit enhancement on the obligation and takes into account the currency in which the obligation is denominated.

Issue credit ratings can be either long-term or short-term (Tables 2.3 and 2.4). Short-term ratings are generally assigned to obligations considered short-term in the relevant market, e.g. in the USA obligations with an original maturity of no more than 365 days, including commercial paper. Short-term ratings are also used to indicate the creditworthiness of an obligor with respect to put features on long-term obligations. The result is a dual rating, in which the short-term rating addresses the put feature, in addition to the usual long-term rating. Medium-term notes are assigned long-term ratings.

Issue credit ratings are based on information furnished by obligors or obtained by S&P from other sources it considers reliable. Note that the rating is not an audit, and typically relies on unaudited financial information such as management accounts. Issue credit ratings are based, in varying degrees, on the following considerations:

- Likelihood of payment: capacity and willingness of the obligor to meet its financial commitment on an obligation in accordance with the terms of the obligation.

Table 2.3   S&P long-term issue credit ratings

AAA	An obligation rated AAA has the highest rating assigned by S&P. The obligor's capacity to meet its financial commitment on the obligation is extremely strong
AA	An obligation rated AA differs from the highest-rated obligations only in small degree. The obligor's capacity to meet its financial commitment on the obligation is very strong
A	An obligation rated A is somewhat more susceptible to the adverse effects of changes in circumstances and economic conditions than obligations in higher-rated categories. However, the obligor's capacity to meet its financial commitment on the obligation is still strong
BBB	An obligation rated BBB exhibits adequate protection parameters. However, adverse economic conditions or changing circumstances are more likely to lead to a weakened capacity of the obligor to meet its financial commitment on the obligation. Obligations rated BB, B, CCC, CC, and C are regarded as having significant speculative characteristics. BB indicates the least degree of speculation and C the highest. While such obligations will likely have some quality and protective characteristics, these may be outweighed by large uncertainties or major exposures to adverse conditions
BB	An obligation rated BB is less vulnerable to non-payment than other speculative issues. However, it faces major ongoing uncertainties or exposure to adverse business, financial, or economic conditions which could lead to the obligor's inadequate capacity to meet its financial commitment on the obligation
B	An obligation rated B is more vulnerable to non-payment than obligations rated BB, but the obligor currently has the capacity to meet its financial commitment on the obligation. Adverse business, financial, or economic conditions will likely impair the obligor's capacity or willingness to meet its financial commitment on the obligation
CCC	An obligation rated CCC is currently vulnerable to non-payment, and is dependent upon favourable business, financial, and economic conditions for the obligor to meet its financial commitment on the obligation. In the event of adverse business, financial, or economic conditions, the obligor is not likely to have the capacity to meet its financial commitment on the obligation
CC	An obligation rated CC is currently highly vulnerable to non-payment
C	A subordinated debt or preferred stock obligation rated C is currently highly vulnerable to non-payment. The C rating may be used to cover a situation where a bankruptcy petition has been filed or similar action taken, but payments on this obligation are being continued. A C will also be assigned to a preferred stock issue in arrears on dividends or sinking fund payments, but that is currently paying
D	An obligation rated D is in payment default. The D rating category is used when payments on an obligation are not made on the date due even if the applicable grace period has not expired, unless S&P believes that such payments will be made during such grace period. The D rating will also be used upon the filing of a bankruptcy petition or the taking of a similar action if payments on an obligation are jeopardised. Plus (+) or minus (–): The ratings from AA to CCC may be modified by the addition of a plus or minus sign to show relative standing within the major rating categories
r	This symbol is attached to the ratings of instruments with significant non-credit risks. It highlights risks to principal or volatility of expected returns which are not addressed in the credit rating. Examples include obligations linked or indexed to equities, currencies, or commodities; obligations exposed to severe prepayment risk, such as interest-only or principal-only mortgage securities; and obligations with unusually risky interest terms, such as inverse floaters
NR	This indicates that no rating has been requested, that there is insufficient information on which to base a rating, or that S&P does not rate a particular obligation as a matter of policy

Source: Standard & Poor's, 2000

Table 2.4 S&P short-term issue credit ratings

A-1	A short-term obligation rated A-1 is rated in the highest category by S&P. The obligor's capacity to meet its financial commitment on the obligation is strong. Within this category, certain obligations are designated with a plus sign (+). This indicates that the obligor's capacity to meet its financial commitment on these obligations is extremely strong
A-2	A short-term obligation rated A-2 is somewhat more susceptible to the adverse effects of changes in circumstances and economic conditions than obligations in higher rating categories. However, the obligor's capacity to meet its financial commitment on the obligation is satisfactory
A-3	A short-term obligation rated A-3 exhibits adequate protection parameters. However, adverse economic conditions or changing circumstances are more likely to lead to a weakened capacity of the obligor to meet its financial commitment on the obligation
B	A short-term obligation rated B is regarded as having significant speculative characteristics. The obligor currently has the capacity to meet its financial commitment on the obligation; however, it faces major ongoing uncertainties which could lead to the obligor's inadequate capacity to meet its financial commitment on the obligation
C	A short-term obligation rated C is currently vulnerable to non-payment and is dependent upon favourable business, financial, and economic conditions for the obligor to meet its financial commitment on the obligation
D	A short-term obligation rated D is in payment default. The D rating category is used when payments on an obligation are not made on the date due even if the applicable grace period has not expired, unless S&P believes that such payments will be made during such grace period. The D rating will also be used upon the filing of a bankruptcy petition or the taking of a similar action if payments on an obligation are jeopardised

Source: Standard & Poor's, 2000

- Nature and provisions of the obligation.
- Protection afforded by, and relative position of, the obligation in the event of bankruptcy, reorganisation, or other arrangement under the laws of bankruptcy and other laws affecting creditors' rights.

The issue rating definitions are expressed in terms of default risk. As such, they pertain to senior obligations of an entity. Junior obligations are typically rated lower than senior obligations, to reflect the lower priority in bankruptcy, as noted above.

Local currency and foreign currency risks

Country risk considerations and currency of repayment can be key factors in the analysis. For example, an obligor's capacity to repay foreign currency obligations may be lower than its capacity to repay obligations in its local currency due to the sovereign government's own relatively lower capacity to repay external versus domestic debt. These sovereign risk considerations are accordingly incorporated in the debt ratings assigned to specific issues.

Rating outlook definitions

S&P's rating outlook assesses the potential direction of a long-term credit rating over the medium to longer term. In determining a rating outlook, consideration is given to any changes in the economic and/or fundamental business conditions:

- Positive means that a rating may be raised
- Negative means that a rating may be lowered
- Stable means that a rating is not likely to change
- Developing means a rating may be raised or lowered
- NM means not meaningful

Moody's Investors Service, Inc.

Background

Moody's and Standard & Poor's comprise the duopoly in the ratings business. Moody's is an NRSRO-approved credit rating agency which publishes credit opinions, research, and ratings on fixed-income securities, issuers of securities and other credit obligations. As with S&P, it also provides a broad range of business and financial information.

Moody's was established in 1900 by John Moody, a financial analyst. Moody's published the first ratings in 1909; it rated approximately 1500 loans of 250 US railway companies which were classified using a rating scale with symbols ranging from Aaa to C, still in use today. Ratings were later expanded to important industrial enterprises as well as regional administrative bodies and later states. Moody's began rating commercial paper and eurobonds in the 1970s and expanded during the 1980s to cover insurance, bank deposits, and structured financing. Moody's international expansion in the 1980s began with the establishment of a Tokyo office (1985), followed by London (1986), Paris (1987), and Sydney (1987).

Moody's local offices primarily sell Moody's publications and rating products to local issuers; a fully independent analysis capability is typically not maintained. Decisions over the classification of issuers are made just like all other business and political decisions—at the seat of the agency in New York. This approach ensures that Moody's guarantees adherence to its American rating standards worldwide, without the influence of local factors.

Moody's has been a 100% owned subsidiary of Dun and Bradstreet Corporation (D&B) since 1962. It was announced in December 1999 that D&B would be spinning off Moody's as a separately quoted company. D&B appoints the president of Moody's and decides on the tenure or removal;

otherwise Moody's operates to a large extent independently of D&B. D&B coworkers are theoretically firewalled from confidential documents of issuers rated by Moody's. Moody's traditional approach has been to cooperate with other rating agencies and, unlike Standard & Poor's, it does not hold participatory shareholdings in other agencies.

John Bohn Jr is a former president of Moody's who left the company in 1996 (just as the US Department of Justice was initiating investigations into Moody's alleged abusive business practices) only to resurface later at Open Source Solutions Inc. (OSS), a Washington Beltway think tank set up by a former CIA intelligence officer. He has noted how 'this is not the manifestation of any specific corporate policy but rather, reflects the lack of suitability of co-operation partners'.

Moody's is no stranger to controversy. Whilst the *Wall Street Journal* said that Bohn strongly denied his departure is in any way connected to the investigation, this adds further colour to the conflict and controversy that Moody's has courted in recent years in its single-minded pursuit of market presence and 'providing investor service' as it sees it, not only in the USA but also in Japan (see later).

Bohn's departure occurred at a time when the US Department of Justice was probing Moody's ratings services for alleged antitrust violations and anticompetitive practices. The probe focused on whether Moody's pressured bond issuers (via unsolicited ratings) to use its services to evaluate their debt or face negative comments and lower ratings that could affect the marketability of their bonds.

Moody's has been criticised frequently in recent years by bond issuers who say the company's ratings are too harsh. Colorado's largest school system sued Moody's in a federal court in Jefferson County, Colorado, alleging that after the district refused to hire Moody's services, the company issued a negative outlook on a 1993 bond sale. The company has also courted controversy in Europe and Japan, something we shall examine later on.

Moody's typically defends its activities by claiming the right to freely express opinions about bond sales even against the wishes of the issuer, without necessarily linking these 'rights' to 'responsibilities' should these 'opinions' (which may not necessarily be fact) result in a negative financial impact—negative not only to public bodies being rated, but also ultimately to the taxpayers who fund these bodies. This begs the question of whom Moody's believes it is 'serving' by its rating activities.

According to the *Wall Street Journal*, the Department of Justice is focusing on Moody's mortgage-backed market and its municipal bond market. The department seems particularly interested in how Moody's decides what fees to charge on bond deals and whether it has pressured bond issuers to hire its rating services.

Internationally, Moody's is known for its straightforward export of the modus operandi it uses on its home turf, which has led to vociferous criticism of its activities in Europe as well as Japan. Indeed, in contrast to other players, Moody's is the McDonald's of the business. Wherever you go, in or out of the USA, the agency's mission is to serve up the same homogenised offering it serves in the USA. This means the agency is predominantly aligned to US markets and methodologies. In Moody's words, 'our objective for the future is to supply the global credit markets with the same independently created analyses that those domestic US financial markets have required since 1909'.

Hence no concession to local aficionados or historical imperatives: the McDonald's formula is appropriate for global roll-out because Moody's deems it so. Regional characteristics and differing historical, economic, or financing infrastructures do not figure in Moody's methodologies that it claims the 'domestic US financial market has required since 1909'.

Furthermore, Moody's has built itself a reputation for strong-arm sales techniques via the development of unsolicited ratings, a practice whereby entities are summarily rated and informed that an unsolicited rating will be issued. The unspoken message has a whiff of the old protection racket in that it is typically understood that better research and a better rating can be the result if the company formally requests a rating and opens its books, whether or not it actually wants or needs the rating.

This proactive marketing technique, however, has not curried favour with everyone and has resulted in the occasional lawsuit from corporates and public bodies. Moody's defends the practice by referring to information flows and freedom of speech provisions under the US Constitution, without necessarily drawing the distinction or identifying the responsibility between, say, slandering an individual or company with relatively limited effects as opposed to adversely impacting a public sector entity which may indirectly result in increased funding costs that are ultimately borne by the taxpayer.

However, there are inevitably other factors influencing the process. Given the increasing competition in the ratings business in the USA, the company is increasingly pinning its hopes on the newly deregulated, mobile, and globalised international capital markets being stimulated by the global growth in privatisation programmes. It is therefore natural to wonder how far Moody's is pinning its hopes on international expansion and how much the unsolicited ratings form a part of this strategy.

Marketing orientation

In a recent 10-K filing with the SEC, Moody's states that it employs some 680 analysts and has a total of more than 1300 associates located around the world. Moody's maintains offices in 12 countries (including London, Paris, Frankfurt, Hong Kong, and Tokyo), and has begun to expand into developing markets through joint ventures or affiliation agreements with local rating agencies. Moody's rates governmental and commercial entities in some 100 countries. Its customers include investors; depositors, creditors, investment banks, commercial banks and other financial intermediaries; and a wide range of corporate and governmental issuers of securities.

Moody's publishes rating opinions, both solicited and unsolicited, on credit obligations which include various US corporate and governmental obligations, international cross-border notes and bonds, domestic obligations in foreign local markets, structured finance securities and commercial paper issuers. Moody's has in recent years diversified beyond its traditional bond ratings activity, assigning ratings to insurance companies' obligations, bank loans, derivative product companies, bank deposits and other bank debt, managed funds, and derivatives in an effort to broaden its market presence and income streams. Ratings are disseminated to the public through a variety of print and electronic media, either by subscription or 'free samples' to gain as wide a readership as possible and propagate the firm's rating activities.

In addition to its rating activities, Moody's publishes 'investor-oriented credit research' as a method of propagating its activities. Moody's has a stable of some 100 publications, including 'research' on major issuers, industry studies, various comments, and summary 'credit opinion' handbooks. The term 'research' is somewhat flattering as, according to a recent market study by Cantwell & Company, typical corporate entities such as banks and corporates pay Moody's for ratings as a prerequisite to accessing the markets but they do not actually consume, as paying entities, a significant portion of Moody's 'research' or consider Moody's various publications as research in the true sense of the word. It may therefore be useful to consider such publications as self-promotional media.

Moody's has also sought to leverage on its market exposure by diversifying into 'educational' activities: Moody's Risk Management Services, Inc. (formerly known as Financial Proformas, Inc.), a wholly-owned subsidiary of Moody's, develops and distributes 'credit education' materials, seminars and computer-based lending simulations. The affiliate also sells financial and risk assessment software for the commercial lending community. Hence not only does the company leverage its skills set into new avenues of profitability, it serves to propagate its methodologies and ideologies as industry standards via the provision of 'educational services'. Ever watchful of cost centres such as credit departments, banks are only too happy to lay off non-essential analysts and delegate the function to an outside entity, thereby abdicating their autonomous decision-making capability and providing a new market for savvy agencies to tap.

Competition

Moody's obviously competes with other credit rating agencies. Moody's most direct competitor in the credit rating business is Standard & Poor's (S&P), a division of the McGraw-Hill publishing empire. Other rating agency competitors are Duff & Phelps and Fitch-IBCA. There are also partial competitors such as Thomson Bank Watch, which specialises in rating banks. Although Moody's and S&P are larger than Duff & Phelps and Fitch-IBCA, these two rating agencies are expected to provide increased competition. Similar to S&P, Moody's has noted the growth in rating agencies for emerging markets and how the evolution in local capital market regulation is favouring their establishment; it sees the eventual acquisition of these fledgling entities as offering an entrée to these new markets.

Moody's notes in its recent 10-K that regulators of financial institutions are attempting to improve their approach to supervision by shifting away from rule-based systems that address only specific risk components and institution-specific protections toward more sophisticated, prudential supervision. This evolving approach includes making qualitative judgements about the sophistication of each financial institution's risk management processes and systems, in terms of both market and credit risk. While such regulatory trends present additional opportunities for the use of Moody's ratings, they may also result in additional competition.

Revenues and growth

Rating fees paid by issuers account for most of Moody's revenues. Therefore, a substantial portion of Moody's revenues depend upon the volume of debt securities issued in the global capital markets. Accordingly, Moody's depends on the macroeconomic prospects of the major world economies and, to some extent, the fiscal and monetary policies pursued by various governments. Fees from arrangements with frequent debt issuers, commercial paper and medium-term note programmes, bank and insurance company financial strength ratings, and mutual fund ratings are less dependent on the volume of debt securities issued in the global capital markets.

Everling Advisory Services (EAS), a specialised consultancy active in the ratings business, estimates that the income from the sales of publications accounts for only about 10% of Moody's total receipts. Hence the service is primarily carried via the fees Moody's charges to issuers for the rating, and the publication arm is essentially a vehicle for self-promotion and market notoriety. Ratings for approximately 700 issuers in the US and euromarkets are published by Moody's corporate credit report service. Other publications distributed to investors include its weekly bond survey and international capital market survey, and *Moody's Short-Term Market Record.* Other publications include *Moody's Bond Record* and *Moody's Manual.*

Moody's marketing strategy is clearly stated in its 10-K. It intends to focus its business strategy on the following sectors.

International expansion

Moody's global network of offices and business affiliations, including rating and marketing operations in the major global financial centres of Frankfurt, Hong Kong, London, Paris, and Tokyo, are designed to position it for expansion in global capital markets and offer the greatest potential for its revenue growth. It also expects accelerated growth of its ratings activities due to the financial market integration under European Monetary Union (EMU) and ongoing global development of non-traditional financial instruments (e.g. derivatives, credit-linked bonds). Moody's will most likely continue its expansion into developing markets via joint ventures or affiliations.

Natural adjacencies

Moody's is pursuing initiatives to expand credit ratings from securities markets to other credit risk exposures. It has committed efforts to extend its opinion franchise to the global bank counterparty sector through emerging market ratings, including bank financial strength ratings. Moreover, insurance financial strength ratings (property and casualty, reinsurance, and life insurance) represent additional growth opportunities. Moody's has introduced issuer ratings for mid-sized corporations not active in the debt markets. It is investigating numerous non-traditional opportunities (e.g. unsolicited ratings) to extend its opinion franchise.

New sectors

The enhancement of risk management processes will hasten the convergence of the loan and capital markets as intermediaries and investors seek additional opportunities for the development of financial markets and a consistent standard of relative risk comparison. Moody's may seek to expand coverage in areas such as rating bank loans. It has also introduced equity mutual fund indices and fund analysers for institutional fund managers.

Securitisation

The repackaging of financial assets has had a profound effect on the US fixed-income market. New patterns of securitisation will emerge in the next decade; commercial assets, principally commercial mortgages, term receivables, and corporate loans, are increasingly being securitised. Securitisation concepts are rapidly being exported to Europe and Asia. In addition, securitisation is evolving into a strategic corporate finance tool. Moody's obviously intends to position itself in these areas.

US methodology

Moody's is predominantly aligned towards the US money and financial markets; this is reflected by its organisational structure, which is divided into several areas:

- The corporate department deals with five areas:
  - industrials
  - utilities
  - financial institutions and sovereigns
  - structured finance
  - international
- The public finance department deals with ratings in the American 'tax exempt' market.
- The international department is responsible for the London, Paris, Sydney, and Tokyo offices.

Within the international department, the interests of non-US issuers are assigned subsections. Within these subsections are individual analysts which examine and observe, among other things, European issuers. Generally speaking, there are hardly any analysts devoted exclusively to European issuers. This is most likely to ensure that Moody's policy of applying US methodologies and criteria is consistently applied across all sectors.

Research by EAS suggests that around 80% of Moody's analysts have academic qualifications, although there is no specific educational programme or professional qualification specifically related to being a rating agency analyst. The average length of service for a Moody's employee is eight years, although approximately 10% of Moody's analysts leave each year and must be replaced via new recruits, typically inexpensive and malleable youngsters who perform grunt work under supervision.

The formalised internal training offered by Moody's is limited to some internal and external courses covering specific topics. Analysts typically absorb their knowledge by cooperating with their colleagues on rating assignments rather than via a formalised training programme. The problem of staff turnover and skills erosion is partially offset by the fact that each rating is processed by at least two analysts.

Moody's does not deny that its rating system is subjective. Moody's long US tradition has led to the development of specific evaluation yardsticks which are closely in line with American business school methodologies and conventions. Quantifiable financial data and mathematical or statistical models assessing creditworthiness are useful analytical tools. EAS, however, notes that Moody's analysts admit these statistical factors are overridden in the rating decision if new factors such as market sector developments are discernible. This means that basing the ratings definition or update on purely historical trends is impossible. The reliability of the rating evaluation therefore depends more on a combination of both quantitative and qualitative criteria rather than purely quantifiable criteria, and is hence a somewhat subjective judgement.

Although the weighting of individual rating criteria is subjective and therefore dependent on available analysts, certain evaluation principles can be established, hence affording guidelines to which Moody's analysts can refer. In the first place, emphasis on risk factors is formalised as a principle: Since creditors do not participate directly in the management of the debtor enterprise, Moody's analyses focus primarily on the vulnerability of the issuer to specific unfavourable developments in the economy or industry sector and possible adverse impact on the creditor position. While share analysts are typically guided by growth prospects, Moody's analysts focus more on the factors of uncertainty.

Peer group analysis

Another analytical technique used by Moody's in assessing issuers accessing the markets is to evaluate as wide a range of issuers as possible (setting the groundwork for unsolicited ratings and possible pay-off on this background work), thereby enabling a comparative peer group analysis to be undertaken. Only by comparing different issuers or issues in a peer group can nuances be precisely identified in the peer group or industry sector. Whilst this is not exclusive to Moody's, they have publicised it more prominently than other agencies.

Moody's analysts typically analyse a relatively broad range of issuers and are involved in several rating procedures, which enables an accumulation of knowledge and identification of possible inconsistencies in the evaluations. Finally, there is the principle of adjusting the analysis based on fundamental factors before issuing the rating. Typically, these are not short-term factors but a multiplicity of regulations which may have an impact on the industry sector's growth trends and market developments.

Political criteria

A rating analysis typically starts off by analysing the general economic situation of the country in which the issuer is domiciled. This includes evaluating both political and economic risks, and basically corresponds to the analysis which is made when rating sovereign entities (national issuers). This classification usually represents the upper limit of possible ratings for issuers in the state concerned (sovereign ceiling). The crux of the matter here arises from the willingness and ability of a state to honour its foreign currency commitments. This not only includes aspects which are regarded as directly relevant such as balance of payments relations, liquidity, and indebtedness, but also criteria such as the unemployment ratio, GDP growth rate, and stability of the government and political system.

Apart from the overall economic analysis, much space is given to industry analysis. Moody's approach is to evaluate the characteristics of the specialised industry segment before focusing on the issuer, and check the performance of the company's sales development against an industry backdrop. Competitive pressures, commercial pressures, barriers to market entry, and industry trends in supply and demand are identified and classified, and possible market strategies noted.

The rating process naturally focuses on the company's financial performance, with emphasis on the earnings of the company vis-à-vis competitors in the same industry sector. The company's positioning and ability to maintain or expand market share is also identified and assessed. Even if Moody's usually gives a bonus to large enterprises endowed with a high market share, this criterion alone does not necessarily produce a favourable rating. Unfavourable cost structures compared to peer averages can lead to rating reductions, just like insufficient effort in research and development. Moody's in particular focuses heavily on evaluating features particular to a given economy (if they do not concern the USA).

Moody's claims to attach high importance to evaluating management as part of the rating process, but this seems considerably at odds with its various pronouncements on the theme of unsolicited ratings (see later). The weight allocated to this subjective criterion contrasts significantly with its highly subjective nature. This evaluation attempts to predict management's ability to formulate as well as execute corporate policies, attain realisable strategic targets, and translate these results into profits. Moody's therefore relies on its accumulated experiences gained in the USA in assessing these subjective criteria, which can lead it to criticisms that it is somewhat ethnocentric in its various pronouncements.

The financial flexibility of the issuer is also considered in the rating. In addition to the status quo and liquidity reserves, Moody's also reviews the company's cost and revenue structures. Interest on future debt requirements and other expenditures and yields are also assessed, in order to forecast additional financing requirements. Since company plans in future will affect the company's future liquidity, relevant financial forecasts and management accounting reports are also included in the assessment if available.

Characteristics of the issue

Moody's rating is determined by criteria which refer to the configuration and provision of security of the individual issue. Long-term ratings are given only for specific debt issues and are defined by the specific features of the rated issue. The short-term rating in contrast represents Moody's opinion of the issuer's ability to repay punctually its priority obligations with original maturities under one year, and avoid a commercial paper issue bind. Structural factors can therefore impact the bond rating, e.g. endorsements, warranties or guarantees of a parent company or an affiliate, backup facilities, and security arrangements.

The rating procedure (except in the case of unsolicited ratings) is in theory initiated by the issuer. Moody's typically starts off the process by explaining the fundamentals of the evaluation process and its rating criteria. If the issuer agrees with the conditions, it signs a request asking Moody's to issue a rating. This request indicates what the precise characteristics of the issue will be, including the amount of capital, the maturity date, the purpose of the loan, etc. The request also commits the issuer to provide all information required by Moody's immediately. It also includes (according to calculation techniques which can include various criteria relating to the company and amount of the debt issue) the rating fee, which can amount to USD 125 000.

At the same time, the issuer (with its signature) can typically be obliged to acknowledge that Moody's does not assume any responsibility for the correctness of the rating and the accuracy of the information spread over the issuers.

Necessary documents

As part of the ratings process, the issuer is required to provide documentation. For example, in the case of industrial enterprises, this can include end-of-year financial accounts of the parent company (consolidated if necessary) as well as those of key subsidiaries typically going back five years, and legal or submitted forms such as articles of incorporation, certification from the stock exchange authorising the proposed issue, copies of all loan agreements, and certificates of non-default.

After examination of the documents, a meeting is arranged with the issuer's management. The typical attendees can comprise four or five representatives of the issuer, as well as a member of the executive committee, and two or more Moody's analysts (senior and junior). The discussions typically last two days, whether a short- or long-term rating was requested. Items on the agenda typically include the industrial addresses for the organisation or the enterprise, the accounting principles in use, the company's strategy, its balance sheets and income statements, its plans, its personnel policy and any other aspects which may specifically relate to the issue.

Rating committee deliberations

The ratings process typically lasts between three and six weeks. While discussions with the issuers are led by analysts which are familiar with the issuer and the language and conditions in the respective country and may be based in those countries, rating decisions are made centrally in New York.

The function of the local analysts, who hold the conversations with the issuers, is limited to ferreting the data to compile the rating analysis report, which forms the basis of the rating committee's *intra muros* decision. The issuer is then informed about the rating committee's judgement and receives a statement notifying them of the decision. If the issuer does not raise any objections, the rating and the underlying rationale are published. The confidential information raised in the meetings and provided by the issuer influences the rating committee's rating, but it is not publicly disclosed. Once the rating has been issued, the rating activity of the agency does not stand still; business reports, press releases, and other data concerning the issuer are disseminated.

Negative corporate messages as well as adverse industry sector developments can trigger off a new review process; this can range from monitoring (announced in *Moody's Review*) to a reassessment of the rating (announced in *Watchlist*) which may lead to a modification of the company's rating. Similarly, favourable data such as the denouement of a blocked situation can give cause for a 'ratings upgrade'. The review process is usually less complex than the initial rating procedure, although this is a generalisation.

Moody's rating principles

In Moody's innocuous words, ratings exist to 'simply help investors determine the relative likelihood that they might lose money on a given fixed-income investment. More technically, it is an opinion of the future ability,

legal obligation, and willingness of a bond issuer or other obligor to make
full and timely payments on principal and interest due to investors'.

Long-term ratings

Obligations with maturities of over one year are rated using Moody's traditional Aaa through C long-term rating symbols:

- At the top of the scale, Moody's Aaa represents the highest or 'gilt edge'
  credit quality, meaning that the obligation ranks highest in its margins of
  investor safety against credit loss, even under severe economic
  conditions.
- In between, obligations rated Baa and above are termed 'investment
  grade'. Those rated Ba and below are 'speculative grade'. Numerical modifiers indicate further gradations of credit risk. Moody's ratings in the US
  municipal bond market use slightly different numerical modifiers, but the
  definitions of each letter rating category are the same across all markets.
- The lowest rating, C, indicates the lowest level of credit quality, meaning
  that the obligation has extremely poor chances of attaining any real
  investment value.

Each rating category can also be defined statistically. Moody's annual bond
default studies track the actual default and credit loss experience by rating
category of corporate bond issuers over the last 78 years.

The most recent study shows that the average one-year default rate for
Aaa-rated bonds during that period is zero. By contrast, 6.8% of bonds rated
B defaulted within one year. The studies also report default experience over
longer periods from 2 to up to 20 years. For instance, over ten-year periods,
the study shows that only 0.82% of bonds rated Aaa missed payments; the
ten-year default rates for bonds rated B is dramatically higher at 43.9%. See
Corporate Bond Defaults and Default Rates, 1920–1997, Moody's Special
Report, February 1998; the study is updated annually.

Note that Moody's long-term ratings measure total expected credit loss
over the life of the security. In other words, they are an assessment of (a) the
likelihood that the issuer will default (i.e. miss payments) on a security, and
(b) the amount of loss after a default occurs. Accordingly, ratings on the
issuers' bonds will also be higher or lower depending on the investor protections in each rated security.

Short-term ratings

Like most other rating agencies, Moody's uses a separate rating system to rate
securities that mature in less than one year, such as commercial paper, bank

deposits, or money market funds. Moody's NP (not prime) rating represents an opinion that the issuer may not have sufficient access to firm bank lines of credit or other forms of backup funding to meet all its short-term obligations in a period of market stress. By contrast, Moody's prime rating indicates the opinion that the issuer does have sufficient access to funds to meet payments on all its short-term obligations under periods of market stress. The three numerical modifiers associated with the prime rating indicate relative degrees of protection against potential default, with prime-1 indicating the highest degree of investor protection.

Use of the rating

Moody's notes that its ratings are intended only to measure risk of credit loss. They are not intended to measure other risks in fixed-income investment, such as market risk (the risk of loss in the market value of a security.) They are also not intended to rise with the business cycle or a company's latest earnings report. Ratings also are not intended to measure a security's potential for price appreciation.

Moody's typically notes as a disclaimer—and it proves to be quite a good definition of a rating—that its ratings are 'opinions, not recommendations to buy or sell, and their accuracy is not guaranteed. A rating should be weighed solely as one factor in an investment decision and you should make your own study and evaluation of any issuer whose securities or debt obligations you consider buying or selling'.

Moody's rating scales and definitions

Long-term rating: Moody's bank financial strength ratings

Moody's bank financial strength ratings represent Moody's opinion of a bank's intrinsic safety and soundness and, as such, they exclude certain external credit risks and credit support elements that are addressed by Moody's traditional debt and deposit ratings. Unlike Moody's debt ratings, bank financial strength ratings do not address the probability of timely payment. Instead, they can be understood as a measure of the likelihood that a bank will require assistance from third parties such as its owners, its industry group, or official institutions. Bank financial strength ratings do not take into account the probability that the bank will *receive* such external support, nor do they address *risks arising from sovereign actions* that may interfere with a bank's ability to honour its domestic or foreign currency obligations. The definitions for Moody's bank financial strength ratings are given in Table 2.5.

Table 2.5 Moody's bank financial strength ratings

A	Banks rated A possess exceptional intrinsic financial strength. Typically, they will be major institutions with highly valuable and defensible business franchises, strong financial fundamentals, and a very attractive and stable operating environment
B	Banks rated B possess strong intrinsic financial strength. Typically, they will be important institutions with valuable and defensible business franchises, good financial fundamentals, and an attractive and stable operating environment
C	Banks rated C possess good intrinsic financial strength. Typically, they will be institutions with valuable and defensible business franchises. These banks will demonstrate either acceptable financial fundamentals within a stable operating environment, or better than average financial fundamentals within an unstable operating environment
D	Banks rated D possess adequate financial strength, but may be limited by one or more of the following factors: a vulnerable or developing business franchise; weak financial fundamentals; or an unstable operating environment
E	Banks rated E possess very weak intrinsic financial strength, requiring periodic outside support or suggesting an eventual need for outside assistance. Such institutions may be limited by one or more of the following factors: a business franchise of questionable value; financial fundamentals that are seriously deficient in one or more respects; or a highly unstable operating environment
Intermediate categories	Where appropriate, a + may be appended to ratings below the A category to distinguish those banks that fall into intermediate categories

Source: Moody's Investors Service, 2000

Factors considered in assigning bank financial strength ratings include bank-specific elements such as financials, franchise value, and business/asset diversification. Although bank financial strength ratings exclude the external factors specified above, they do take into account other risk factors in the bank's operating environment, including the strength and prospective performance of the economy, as well as the structure and relative fragility of the financial system, and the quality of banking regulation and supervision.

Long-term rating: Moody's issuer ratings

● *Foreign currency.* Moody's foreign currency issuer ratings are opinions of the ability of entities to honour senior unsecured financial obligations and contracts denominated in foreign currency. Issuer ratings are unlike long-term debt ratings in that they are assigned to issuers rather than specific debt issues. Specific debt issues of the issuer may be rated differently, and are considered unrated unless individually rated by

Moody's. Unless specified, obligations guaranteed by the issuer are considered unrated and are not covered by the issuer rating.

- *Domestic currency*: Moody's domestic currency issuer ratings are opinions of the ability of entities to honour senior unsecured financial obligations and contracts denominated in their domestic currency.
- *Derivative product companies*: Issuer ratings that are assigned to derivative product companies are opinions of the financial capacity of an obligor to honour its senior obligations under financial contracts, given appropriate documentation and authorisations.

Moody's rating symbols for issuer ratings (Table 2.6) are identical to those used to show the credit quality of bonds. These rating gradations provide creditors with a simple system to measure an entity's ability to meet its senior financial obligations.

Table 2.6 Moody's issuer ratings

Aaa	Issuers rated Aaa offer exceptional financial security. While the creditworthiness of these entities is likely to change, such changes as can be visualised are most unlikely to impair their fundamentally strong position
Aa	Issuers rated Aa offer excellent financial security. Together with the Aaa group, they constitute what are generally known as high-grade entities. They are rated lower than Aaa entities because long-term risks appear somewhat larger
A	Issuers rated A offer good financial security. However, elements may be present which suggest a susceptibility to impairment sometime in the future
Baa	Issuers rated Baa offer adequate financial security. However, certain protective elements may be lacking or may be unreliable over any great period of time
Ba	Issuers rated Ba offer questionable financial security. Often the ability of these entities to meet obligations may be moderate and not well safeguarded in the future
B	Issuers rated B offer poor financial security. Assurance of payment of obligations over any long period of time is small
Caa	Issuers rated Caa offer very poor financial security. They may be in default on their obligations or there may be present elements of danger with respect to punctual payment of obligations
Ca	Issuers rated Ca offer extremely poor financial security. Such entities are often in default on their obligations or have other marked shortcomings
C	Issuers rated C are the lowest-rated class of entity, are usually in default on their obligations, and potential recovery values are low
Note	Moody's applies numerical modifiers 1, 2, and 3 in each generic rating category from Aa to Caa in the corporate finance sectors, and from Aa to B in the public finance sectors. The modifier 1 indicates that the issuer is in the higher end of its letter rating category; the modifier 2 indicates a mid-range ranking; the modifier 3 indicates that the issuer is in the lower end of the letter ranking category

Source: Moody's Investors Service, 2000

Table 2.7 Moody's short-term prime rating system

Prime-1	Issuers rated prime-1 (or supporting institutions) have a superior ability for repayment of senior short-term debt obligations. Prime-1 repayment ability will often be evidenced by many of the following characteristics:

- Leading market positions in well-established industries
- High rates of return on funds employed
- Conservative capitalisation structure with moderate reliance on debt and ample asset protection
- Broad margins in earnings coverage of fixed financial charges and high internal cash generation
- Well-established access to a range of financial markets and assured sources of alternate liquidity

Prime-2	Issuers rated prime-2 (or supporting institutions) have a strong ability for repayment of senior short-term debt obligations. This will normally be evidenced by many of the characteristics cited above but to a lesser degree. Earnings trends and coverage ratios, while sound, may be more subject to variation. Capitalisation characteristics, while still appropriate, may be more affected by external conditions. Ample alternate liquidity is maintained
Prime-3	Issuers rated prime-3 (or supporting institutions) have an acceptable ability for repayment of senior short-term obligations. The effect of industry characteristics and market compositions may be more pronounced. Variability in earnings and profitability may result in changes in the level of debt protection measurements and may require relatively high financial leverage. Adequate alternate liquidity is maintained
Not prime	Issuers rated not prime do not fall within any of the prime rating categories

Source: Moody's Investors Service, 2000

Moody's short-term prime rating system

Moody's short-term debt ratings are opinions of the ability of issuers to repay punctually senior debt obligations. These obligations have an original maturity not exceeding one year, unless explicitly noted. Table 2.7 shows the three designations Moody's employs to indicate the relative repayment ability of rated issuers; all three are judged to be investment grade.

Obligations of a branch of a bank are considered to be domiciled in the country in which the branch is located. Unless noted as an exception, Moody's rating on a bank's ability to repay senior obligations extends only to branches located in countries which carry a Moody's sovereign rating for bank deposits. Such branch obligations are rated at the lower of the bank's rating or Moody's sovereign rating for bank deposits for the country in which the branch is located.

When the currency in which an obligation is denominated is not the same as the currency of the country in which the obligation is domiciled, Moody's ratings do not incorporate an opinion as to whether payment of the obligation will be affected by actions of the government controlling the currency of denomination. In addition, risks associated with bilateral conflicts between an investor's home country and either the issuer's home country or the country where an issuer's branch is located are not incorporated into Moody's short-term debt ratings.

Moody's makes no representation that rated bank or insurance company obligations are exempt from registration under the US Securities Act of 1933 or issued in conformity with any other applicable law or regulation. Nor does Moody's represent that any specific bank or insurance company obligation is legally enforceable or a valid senior obligation of a rated issuer.

If an issuer represents to Moody's that its short-term debt obligations are supported by the credit of another entity or entities, then the name or names of such supporting entity or entities are detailed. In assigning ratings to such issuers, Moody's evaluates the financial strength of the affiliated corporations, commercial banks, insurance companies, foreign governments or other entities, but only as one factor in the total rating assessment.

Fitch (formerly Fitch-IBCA)

Background

Fitch (the Fimalac-Euronotation-IBCA-Fitch-Duff & Phelps quilt) is the new kid on the block striving to enter into the first-tier category of rating agencies, and regarded by some aficionados as a competitor to the US duopoly of Standard & Poor's and Moody's. Compared to the US agencies, IBCA's history is somewhat briefer and more complex. Its rapid expansion, in light of its difficulties to penetrate the US market due to its inability to obtain NRSRO status, has been primarily acquisition driven, as evidenced by its takeover of the Fitch Rating agency in 1997 and Duff & Phelps in early 2000.

IBCA, or International Bank Credit Analysis, before the Fitch acquisition, is basically an amalgam of French money and British know-how. Its story dates back to the late 1970s. Originally brokers providing bank research for the World Bank (in light of certain criticisms which had been levelled at Moody's), Robin Monro Davies established International Bank Credit Analysis Ltd (IBCA) in order to make the analyses available to interested parties and accordingly increase revenues.

As part of its international expansion, IBCA entered into certain cooperative ventures and agreements. In 1981 IBCA partnered with Australian Ratings Pty Ltd; the agency also established IBCA Corporate Ratings with its seat in London, and established IBCA Inc. in New York. In 1989 IBCA opened a representative office in Tokyo. The agency operated throughout the 1980s primarily by rating banks and sovereigns in the international banking market and providing these reports to interested parties. IBCA did not attack the US markets until 1985, when it began to issue ratings on US banks. IBCA has only rated corporates since 1987, albeit without NRSRO status.

A privately held UK-based concern owned by Monro Davies and certain key employees, IBCA sought to reinforce and expand its positioning against the backdrop of European integration and EMU, whilst maintaining its private ownership structure. The agency found a willing partner in the French venture capitalist and Bilderberger Marc Ladreit de Lacharrière, prime mover behind French holding company Fimalac (Financière Marc Ladreit de Lacharrière). Hoover's 1999 Company Capsule describes Fimalac as follows:

> Holding company Fimalac s.a. has some strange bedfellows in its corporate structure. Engelhard-CLAL, the company's 50/50 joint venture with Engelhard, which accounts for nearly 85% of Fimalac's sales, manufactures products that incorporate precious metals and are themselves used to make auto parts, aerospace products, and related items. Other subsidiaries include Secap, which makes French postal meters; Fitch-IBCA, the world's #3 bond rating agency; LBC, which stores chemicals at US and European seaports; and Clal-MSX, a metal fabricator of nickel and copper alloys.

Other entities include the Paris-based Journal de la Finance and FACOM, a French machine tool manufacturer. Fimalac merged the Paris-based Euronotation rating agency (which was active only in France, a not unusual case with French companies adopting the Euro moniker) with IBCA. Euronotation, as a home-grown agency, had few aficionados outside of France, and so was absorbed into IBCA. IBCA's British management lost no time in sweeping out Euronotation's French management and analysts, and imposing its own UK staff to oversee the day-to-day management of the Paris office. The Franco-British entity provided itself with a respectable Frenchman to front on the board of directors, septuagenarian Bernard Mirat, a former head of the Paris Stock Exchange and a member of the executive board of Elf-Gabon. Elf-Gabon is alleged to have links with electoral slush funds in France, Francophone Africa, and more recently Germany via the Mitterrand–Kohl scandal which resulted in the recent resignation of Roland Dumas, another Elf alumnus, from France's Constitutional Council and smearing of Germany's CDU, Kohl's political party. Management in contrast resided in London, focusing on the more mundane business of ratings.

IBCA has been recognised as a rating agency by UK supervisory agencies since 1987, but only for banks, building societies, and security houses. Franco-British IBCA had for a long time sought the SEC's coveted NRSRO status for both banks and corporates via the front door (direct albeit unsuccessful requests to the SEC) and, it is rumoured, via the back door (via Mirat's political connections and string pulling with Jean Artuis, minister of industry in the Juppé government). Its front-door efforts bore no fruit and the Juppé government was soundly trounced at the polls.

Franco-British IBCA found itself the entry ticket via purchase of the privately held US-based Fitch Investors Service rating agency. In the past Fitch had sought to expand into Europe via the failed London-based Euroratings service in 1989, in which it was a major shareholder, but these efforts were unsuccessful and the company remained a primarily US-oriented affair.

However, for IBCA, whatever synergies Fitch might offer were clearly outweighed by the frosting on the cake, namely Fitch's NRSRO status for rating corporate issues in the US. It was a match made in heaven: Fitch's US-based corporate analysis capabilities could avail themselves of IBCA's European connections for expansion, while IBCA could circumvent traditional lengthy NRSRO entry criteria for corporate ratings by buying its way into the SEC's club of corporate-approved NRSROs by taking over Fitch, thereby adding the precious corporate NRSRO status to its own bank NRSRO status. The result yields a vessel with the French at the helm, and the British in the engine room, under a US flag of convenience. This acquisition-created entity, moreover, has just added Duff & Phelps to its structure, further enlarging the scope and heterogeneity of its business, as well as rating scales.

In contrast to the plethora of home-grown agencies attempting to carve a niche in recent years, IBCA has become the prime competitor to the large and established US rating agencies Standard & Poor's and Moody's. Compared to the time taken by Standard & Poor's and Moody's to establish their market position, the acquisition-driven status won by IBCA within a short time frame is considerable.

Acquisition of Fitch, market coverage, and expansion

In contrast to the US agencies who are seeking to supplement their revenues and market position by expanding internationally, often using strong-arm techniques such as unsolicited ratings, IBCA in Europe is looking at the obverse of the coin. The agency had long sought to expand its coverage and credibility by entering the USA's lucrative corporate rating market. But IBCA's moves to obtain the SEC's coveted NRSRO status, enabling it to tap this market, had been to no avail. The entry ticket to expanded market coverage, so to speak, lay with the acquisition of US-based Fitch Investors Service.

In a press release dated October 1997, Fimalac announced that it was acquiring Fitch: 'In a move that will create the world's third largest credit rating agency, Fimalac of France today announced an agreement to acquire Fitch Investors Service, L.P. from the Van Kampen Group of Grand Haven, Michigan and other investors, and merge it with IBCA Limited, the London-based rating agency controlled by the French company. The new entity will

be known as Fitch IBCA, Inc.'. Fimalac noted that 'Fitch IBCA management
will have a significant equity-based participation in the new company'. The
newly combined Fitch-IBCA will have combined revenues of USD 105 million and over 550 employees in 18 offices worldwide.

Fimalac's Paris-based chairman, Mr Ladreit de Lacharrière, a complete
outsider to the ratings business, not surprisingly secured the position of
chairman of Fitch-IBCA; London-based Monro Davies was appointed IBCA's
chairman, vice chairman, and chief executive officer; whilst Fitch's US-based
president, Stephen W. Joynt, was appointed as president and chief operating
officer to maintain the US leg of the triumvirate.

Mr Ladreit de Lacharrière noted in the press release, 'This merger constitutes
a unique opportunity to bring much needed competition and an international
perspective to the global ratings business'. One may wonder whether Mr
Ladreit de Lacharrière is implying that a rating agency under French ownership
is in some way more competitive and international than one under US ownership, or whether he is implying that the business is in need of more open
competition. Lacharrière's comment that the acquisition 'also reflects Fimalac's
commitment to expanding its role as an international group and to pursuing its
global development strategy' could mean anything, and could lead one to
wonder what could possibly be the underlying strategy of a holding company
present in metals, machine tools, printing, journalism, and ratings.

Monro Davies states, 'There is a compelling logic to this merger,' and adds
hopefully, 'Fitch IBCA is certain to be a formidable player in the global ratings
business'. He accurately notes that 'our strengths are highly complementary,
and there is virtually no overlap in our ratings coverage'; but there is no
mention of the coveted NRSRO status, enabling Fitch-IBCA to penetrate the US
corporate ratings market. Fitch's Joynt adds, 'The combined company will
benefit from IBCA's international coverage and reputation and Fitch's strong
market recognition in the US and leading position in securitisation markets'.

The combination of the two agencies indeed creates an entity present
across the breadth of the ratings business with US and international
coverage; however, many hurdles remain before the group can operate on
the same level of credibility and acceptance as the US duopoly. For example,
it should be interesting to see how the quiltwork entity proposes to integrate
heterogeneous rating scales and possibly split ratings from the diverse
heritage of Euronotation-IBCA-Fitch-Duff & Phelps, and explain the underlying rationale to the investor-creditor community.

Competition and marketing orientation

IBCA possesses certain competitive advantages over its US rivals, and is
acting on them to support its expansion efforts. The management and

analysis team, at least in the pre-Fitch era, is based in London and therefore has a higher proximity to European issuers. IBCA, moreover, has a small but efficient organisation and is free from the bureaucratic excesses, ethnocentrism, and innate arrogance of the US agencies. IBCA analysts have the credibility of the London market behind them and are relatively more in tune with European economic, political, cultural, and social conditions, thereby enabling them to establish a greater degree of trust than obtained by the US agencies from European issuers and investors. The heavy-handed and arrogant US approach, particularly Moody's use of unsolicited ratings, has not curried favour in the Old Continent.

IBCA is obviously quick to pick up and build on the fact that an agency based in Europe (in this case the UK is considered as being in Europe although in an EMU sense it is not in Europe), specialised in the rating of European issuers, will achieve a higher international acceptance on a long-term basis with European market users than that granted to the US or indeed Japanese agencies. For the US markets, it is difficult to see how IBCA can seriously compete against the US agencies but it is likely that IBCA sees good chances to participate in the lucrative ratings business by integrating its recent acquisition of Fitch to build up credibility and thereafter perhaps gaining market share by undercutting the US agencies' issuer fees.

Nevertheless, the matter of historical and statistical continuity and winning acceptance with an initially weaker position is a substantial challenge. The US economy is replete with stories of French investors attempting to buy their way in, only to later pack their bags and make a precipitous exit. Moreover, the track record of French shareholders successfully managing their overseas acquisitions, especially in Anglo-Saxon markets, gives one food for thought. Whether Franco-British-US Fitch-IBCA can be successfully promoted in the world's most competitive and mature market with French ownership, a new logo, and intensified marketing, remains an open and interesting question.

Rating methodology and committee deliberations

IBCA's rating process typically begins when the issuers who require a rating are visited by two analysts; the meeting can last around two to three hours. The research derived from documentation, other research, and the meetings form the basis of the ratings report. This report is in turn submitted to a rating committee which typically includes the two analysts working on the dossier (who are expected to answer or elaborate on matters which the credit committee may query) and senior members of the committee, based in the local office and in London.

The committee may then pronounce its ratings decision which can be provisional, contingent on further information or conditions, or final, in which case it is typically communicated to the issuer for final approval and corrections if necessary. Once this stage has been completed, the rating decision is communicated via press releases to IBCA's subscriber base and the investor-creditor community.

The rating procedure is to a large extent comparable to that of the duopoly; however, industry sources cast certain doubts about the thoroughness of IBCA's procedures. The fact that IBCA is the new kid on the block means it is eager to conquer market share and may therefore be vulnerable to issuer preferences to be less than forthright with the provision of confidential information, as in the case of honeymoon audits.

Various market research and questionnaires provided by specialised entities such as Cantwell & Company, Everling Advisory Services, and the Japan Centre for International Finance suggest that IBCA often short-steps this issue, since it cannot operate with the same negotiation power as Standard & Poor's and Moody's, who firmly occupy the lion's share of what is effectively a captive market.

Publications service

As with most other agencies, Fitch-IBCA provides a range of publications. IBCA's list of ratings is typically distributed free of charge, as a method of diffusing and furthering the visibility and notoriety of its rating scales and techniques. In addition, Fitch-IBCA also has a full service range of publications which can either be distributed on paper or by CD-ROM with search and query facilities.

The company also diffuses a CD-ROM database called BankScope. BankScope contains a database of financial statements, shareholder information, ratings from the major rating agencies, and Reuters news database on over ten thousand banks, all linked with a search tool. BankScope also enables detailing of certain items in the financial statements and the compilation of peer group indicators for comparative purposes. The financial element contains a database on the banks' financial statements typically going back five years or more. A Bankscope bank report typically contains these four items:

- A cover sheet with summary financial data and ratings
- A complete set of financial statements with ratios that enable international comparisons
- A sheet with lists of shareholders and subsidiaries
- A database of Reuters news articles going back two years relating to the bank in question

IBCA rating definitions

IBCA's rating scales incorporate certain unique features. In addition to the well-known traditional rating scales which hardly differ from those of the market leaders, e.g. AAA, AA, A, BBB down to C (with enhancements of + or –) for long-term as well as A1+, A1, A2, B1, B2, C1 and D1 for short-term financial titles, the company also offers individual ratings, which measure the yield capacity of the issuer, and legal ratings which attempt to measure support in the case of insolvency by deficiency guarantee, guarantor, etc. The five-stage scales (plus intermediate stages) range from A to E for the individual ratings and from 1 to 5 for the legal ratings. For example, IBCA's users, when consulting the ratings for a bank, will find four ratings: a rating for long-term issues, one for short-term issues, one for the individual rating and one for the legal rating.

As with other ratings, Fitch-IBCA credit ratings represent an 'opinion on the ability of an entity or of a securities issue to meet financial commitments, such as interest, preferred dividends, or repayment of principal, on a timely basis'. Fitch-IBCA credit ratings apply to a variety of entities and issues, such as sovereigns, governments, structured financings, and corporations; and issues such as debt, preferred/preference stock, bank loans, and counterparties; as well as the claims-paying ability of insurance companies and financial guarantors. Entities or issues carrying the same rating are of similar but not necessarily identical credit quality since the rating categories do not fully reflect small differences in the degrees of credit risk.

Fitch-IBCA notes with the typical disclaimer that its credit and other ratings are not

> recommendations to buy, sell, or hold any security. Ratings do not comment on the adequacy of market price, the suitability of any security for a particular investor, or the tax-exempt nature or taxability of any payments of any security. The ratings are based on information obtained from issuers, other obligors, underwriters, their experts, and other sources Fitch IBCA believes to be reliable. Fitch IBCA does not audit or verify the truth or accuracy of such information. Ratings may be changed or withdrawn as a result of changes in, or the unavailability of, information or for other reasons.

International credit ratings

Fitch-IBCA's international credit ratings are applied to corporate, structured, and public finance. They cover sovereign (including supranational and subnational), financial, bank, insurance, and other corporate entities and the securities they issue, as well as municipal and other public finance entities, and securities backed by receivables or other financial assets, and counterparties. When applied to an entity, these long- and short-term ratings assess its general creditworthiness on a senior basis. When applied to specific issues and programmes, these ratings take into account the relative preferential position of the holder of the security and reflect the terms, conditions, and covenants attaching to that security.

International credit ratings assess the capacity to meet foreign currency or local currency commitments. Both 'foreign currency' and 'local currency' ratings are internationally comparable assessments. The local currency rating measures the probability of payment within the relevant sovereign state's currency and jurisdiction and therefore, unlike the foreign currency rating, does not take account of the possibility of foreign exchange controls limiting transfer into foreign currency.

Other ratings

Fitch-IBCA also provides specialised ratings of services of performing and non-performing multifamily and commercial mortgages, cash flow bond ratings, and volatility ratings of collateralised mortgage obligations and bond funds. The agency also provides individual and support ratings of banks, which assess the likelihood that they will get into difficulties and, in the event of this actually happening, whether they would indeed receive support.

In particular cases, Fitch-IBCA offers national ratings, which are an assessment of credit quality relative to the rating of the relevant sovereign state in that country's national market. For particular countries, Fitch-IBCA also assigns national insurance claims-paying ability ratings using a scale unique to such ratings.

The author was unable to obtain permission from Fitch-IBCA to include its tables in this book. The author can, however, make the following observations at the time of going to press.

Long-term ratings

Fitch-IBCA long-term ratings are comparable to the typical layering of risk levels used by the other credit ratings companies. Here they are in increasing order of risk:

AAA
AA
A
BBB
BB
B
CCC
CC
C

Short-term ratings (up to 12 months)

Fitch-IBCA short-term ratings are comparable to the typical layering of risk levels used by the other credit companies. Here they are in increasing order of risk:

A1
A2
A3
B
C

Support ratings

IBCA support ratings do not assess the quality of a bank. Rather, they represent Fitch-IBCA's assessment of whether it would receive support should this be necessary. Note that these ratings constitute Fitch-IBCA's *opinions*, as opposed to legal facts or formal policy pronouncements by state or regulatory agencies.

Individual ratings

IBCA individual ratings, which Fitch-IBCA notes are internationally comparable, attempt to assess how a bank would be viewed if it were entirely independent and could not rely on external support. They represent IBCA's view on the likelihood that the bank would run into significant difficulties such that it would require support. The principal factors examined with a view to the rating include profitability and balance sheet integrity, franchise, management, operating environment, and prospects. The agency looks favourably on consistency.

Duff & Phelps

Background

Duff & Phelps Credit Rating Co. (DCR) is an NRSRO-approved credit rating agency, and as this book goes to press, the latest addition to the Fimalac-Euronotation-IBCA-Fitch conglomerate owned by the French Fimalac holding company. Therefore it is no longer an autonomous entity but a component of the Fimalac quilt. The credit rating business was an outgrowth of the fixed-income research services provided by the firm, and its predecessors. The origins date back to 1932, when William Duff and George Phelps founded Duff & Phelps with the aim of offering institutional investors and dealers a news service, since at that time many suppliers were being confronted with financial difficulties.

DCR was incorporated in Illinois in 1987 as a wholly-owned subsidiary of Duff & Phelps Corporation, at which time Duff & Phelps Corporation contributed substantially all of the assets and liabilities of its credit rating business to DCR. As a result, DCR owns and operates the credit rating business as an independent public company. On 31 October 1994 the spin-off of DCR from its parent company, Phoenix Investment Partners Ltd, formerly Duff & Phelps Corporation (D&P), was finalised. This resulted in DCR operating as a free-standing entity whose common stock is publicly traded on the New York Stock Exchange under the ticker symbol DCR.

The company, which is headquartered in Chicago, conducts its operations through offices located in Chicago, New York, London, and Hong Kong. As of 31 December 1998, DCR employed 318 persons. The executive officers of the company are elected annually and serve at the discretion of the board of directors. DCR's 1998 10-K filing notes that Paul McCarthy has been chairman of the board since December 1995 and chief executive officer and a director of DCR since February 1991 as well as chief financial officer since November 1994.

Marketing orientation

DCR has affiliate offices in Argentina, Bangladesh, Brazil, Canada, Chile, Colombia, Costa Rica, Czech Republic, India, Indonesia, Italy, Korea, Malaysia, Mexico, Pakistan, Peru, Singapore, South Africa, Spain, Turkey, Venezuela, and Zimbabwe and is pursuing joint venture relationships in several other countries. Additionally, DCR maintains its designation as a rating agency in Japan, which was granted in October 1992 by the minister of finance of Japan.

In July 1994 DCR organised Duff & Phelps Credit Rating Co. of Europe, a US wholly-owned subsidiary with an office in London, to provide rating services in the United Kingdom and throughout Europe, as well as Africa. In July 1996 the company organised Duff & Phelps Credit Rating Co. of Asia, a wholly-owned US subsidiary with an office in Hong Kong, to provide rating services in Hong Kong and throughout Asia.

Competition

DCR competes primarily with three other full-service NRSRO-approved credit rating agencies. Moody's Investors Service, Inc. and Standard & Poor's dominate the market and are much larger than DCR. As with S&P and Moody's, DCR believes that significant growth opportunities exist in the credit rating market for the following reasons:

- Multiple agencies are increasingly used for ratings in the domestic and international markets
- Securities issuance continues to grow globally
- Certain securities issued in the marketplace have become more complex
- New and innovative asset-backed securities continue to be introduced into the capital markets
- More international issuers now have the ability to access the US capital markets for financing than in the past
- Global markets continue to experience disintermediation

DCR penetrates international markets through joint ventures and its US, London and Hong Kong offices. As part of its marketing efforts, DCR attempts to identify new financial products or emerging markets not fully covered by other rating agencies. This strategy has allowed DCR to gain market presence in rating domestic and international structured financings. DCR believes that since structured finance ratings are transaction specific, there remains the potential for further growth through penetration and continued development of the structured finance markets, especially internationally.

Marketing strategy and international expansion

DCR, as with other agencies, has sought to expand its activities and profits by providing credit ratings in developing economies. This has led it to rate innovative issues, such as those with future-flow structures and unique receivables as collateral. DCR's marketing slogan of 'local expertise, global reach' describes how it likes to see itself in the global ratings market.

Inspired by the Moody's model of overseer and grunt analyst, industry-specific analysts in DCR's local-market offices provide local insight into debt issues, while regional rating offices in the US, the UK and Hong Kong are responsible for undertaking the rating analyses. DCR believes that this local–global arrangement enables it to objectively evaluate each credit rating on its own merits, laying the groundwork for what it calls 'thorough monitoring of credit quality and timely dissemination of in-depth research', and avoiding analysts getting enamoured with local customs.

North America

DCR's home market, the US, is the largest fixed-income marketplace in the world and the core of DCR's business. From its debut in analysing the US utility industry, DCR has expanded into rating numerous US industry sectors, including corporates, structured, and project finance. DCR is striving to further expand its activities into sectors such as the asset-backed, financial services, industrial, project finance, real estate, telecommunications and utility sectors. DCR runs its North American activities from regional rating offices in Chicago and New York and it operates in Canada via a partnership with Canadian Bond Rating Service, a local rating agency.

Latin America

DCR has some 100 analysts focused on the region. DCR's Latin America analysts cover the region from offices in Chicago and New York. Local staff in Argentina, Brazil, Chile, Colombia, Costa Rica, Mexico, Peru, and Venezuela provide the grunt work by producing local ratings and research and providing a local perspective on cross-border issues.

Europe, Middle East, and Africa (EMEA)

DCR's EMEA relies on local-market offices and London-based staff. DCR is striving to expand its market presence and establish credibility in these markets. DCR rates some 20 EMEA countries (including the debt markets of Central and Eastern Europe). DCR's London office manages DCR's presence in the EMEA region, via local outposts in the Czech Republic, Hungary, Italy, Spain, Turkey, and South Africa.

Asia

DCR believes that the economic volatility in Asia underscores the value of having local-market expertise to effectively evaluate credits. DCR claims that it has more local-market offices in Asia than any other rating agency, and it believes this to be a strong selling point. DCR's Hong Kong office manages its coverage in the region, which includes local outposts in Bangladesh, India, Indonesia, Korea, Malaysia, Pakistan, and Singapore.

Revenues and growth

DCR notes in its 10-K filing that while precise statistics are not available on industry revenues (since DCR's competitors are privately owned or are part of larger corporations), it believes that its 1998 revenues equal approximately 17% of the revenues of its largest competitor. DCR's market penetration, however, varies significantly depending on market sector. For example, it has an inconsequential share of the municipal, mutual fund, and high-yield rating market. However, DCR's share of the rating business for insurance company claims-paying ability, structured financings, and certain segments of the corporate market are stronger. In its recent 10-K filing, DCR summarises its market presence in the US markets as follows:

- 85% of the top 100 life insurance companies
- 70% of the companies in the investor-owned electric utility industry
- 80% of the 50 largest telecom and cable TV companies
- 81% of the debt issued by the top 25 US banks
- 21 of the top 25 US finance companies
- 48% of Fortune 100 companies

In structured finance, DCR rates the majority of privately placed asset-backed securities transactions and rates 13 of the top 25 public issuers of asset-backed securities. Market share penetration for the commercial mortgage-backed securities market is approximately 30% and about 44% for the residential mortgage-backed securities market. DCR believes that significant growth opportunities exist due to the generally low market penetration described above, as well as the growing practice of obtaining multiple ratings, the increasing number of new financial instruments that require ratings, and the growth of international financial markets. Moreover, DCR has sought to stimulate growth by establishing joint ventures in certain North American, South American, European, African, and Asian countries.

DCR publications

As with the other rating agencies, DCR has its publications wing, diffusing promotional literature and various studies to interested parties. Here are some of its publications:

- *D&P bond lists* give all ratings for bonds with selected statistical data as well as previous rating modifications.
- *D&P preferred stock ratings* adopt the above formula but for preferred stock issues.
- *Fixed Income Summary* is a quarterly publication summarising qualitative and quantitative factors underlying the rating.
- *New Financing Report* focuses on shelf registrations and pending issues.
- *Short Term Ratings & Research Guide* is a monthly publication with all ratings (and a short profile of the issuer) of commercial paper, certificates of deposit, backed commercial paper, and insurance company solvencies.
- *Credit Decisions* is a weekly publication that focuses on recent rating modifications.

In most of DCR's publications the ratings awarded by Standard & Poor's and Moody's are also adjacently displayed, facilitating comparison and obviating the need to subscribe to those agencies' publications. More recently, many of these updates and reports are provided on the company's web site

DCR methodology

DCR likes to consider its modus operandi and thoroughness as its main selling point. This image for quality is somewhat echoed in the various market research reports that have been realised by specialised consultants monitoring the ratings business, such as Cantwell & Company or the Japan Centre of International Finance.

DCR's analytical methodology involves preparing a summarised analysis incorporating performance assessments, performance improvement overviews, the yield and cash position of the issuer, and the financial history and projections that its analysts prepare, based on both publicly available and confidential information. DCR understands that a rating is a particularly efficient instrument of communication between issuers and investors.

D&P developed the implemented rating concept in the early 1970s for loans and preferred stock. Institutional investors availed themselves of DCR's ratings as an item substituting the internal decision-making process. DCR was recognised as an official rating agency by a laboratory for ERISA guidelines; other US supervisory authorities also avail themselves of DCR's ratings.

Rating procedure

The rating procedure, typically requested by the issuer, begins with a provisional analysis by the analysts. The analysts rely first on official sources of information dealing with the rating, in particular, information about the development of the industry, and the end-of-year accounts of the company. The issuer is next typically required to provide information such as an obligatory assertion stipulating the purpose as to which the issue is committed, explanations concerning the use of moneys over the last twelve months, cash flow forecasts for the next six months, detailed information regarding all of the issuer's banks, particularly banks which provide backup lines. After DCR's analysts have analysed the data, a meeting is arranged with the management of the issuing company, to explore aspects such as marketing, production procedures, strategic planning, the financial plan, and other industry-specific matters. The discussion also enables the analysts to assess the quality of management.

Once the process has been completed, the analysts communicate their analyses and findings in a report which is then submitted to DCR's rating committee. The rating committee then meet with the management of the issuer, in order to clarify final outstanding matters before preparing the decision to assign a rating. Finally, the rating committee convenes in a meeting and the decision to attribute a rating is finalised and confirmed. The attendance of the issuer's management occurs annually; moreover, every quarter each issuer is contacted by telephone and queried as to the most recent developments, and the feedback is tallied against the rating committee's rating evaluation. Even if the rating procedure is not requested by the issuer, DCR strives to maintain regular contacts with the issuer.

Rating committee deliberations

DCR's rating committee may consist of up to ten analysts, and is therefore larger than most other rating agencies' committees. The rating, however, is decided only by those three analysts which visited the issuer and dealt with them in detail. While Standard & Poor's and Moody's ratings are usually anonymous, DCR's decisions are attributable to the analysts which dealt with the issuer and recommended the rating. DCR relies considerably on the knowledge and the experience of its analysts; however, confidential information, passed on in the context of a rating procedure by an issuer to the analysts, is only made available to the members of the rating committee.

DCR's rating fees vary according to the type of issue being rated: loans, commercial paper or certificates of deposit, classifications of insurance companies, or securitised loans. While some fees may, at minimum, total around USD 10 000, some issues can result in a fee as high as USD 160 000. The upper and lower bands of the fee are usually calculated based on a percentage of the issue's volume (e.g. 0.02%); in subsequent years the review fee can be lower.

DCR's rating scales and definitions

At the time of going to press, DCR's rating scales have been amalgamated into the Fitch-IBCA-Euronotation quilt. This raises the interesting question of how split ratings and heterogeneous rating scales will be incorporated into a coherent system.

Thomson Bank Watch

Background

Keefe Bank Watch, founded in the early 1960s, was a department of Keefe, Bruyette, and Woods until March 1989. The rating agency primarily targeted US banks. This coverage expanded to rating international banks in 1979 and US savings banks in 1984. Keefe Bank Watch operated to a large extent autonomously, it was spun off into its own legal entity, which was then sold off during a corporate reorganisation in March 1989. With a new parent company but unchanged management, the agency was renamed Thomson Bank Watch (TBW) to reflect its new parent's ownership, the Canadian-based media conglomerate Thomson Corporation Ltd.

With the Fimalac-Euronotation-IBCA-Fitch-Duff & Phelps collective resulting in IBCA's swapping the title of 'world's leading international bank rating company' in favour of 'world's leading international credit rating agency', TBW has by default inherited the title 'world's largest bank credit rating agency'. TBW rates around 1000 financial institutions in over 95 countries. TBW is a division of Thomson Financial, a diversified holding company selling products such as *American Banker* newspapers and newsletters, economic research, and financial analysis software to the international investor-creditor community. TBW is ultimately owned by the Canadian-based Thomson Corporation. Thomson Financial employs nearly 4500 people in 40 offices worldwide.

Marketing orientation

TBW has offices in New York, London, Hong Kong, Moscow, Kuala Lumpur, Cyprus, and Sydney, and representative offices in Beirut, Brazil, Chile, India, Israel, Japan, Malaysia, Turkey, and Venezuela. TBW has also made equity investments in Focus Rating Agency in Hungary, the Central European Rating Agency in Warsaw, Magister/Bank Watch in Buenos Aires, Equilibrium/Bank Watch in Lima, Bank Watch Ratings del Ecuador in Quito and Bank Watch Ratings de Colombia in Bogotá.

While the duopoly favours a broad public, TBW favours catering to a specialised segment of the investor-creditor community. For example, TBW's ratings typically do not appear in press headlines as frequently as the duopoly's, since they are mainly communicated to the agency's subscribers. S&P's and Moody's publication practices are geared to fostering and encouraging broad diffusion of their information and use of ratings to as wide a public as possible in the investor-creditor community, whereas, TBW's approach is more specifically oriented towards the needs and demands of its subscribers and clients.

After each issue or modification of a rating, TBW's customers are notified of the decision directly and provided with the reasons underlying the decision. TBW's strength as an agency is situated in its knowledge of the management, business philosophy, and character of the financial establishments which appear in its lists. Subscribers to the industry sector comparisons are assisted by a uniform rating scale kept as simple as possible. Each rating includes quantitative and qualitative aspects of industry sector evaluation, and further emphasis has focused on the estimated future yield capacity of the issuer.

A TBW rating therefore does not represent only 'an opinion over the probability of the payment of interest and repayment for a certain loan', but rather 'is a general judgement of the susceptibility of the bank to be subjected to unfavourable business developments, which can be linked to the bank's liquidity and asset quality'. The rating of issuers (instead of issues), however, is not without problem; for example, individual debt issues can be more favourable to judge than other issues due to their specific security structures. Likewise, loans of financial establishments from which the parent company extracts itself, end up having a higher risk than loans residing with the remaining group. TBW ratings therefore cannot be used in a decision-making process in the same way as ratings issued by Standard & Poor's or Moody's.

TBW's products are available in printed reports, in CD-ROM format updated 40 times per year, or via First Call's Bond Call Direct. As part of its cross-marketing data used in its rating activities, TBW also produces Bank Stat, a competitor product to Fitch-IBCA's BankScope, which is a database containing current and historical financial information (financial statements going back several years) on over 10 000 banks in 190 countries. Bank Stat includes software enabling the manipulation of current and historical financial data such as spreadsheets by bank credit analysts for purposes such as evaluating potential mergers or calculating bank guidelines as a percentage of equity.

TBW ratings process

Except in the case of the unsolicited CE (credit evaluation) ratings, TBW's rating procedure is typically initiated not by the issuer but by its subscribers. There are exceptions to this; for example, a foreign bank wanting to gain a foothold in the USA and therefore approaching TBW in order to be able to introduce itself to investors. TBW, however, cannot rely solely on the demand of issuers.

EAS research has noted that TBW's list of ratings reflects the information needs of its subscribers. About 90% of TBW's subscribers are based in the USA, only a small portion has been allotted to Asia and Australia; the bulk of foreign subscribers are European entities. Some 73% of the foreign customers are banks; in the USA some 30% of subscribers are banks, 25% are other financial establishments and national authorities, and 45% are industrial enterprises.

TBW supplies ratings for approximately 300 banks and 50 savings banks in the USA, beyond that for 110 banks, which have their seat outside of the USA. These relatively low numbers should be considered in light of the fact that the major rating agencies assign ratings not only for issuers but also their subsidiaries as well as specific issues.

Each TBW rating is decided by a rating committee composed of in-house analysts. Most analysts have already been involved with each bank in the ratings evaluation process, and may come from other rating agencies, or the credit departments of banks or securities houses. The rating procedure for larger banks typically starts off with a statistical analysis, which creates a basis for discussions between TBW analysts and the issuer's management. The discussions typically focus on developments which can impact adversely the issuer's future yield capacity.

The ratings meeting's raison d'être, within the scope of the ratings procedure, is to obtain quantitative and qualitative information which is not normally available in publicly diffused media. The quantitative analyses focus on traditional areas such as asset quality, availability of capital resources, balance sheet structure, profitability, cash flow, and liquidity ratio. These in turn are compared with peer group averages in TBW's database and trend deviations are noted. The qualitative analysis focuses on issues such as the management structure and quality, the suitability and effectiveness of management control structures, organisational flexibility, and risk diversification.

TBW rating characteristics and methodology

TBW employs a rating methodology which, as with the other rating agencies, has developed over time. TBW provides several types of rating:

- TBW issuer ratings are based on the overall health and financial condition of the rated company on a consolidated basis.
- TBW debt ratings are applied to specific short- and long-term debt issues.
- TBW sovereign risk ratings represent assessments of the long-term business environments in developed and emerging countries.

Both issuer and debt ratings are further subdivided into ratings for global comparison and ratings for local currency operations.

TBW issuer ratings

TBW has traditionally focused on the rating of financial institutions. TBW issuer ratings are based on the overall health and financial condition of the rated company on a consolidated basis. They give an indication of the likelihood of future problems arising and the ability of the company to address such adversity. Issuer ratings combine pure credit risk (timely payment in full of principal and interest) with performance risk. Issuer ratings also incorporate the relative strengths and weaknesses of each of the major operating units within the consolidated group, as well as the company's legal structure, in order to arrive at a final decision.

TBW issuer ratings are based on a nine-point scale from A, A/B, B through E. For institutions domiciled in emerging markets there is a separate intra-country issuer rating. These ratings do not reflect the credit rating of the sovereign country and therefore they are not directly comparable from country to country when considering the risk associated with foreign currency operations. The scale is IC-A, IC-A/B through IC-E. One issuer rating is assigned to each company. The primary underlying assumption for this approach is that when analysing the creditworthiness of a bank or securities firm—regulated entities which rely on the confidence of the marketplace for their funding—the focus must be on the group as a whole rather than simply on any one segment of the organisation.

TBW's experience has led it to conclude that the parent company will support its affiliates as long as the parent company itself has the capacity to offer such assistance. Countless times over the years, parent companies have aided their affiliates, despite there being no legal obligation which required such action. This rating approach is applied only when there is a thorough understanding of the management of the institution as well as the regulatory framework within which the entity operates.

TBW debt ratings

TBW's publicly diffused documentation explains that debt ratings are applied to specific short- and long-term debt issues. Debt ratings represent pure credit risk and are defined as an assessment of the likelihood of an untimely or incomplete payment of principal or interest.

- *Short-term debt ratings* are based on a scale from TBW-1 (with 1 being the highest) through TBW-4 (non-investment grade or speculative). They can be restricted to local currency (LC) debt.

- *Long-term debt ratings* are based on a scale from AAA, AA, A through D (default). They can be restricted to local currency (LC) debt.

TBW sovereign risk ratings

TBW sovereign risk ratings represent assessments of the long-term business environments in developed and emerging countries. TBW's focus on the financial sector evaluates how the various economic and political forces in the country affect the banking environment. Sovereign risk ratings are sovereign ceilings; they do not apply to sovereign paper. Ratings are based on a scale from AAA, AA, A through D.

TBW rating methodology

These rating scales and definitions reflect official pronouncements of TBW at the time of writing. All TBW ratings are arrived at by a committee process. The foundation for the ratings is an analysis of quantitative and qualitative factors which may impact the company's ability to meet or service its obligations. TBW ratings are prospective. A prospective analysis is accomplished by building a thorough knowledge of the market in which the company operates and evaluating the skills of the institution's management. This insight is gained by an ongoing dialogue with management and regular due diligence visits.

Quantitative factors

The starting point of a rating decision is a detailed review of key statistical measures of financial performance and stability. TBW analysts look at the most recent financials, and they perform comprehensive trend and peer group analysis. These four items are among the first to be reviewed:

- Asset quality
- Capital adequacy
- Profitability
- Liquidity

Several ratios in each of the respective areas are considered with the numbers adjusted to exclude any non-recurring items. The goal is to determine core recurring measures of performance.

Qualitative factors

Following an exhaustive statistical review, the next step incorporates all relevant qualitative factors deemed critical to the rating process. Qualitative considerations become increasingly important in times of rapid change and in difficult operating environments. Also, because TBW ratings are meant to be prospective and predictive of what the future might hold, various non-numerical factors must be considered:

● Environment
● Management quality
● Business franchise
● Hidden strengths and reserves
● Hidden weaknesses and overvalued assets

To understand all these issues and incorporate them into the rating process, TBW analysts spend a great deal of time directly with bank management. Their due diligence process includes frequent visits and phone conversations.

TBW rating scales and definitions

TBW sovereign risk ratings

TBW sovereign risk ratings represent long-term assessments of the business environments in over 94 countries (Table 2.8). Their focus is on the financial sector and how the various economic and political forces in the country affect the sector. TBW arrives at its assessments after carefully weighing several factors, including recent economic performance; the quality of economic and financial management; the depth and sophistication of markets; the stability of economic policy; the stability and effectiveness of the political

Table 2.8   TBW sovereign risk ratings

AAA	Most creditworthy
AA	Highly creditworthy
A	Creditworthy
BBB	Less creditworthy but investment grade
BB	Low-risk speculative
B	High-risk speculative
CCC	High default risk, good recovery potential
CC	High default risk, moderate recovery potential
C	Imminent default, low recovery potential
D	Imminent default, no recovery potential

Source: TBW, 2000

system; and long-term trends and expected future performance. Particular emphasis is given to the quality of economic management, the stability of policy, and the depth and sophistication of local markets, all of which are fundamental to the operation of a national financial system. TBW assigns these ratings in two steps:

1. Countries are graded according to their broad level of creditworthiness: AAA, AA through D.
2. Countries are ranked within these levels on a comparative basis, with + indicating the highest and – the lowest within each level (except for CCC, CC, C, and D).

TBW global issuer and intra-country issuer ratings

TBW's global issuer ratings are comparable worldwide and combine credit risk with performance risk over an intermediate time horizon (Table 2.9). These ratings indicate the likelihood of receiving timely payment of principal and interest, and an opinion on the company's vulnerability to negative events that might alter the market's perception of the company and affect the marketability of its securities.

For institutions domiciled in emerging markets, a separate intra-country issuer rating is issued. The approach is the same as for global issuer ratings, except intra-country issuer ratings do not reflect the credit rating of the sovereign country and therefore they are not directly comparable from country to country. However, a company rated IC-B in one country is thought to be of the same relative fundamental quality as a company rated IC-B in another. Intra-country issuer ratings incorporate systemic risks within certain banking systems that may preclude any bank within the system from achieving the top rating.

TBW short-term debt ratings

TBW assigns short-term debt ratings to specific debt instruments with original maturities of one year or less (Table 2.10). These ratings basically incorporate the same factors used for TBW's issuer ratings. There is one major difference, however: the short-term debt ratings put a greater emphasis on the likelihood of government support. TBW ratings represent an assessment of the likelihood of an untimely payment of principal and interest. Factors that may influence this assessment are the overall financial health of the issuer, and the probability that the government will come to the aid of a troubled institution in order to stave off a default or failure. The probability of government intervention stems from four primary factors:

Table 2.9   TBW global issuer and intra-country issuer ratings

A IC-A	Company possesses an exceptionally strong balance sheet and earnings record, translating into an excellent reputation and very good access to its natural money markets. If weakness or vulnerability exists in any aspect of the company's business, it is entirely mitigated by the strengths of the organisation
A/B IC-A/B	Company is financially very solid with a favourable track record and no readily apparent weakness. Its overall risk profile, while low, is not quite as favourable as for companies in the highest rating category
B IC-B	Company is strong with a solid financial record and is well received by its natural money markets. Some minor weaknesses may exist, but any deviation from the company's historical performance levels should be limited and short-lived. The likelihood of significant problems is small, yet slightly greater than for a higher-rated company
B/C IC-B/C	Company is clearly viewed as a good credit. While some shortcomings are apparent, they are not serious and/or are quite manageable in the short term
C IC-C	Company is inherently a sound credit with no serious deficiencies, but financials reveal at least one fundamental area of concern that prevents a higher rating. Company may recently have experienced a period of difficulty, but those pressures should not be long-term in nature. The company's ability to absorb a surprise, however, is less than that for organisations with better operating records
C/D IC-C/D	While still considered an acceptable credit, the company has some meaningful deficiencies. Its ability to deal with further deterioration is less than that of better-rated companies
D IC-D	Company financials suggest obvious weaknesses, most likely created by asset quality considerations and/or a poorly structured balance sheet. A meaningful level of uncertainty and vulnerability exists going forward. The ability to address further unexpected problems must be questioned
D/E IC-D/E	Company has areas of major weakness that may include funding and/or liquidity difficulties. A high degree of uncertainty exists about the company's ability to absorb incremental problems
E IC-E	Very serious problems exist for the company, creating doubt about its continued viability without some form of outside assistance, regulatory or otherwise

Source: TBW, 2000

- Government guarantees
- Government or quasi-government ownership or control
- The degree of concentration in the banking system
- Government precedent

As with issuer ratings, short-term debt ratings incorporate both qualitative and quantitative factors. The ratings are not meant to be pass/fail but rather to provide a relative indication of creditworthiness. Therefore, obligations rated TBW-3 are still considered investment grade. These short-term debt ratings can also be restricted to local currency instruments; then the ratings will be preceded by the designation LC for 'local currency'.

Table 2.10   TBW short-term debt ratings

TBW-1 LC-1	The highest category; indicates a very high likelihood that principal and interest will be paid on a timely basis
TBW-2 LC-2	The second highest category; while the degree of safety regarding timely repayment of principal and interest is strong, the relative degree of safety is not as high as for issues rated TBW-1
TBW-3 LC-3	The lowest investment-grade category; indicates that while the obligation is more susceptible to adverse developments (both internal and external) than those with higher ratings, the capacity to service principal and interest in a timely fashion is considered adequate
TBW-4 LC-4	The lowest rating category; this rating is regarded as non-investment grade and therefore speculative

Source: TBW, 2000

TBW long-term debt ratings

TBW's long-term debt ratings also weigh heavily government ownership and support. The quality of the company's management and franchise is of even greater importance in long-term debt rating decisions (Table 2.11). The ratings look out over a cycle and are not adjusted frequently for short-term performance aberrations. Long-term debt ratings can be restricted to local currency debt and given the designation LC. In addition, they may include a + or – to indicate where within the category the issue is placed. TBW issuer and debt ratings are shown in Table 2.12.

TBW unsolicited rating (credit evaluation) score definitions

TBW's interpretation of the unsolicited ratings theme materialises in its credit evaluation (CE) scores (Table 2.13). CE scores are scores on banks that are not 'fully rated'. In other words, the agency is not paid a rating fee by the issuer and the CE ratings obviously do not include the same research that TBW performs on the banks to which it assigns global issuer or intra-country issuer ratings (and are paid a rating fee). In other words, the research is based on publicly available information and does not benefit from confidential meetings and information provided by the issuer's management. It is not clear what the selection criteria are in TBW selecting an entity to be summarily rated.

Banks which are assigned a CE score are rated by analysing publicly available information (which leads one to wonder where the added value lies). CEs analyse the usual criteria in other ratings (capital adequacy, profitability, asset quality, earnings, liquidity, sovereign risk, and banking system issues) but without the benefit of internal information such as detailed asset

Table 2.11 TBW long-term debt ratings

Investment grade

AAA LC-AAA	Indicates that the ability to repay principal and interest on a timely basis is extremely high
AA LC-AA	Indicates a very strong ability to repay principal and interest on a timely basis, with limited incremental risk compared to issues rated in the highest category
A LC-A	Indicates the ability to repay principal and interest is strong. Issues rated A could be more vulnerable to adverse developments (both internal and external) than obligations with higher ratings
BBB LC-BBB	The lowest investment-grade category; indicates an acceptable capacity to repay principal and interest. BBB issues are more vulnerable to adverse developments (both internal and external) than obligations with higher ratings

Non-investment grade[a]

BB LC-BB	While not investment grade, the BB rating suggests that the likelihood of default is considerably less than for lower-rated issues. However, there are significant uncertainties that could affect the ability to adequately service debt obligations
B LC-B	Issues rated B show a higher degree of uncertainty and therefore greater likelihood of default than higher-rated issues. Adverse developments could negatively affect the payment of interest and principal on a timely basis
CCC LC-CCC	Issues rated CCC clearly have a high likelihood of default, with little capacity to address further adverse changes in financial circumstances
CC LC-CC	CC is applied to issues that are subordinate to other obligations rated CCC and are afforded less protection in the event of bankruptcy or reorganisation
D LC-D	Default

[a]May be speculative in the likelihood of timely repayment of principal and interest.
Source: TBW, 2000

portfolio breakdowns and information on provisioning for substandard loans detailed in management meetings, for example.

TBW states that its evaluation of the bank incorporates qualitative factors such as effectiveness of regulatory supervision, disclosure in financial statements and annual reports, diversification, ownership, management experience and expertise. This implementation of unsolicited ratings, as with the other agencies who provide unsolicited ratings such as Moody's, seems to be a heavy-handed marketing technique designed to expand market share based on the quasi-monopolistic position occupied by the rating agencies. The implications of this will be treated in a later chapter.

Table 2.12   TBW issuer and debt ratings

Issuer	Debt
Characteristics	**Characteristics**
One per company	Assigned to specific obligations
Based on the consolidated financial institution	Evaluates pure credit risk
Combination of credit and performance risk	Indicates likelihood of timely repayment of principal and interest
Global issuer ratings	**Short-term debt ratings**
(for international comparisons)	(maturities up to one year)
A	TBW-1
A/B	TBW-2
B	TBW-3
B/C	TBW-4
C	
C/D	
D	
D/E	
E	
	Short-term local currency debt ratings
	LC-1
	LC-2
	LC-3
	LC-4
Intra-country issuer ratings	**Long-term debt ratings**
(does not reflect sovereign risk)	(for maturities beyond one year)
IC-A	AAA
IC-A/B	AA
IC-B	A
IC-B/C	BBB
IC-C	BB
IC-C/D	B
IC-D	CCC
IC-D/E	CC
IC-E	D
	Long-term local currency debt ratings
	LC-AAA
	LC-AA
	LC-A
	LC-BBB
	LC-BB
	LC-B
	LC-CCC
	LC-CC
	LC-D
	Ratings may include a + or a – to indicate where within the category the issue is placed

Source: TBW, 2000

Table 2.13   TBW credit evaluation (CE) scores

1.0	Company possesses a very strong balance sheet and earnings record. If weakness or vulnerability exists in any part of the company's business, it is entirely mitigated by the financial strengths of the organisation
1.5	Company is financially very solid with a favourable track record and no readily apparent weakness. Its overall risk profile, while low, is not quite as favourable as for companies in the highest category
2.0	A strong company with a solid financial record. Some minor weaknesses many exist, but any deviation from the company's historical performance levels should be both limited and short-lived. The likelihood of a problem developing is small
2.5	Company is clearly viewed as a good credit. While some shortcomings are apparent, they are not serious and/or are manageable in the short term
3.0	Company is inherently a sound credit with no serious deficiencies, but financials reveal at least one fundamental area of concern. Company may have recently experienced a period of difficulty, but those pressures should not be long-term in nature. The company's ability to absorb a surprise, however, is less than that for organisations with better operating results
3.5	While still considered an acceptable credit, the company has some meaningful deficiencies. Its ability to deal with further deterioration is less than that of companies with higher evaluations
4.0	Company's financials suggest obvious weaknesses, most likely created by asset quality considerations and/or a poorly structured balance sheet. A meaningful level of future uncertainty and vulnerability exists
4.5	Company has areas of major weakness that may include funding and/or liquidity difficulties. A high degree of uncertainty exists about the company's ability to absorb incremental problems
5.0	Very serious problems exist for the company, creating doubt about its continued viability, without some form of outside assistance

Source: TBW, 2000

Capital Intelligence Ltd

Background

Capital Intelligence Ltd (CI) is a rating agency based in Limassol, Cyprus. CI is unique in that it covers a specific information need required by bank creditors which to a large extent has been bypassed by the traditional larger rating agencies. CI is not a domestic agency in an emerging market but a full-blown agency with an international remit. CI presently rates 400 entities in emerging markets such as the Middle East, North Africa, the Far East, South-east Asia, Central/Eastern Europe, the Baltic states and South Africa.

CI's founder, Robert Pouliot, a journalist active in the Middle East, identified an unsatisfied demand from banks to have reliable industry sector evaluations of banks in the Middle East and in 1982 he started up an information services company known as Presscan. Early in 1985 the company restructured its capital with the entry of new investors. Its name changed to Capital Intelligence.

CI's Gulf/Mediterranean coverage has increased from 60 banks to encompass presently nearly 180 banks in fifteen countries—Bahrain, Cyprus, Egypt, Greece, Jordan, Kuwait, Lebanon, Morocco, Oman, Qatar, Saudi Arabia, Tunisia, Turkey, United Arab Emirates and Yemen—by far the most comprehensive coverage of any rating agency.

In 1986 CI diversified by providing a new service to cover the emerging markets of the Asia-Pacific region. This regional service has also grown significantly and today it comprises nearly 180 banks in fourteen countries: China, Hong Kong, India, Indonesia, Macau, Malaysia, Pakistan, Philippines, Singapore, South Korea, Sri Lanka, Taiwan, Thailand and Vietnam. In 1997/98 CI expanded into rating banks in Central and Eastern Europe (Czech Republic, Hungary, Poland, Romania, Slovakia and Slovenia), the Baltic states (Estonia, Latvia and Lithuania), and South Africa. The total number of banks covered in these markets is over 60.

The major rating agencies, whilst striving to develop their international activities, essentially remain focused on ratings for debtors in the USA, Europe, Japan, and other mature markets, and typically bypass banks located in markets such as Egypt, Bahrain, Jordan, Kuwait, Oman, Saudi Arabia, or in China, Hong Kong, Indonesia, Malaysia, Singapore, Taiwan, Thailand and other states in Asia.

CI operates principally from its head office in Cyprus but it also maintains a branch office in Hong Kong and a representiative office in India, which supply rating services for customers such as banks who need information on their counterparts in these emerging markets. CI's analysts are typically international and multilingual, and they do not conform to the typical homogeneous profile of analysts found in the US and Eurpoean banks or rating agencies. The agency is privately held, and investors include current and former analysts as well as other investors. There are no financial institutions among the shareholders, hence the analysts are theoretically exempt from conflicts of interest with shareholders.

Marketing orientation and revenue structure

A large part of CI's income is derived from sales of publications and research. CI's subscriber base provides the core of the agency's income base, which is primarily comprised of banks requiring information on trading counterparties in emerging markets. EAS, for example, cites among CI's customers in Germany BHF Bank, Dresdner Bank, Hypo Bank, NordLB and WestLB.

CI's publications include country banking reports as well as individual bank reports. The individual bank reports include positive and negative factors on each rated bank along with detailed reasons underlying the rating. Additionally, CI offers comparative analysis in each market covered, enabling the banks to be compared against a matrix incorporating some 450 financial ratios. CI's country banking reports give a concise overview of a country's banking system. They analyse the economic, political and operating environment of the country's banking system. CI also publishes bank reports, rating reports, rating assessments, spreadsheets and ratios, bank credit ratings and corporate memoranda.

CI has yet to achieve official recognition from market supervisory authorities, such as the SEC's NRSRO status, although one might argue that this objective is peripheral to CI given its area of geographic activity. Indeed, EAS research indicates that CI admits it has not gone out of its way to seek such official status because it is not necessarily relevant to the type of business it is conducting nor an impediment to the development of its subscriber base. CI in effect is carried by the acceptance conferred upon it by its customers, the banks, whose subscribership is proof of a satisfied customer base. Moreover, CI's regional specialisation effectively insulates it from the competition offered by the major rating agencies, who are more interested in pursuing different markets and revenue streams.

CI methodology

CI's ratings represent a 'total classification' of the issuer, as opposed to the Moody's or Standard & Poor's approach of rating individual issues. CI's ratings process regularly includes a discussion between analysts of the agency and management of the bank being rated. As part of the annual review procedure, CI's analysts do considerable amounts of travelling in order to conduct face-to-face meetings with representatives of the banks, central banks, ministries of finance, as well as auditors and other market participants in the countries covered.

CI's rating decision does not rely solely on accounting data and financial statements but also on information from other sources which may be supplied by the bank being analysed (e.g. end-of-year procedures) insofar as they are considered reliable. The financial situation of each bank is monitored at regular intervals throughout the year. Since CI is acting only in the interests of the parties buying CI's research, the banks being rated may have varying levels of cooperation in the process.

Given the focus of CI's analysis in emerging markets, it is important to bear in mind that, by definition, the markets, and thus often the banks themselves, are still developing. Consequently, norms and standards of analysis applied to developed financial markets may not be so readily applicable, perhaps not at all applicable, in some of these emerging markets. The aim therefore has to be to assimilate as far as possible the analysis of a bank into more commonly understood parameters.

Bearing this in mind, the financial and non-financial evaluation of a bank's performance should address a number of key factors. These would include in the main, but should not be limited to, an evaluation of a bank's performance (profitability) and overall risk (capital adequacy). The different aspects of risk can be broken down into several subcategories: credit and other asset quality, liquidity (including interest rate and currency exposure), capital adequacy, profitability, fraud, and operating risks. These topics should be integrated into the overall analysis when evaluating a bank credit by using the conventional CAMEL model (capital, asset quality, management quality, earnings quality, and liquidity).

The evaluation of a bank's overall performance and an assessment of its risk profile should be achieved through a combination of quantitative and qualitative analysis, with the qualitative analysis given significant emphasis. However, prior to accomplishing this, it is essential to establish a common platform for the analysis of a particular banking market. This necessitates undertaking an overall evaluation not only of sovereign risk but also of the regulatory and supervisory regime, as well as the accounting and auditing practices of the relevant market. In essence, these facets of analysis are all of an external nature, being traits of a country's banking system, but they can have a significant impact on the bank.

CI's remit is characterised by the difficulty inherent in being able to apply a consistent yardstick enabling comparison of the creditworthiness of banks across a spectrum of widely varying banking systems and differing economic as well as legal conditions. CI's rating system therefore incorporates into the analysis both financial and non-financial aspects of the industry sector evaluation. The quantitative analysis focuses on particular financial ratios for evaluating banks. CI uses 45 different ratios for each year, although it is recognised that not all are appropriate for particular institutions or countries.

The qualitative factors considered include the impact of market conditions and the quality of regulation and supervision. The cumulative experience of the institution in its present structure is reviewed, as well as the quality and credibility of management together with an assessment of the reliability of the financial and any other information received. Important criteria in CI's qualitative analysis include the extent to which one can rely on government support of the bank, the support by the owners or the parent company, the effectiveness of state supervisory structures, the quality and reliability of management, and the bank's track record in international banking transactions. CI's questionnaire can be influenced by special factors, which must receive individual attention, likewise the weightings of the responses can vary to reflect this.

In some cases the information supplied by the analysed bank may be insufficient. For example, ambiguous responses can result in individual aspects being subjected to estimations or approximations. This may result in certain categories being subject to a blocked judgement; then a resolution is made to determine 'full rating' as soon as possible and in the meantime a qualified rating is assigned.

A weak point of CI's rating system, not surprisingly, is the insufficient sector risk analysis; this is to be expected given the heterogeneous nature of the markets in question as well as the lack of statistical data going back over time. Besides primary sources, CI also uses secondary sources and it issues a disclaimer to this effect. Banks subscribing to CI's reports are of course free to supplement their particular information requirements with information from other sources.

Rating scales and definitions

CI's counterparty ratings summarise the probability that a bank will require external assistance to overcome adversities. These ratings are presented in long-term and short-term ratings tables.

CI's foreign currency ratings assess the likelihood that obligations will be repaid in a timely manner (Tables 2.14 and 2.15). CI foreign currency ratings take into account all sovereign risk factors and are subject to the sovereign ceiling of the host country. CI assigns sovereign ratings to every country where an institution is rated. Foreign currency ratings assigned to an institution will not normally breach the sovereign rating assigned to the country by CI. However, it may be possible to achieve a rating above the sovereign ceiling through financial or legal structuring or through an institution possessing a significant transnational asset profile. CI's long- and short-term foreign currency ratings take into account the full impact of transfer risk and the risk that the host country may be unable or unwilling to service its foreign currency obligations.

CI's domestic strength ratings indicate CI's opinion of a bank's inherent financial strength and risk profile (Table 2.16). CI's domestic strength ratings exclude, as far as possible, the impact of transfer risk, i.e. the risk that the host country may be unable or unwilling to service its foreign currency obligations. Domestic strength ratings also exclude support factors. As transfer risk is excluded, the domestic strength ratings are based on local currency.

Table 2.14 CI foreign currency ratings: long-term

Investment grade

AAA The highest credit quality. Exceptional capacity for timely fulfilment of financial obligations and most unlikely to be affected by any foreseeable adversity. Extremely strong financial condition and very positive non-financial factors. Very strong and stable operating environment

AA Very high credit quality. Very strong capacity for timely fulfilment of financial obligations. Unlikely to have repayment problems over the long term and unquestioned over the short and medium terms. Strong operating environment. Adverse changes in business, economic, and financial conditions unlikely to affect the institution significantly

A High credit quality. Strong capacity for timely fulfilment of financial obligations. Possesses many favourable credit characteristics but may be vulnerable slightly to adverse changes in business, economic, and financial conditions. However, operating environment is solid

BBB Good credit quality. Satisfactory capacity for timely fulfilment of financial obligations. Acceptable credit characteristics but some vulnerability to adverse changes in business, economic, and financial conditions. Medium-grade credit characteristics and the lowest investment-grade category

Speculative grade

BB Speculative credit quality. Capacity for timely fulfilment of financial obligations vulnerable to adverse changes in internal or external circumstances. Financial and/or non-financial factors do not provide significant safeguard and the possibility of investment risk may develop. Unstable operating environment

B Significant credit risk. Capacity for timely fulfilment of financial obligations very vulnerable to adverse changes in internal or external circumstances. Financial and/or non-financial factors provide weak protection; high probability for investment risk exists. Weak operating environment

C Substantial credit risk is apparent and the likelihood of default is high. Considerable uncertainty as to timely repayment of financial obligations. Credit is of poor standing with financial and/or non-financial factors providing little protection

D Obligations are currently in default

Source: Capital Intelligence, 1999

Domestic strength ratings do not assess the likelihood that specific obligations will be repaid in a timely manner. The domestic strength ratings summarise the probability that an institution will require external assistance from third parties to overcome adversities. Domestic strength ratings do not measure the likelihood that the bank will receive such external support, nor do they address sovereign risk factors which may affect an institution's capacity to honour its financial obligations, be they domestic or foreign currency.

In assigning a domestic strength rating, CI considers both internal and external factors. Internal factors include financial fundamentals, business operations, and market position. Although specific transfer risk is excluded, CI's domestic strength ratings take into account the bank's operating

Table 2.15   CI foreign currency ratings: short-term (investment grade)

A1	Superior credit quality. Highest capacity for timely repayment of short-term financial obligations that is extremely unlikely to be affected by unexpected adversities. Institutions with a particularly strong credit profile have a + affixed to the rating
A2	Very strong capacity for timely repayment but may be affected slightly by unexpected adversities
A3	Strong capacity for timely repayment that may be affected by unexpected adversities. Speculative grade
B	Adequate capacity for timely repayment that could be seriously affected by unexpected adversities
C	Inadequate capacity for timely repayment if unexpected adversities are encountered in the short term
D	May be in an untenable position and is likely to default if it does not receive immediate external support

Source: Capital Intelligence, 1999

Table 2.16   CI domestic strength ratings (investment grade)

AAA	Financially in extremely strong condition with positive financial trends; significant strengths in other non-financial areas. Operating environment highly attractive and stable
AA	Financially in very strong condition and significant strengths in other non-financial areas. Operating environment likely to be very attractive and stable
A	Strong financial fundamentals and very favourable non-financial considerations. Operating environment may be unstable but institution's market position and/or financial strength more than compensate
BBB	Basically sound overall; slight weaknesses in financial or other factors could be remedied fairly easily. May be limited by unstable operating environment
BB	One or two significant weaknesses in the bank's financial make-up could cause problems. May be characterised by a limited franchise; other factors may not be sufficient to avoid a need for some degree of temporary external support in cases of extraordinary adversity. Unstable operating environment likely
B	Fundamental weaknesses are present in the bank's financial condition or trends, and other factors are unlikely to provide strong protection from unexpected adversities; in such an event, the need for external support is likely. Bank may be constrained by weak market position and/or volatile operating environment
C	In a very weak financial condition, either with immediate problems or with limited capacity to withstand adversities. May be operating in a highly volatile operating environment
D	Extremely weak financial condition and may be in an untenable position

Source: Capital Intelligence, 1999

environment, including the economy, the structure, strength and stability of the financial system, the legal system, and the quality of banking regulation and supervision. CI maintains global consistency in its domestic strength rating methodology.

CI support ratings assess the likelihood that a bank would receive support in case of difficulties (Table 2.17). Although subjective, they are based on an assessment of a bank's ownership, market position, and importance within the sector and economy, as well as the country's regulatory and supervisory framework. Support ratings do not address the financial soundness of an institution. CI's support ratings also do not specifically address transfer risk as a result of economic and/or political events. A variety of qualifiers may also be used with CI ratings (Table 2.18).

Table 2.17 CI support ratings (investment grade)

1	Government-owned or clear legal guarantee on part of the state, or of such importance to the country that the state would provide support in case of need. The state must clearly be able, and willing, to provide support
2	Government support extremely likely despite absence of written guarantee. There may be some uncertainty regarding the state's willingness or ability to provide support. A private bank which has extremely strong ownership
3	Owners of very good reputation and resources, and which can provide clear support
4	Support is likely but not certain
5	No clear support and/or support cannot be relied upon

Source: Capital Intelligence, 1999

Table 2.18 CI qualifiers (investment grade)

Plus (+) and minus (–)	Foreign currency long-term, and domestic strength ratings from AAA to C may be modified by the addition of a plus or minus sign to indicate that the strength of a particular institution is, respectively, slightly greater or less than that of similarly rated peers
Outlook	Expectations of improvement, no change, or deterioration in a rating over the 12 months following its publication are denoted by letters added to each set of ratings: P (positive), S (stable), N (negative)
Qualified	In cases where data and/or cooperation are such that it is not possible to formulate ratings to CI's high standards of robustness and reliability, the letter Q is appended to the ratings

Source: Capital Intelligence, 1999

The rating process

CI's bank analysts make written and oral presentations to CI's rating committee, which meets weekly or more frequently if required. While analysts recommend specific ratings for banks in their portfolios, it is the committee's decision which determines the credit ratings assigned to each institution. Ratings are based on the collective judgement of CI's analysts, combined with quantitative and qualitative factors. However, the process is ultimately one of subjective judgements.

Quantitative analysis focuses on the typical matrix of financial ratios used by bank analysts worldwide. The use of computer spreadsheets enables the calculation of some 150 ratios going back over the last four years of financial statements. It is recognised, however, that this number crunching approach has a limited relevancy given the particular accounting standards and quality of financial statements being provided in the various countries where CI operates. The ratios typically cover asset quality, capital adequacy, liquidity, and profitability; in other words, they are the standard assortment found in any training textbook. These ratios are further subjected to peer group and trend analysis, again based on the quality of the financial statements available in the markets where CI operates.

Qualitative factors include the impact of market conditions and the quality of regulation and supervision. The cumulative experience of the institution in its present structure is reviewed, as well as the quality and credibility of management together with an assessment of the reliability of the financial data and any other information received. While this is relatively qualitative, it perhaps best represents CI's 'value added' input to the process given the agency's experience in these markets.

CI reports and publications

Reports are distributed by CI in hardcopy form as well as on CD-ROM subscription to BankScope and via CI's web page, Capital Web (http://www.ciratings.com). Subscription to the service can be tailored to suit individual needs from buying a single report, a mixed choice of reports, or country packages, to a regional or full global subscription. Delivery is also through a variety of methods to suit the requirements of different organisations.

Bank reports

Bank reports are annual qualitative and quantitative studies of individual financial institutions based in the emerging markets of North Africa, the Gulf/Mediterranean, Asia, Southeast Asia, Central and Eastern Europe, the Baltic States, and South Africa. They include an analysis of each rated bank's audited financial accounts supplemented by information gained through meetings between CI's analysts and the banks' senior management. CI also meets with other market participants and observers such as central banking authorities and external auditors. In addition to a concise executive summary, each

CI report includes sections covering ownership, management, institutional history, and market background as well as specific operational and business development strategies.

Bank reports also include CI's long- and short-term foreign currency ratings, domestic strength rating, and support rating in addition to spreadsheets and ratios covering the most recent four years of operating results for each rated bank. CI rating reports are either edited versions of the bank reports or shorter credit analysis reports. Rating reports include an institution's ratings, an appraisal of its positive and negative factors, a summary financial analysis and an overall assessment of the institution's financial performance and condition, as well as its prospects. They include spreadsheets and ratios covering the most recent four years of operating results.

Rating assessments

Rating assessments are CI's implementation of the unsolicited ratings theme. They are similar to rating reports but rely on publicly available information not internal contacts and confidential information provided by the issuer. Whilst CI endeavours to apply the same analytical methodologies as in its rating reports, rating assessments do not benefit from the same extent of data or management involvement. Although CI uses the same rating scale as in its bank reports, the symbols for rating assessments are written in lower case characters, e.g. bb+/a–2. They include spreadsheets and ratios covering the most recent four years of operating results, based on publicly available information.

Country banking reports

Country banking reports are annual evaluations of each of the emerging banking markets covered by CI. They look at banking, economic, political, and operational factors. Country banking reports also include discussions on the prevailing supervisory and regulatory regimes as well as accounting standards practised in each national market. They highlight changes in any one of these market aspects, and they assess the likely impact on the financial performance and condition of each national banking sector.

Spreadsheets and ratios

Spreadsheets and ratios contain the most recent four years of audited financial data as presented in published balance sheets and income statements for each rated bank in CI's standardised. They include key performance ratios which focus on profitability, asset quality, capital adequacy, and liquidity. A peer group comparison table is provided for each country.

Bank credit ratings

Bank credit ratings are issued monthly by country; they list the latest long-
and short-term credit ratings for each financial institution monitored by CI. A
ratings history for each bank is also provided.

Bonds and debt instruments

Capital Intelligence recently began rating bonds and debt instruments. Its
long-term bond and debt ratings (Table 2.19) are applicable to specific

Table 2.19   CI definitions for long-term bond and debt rating

Investment grade

AAA	Bonds and obligations that are rated AAA are considered to be of the highest quality. They carry the smallest degree of investment risk. Interest payments are protected by a significant and exceptionally stable margin, and the principal is extremely secure. There are unlikely to be significant changes in the various protective elements. In any case, such possible changes are very likely to weaken the fundamentally strong position of such issues
AA	Bonds and obligation that are rated AA are considered to be of very hight quality by all criteria. These are high-grade bonds, but are rated lower than AAA bonds as the elements of protection may not be as large and there may be slightly greater fluctuation within the margin of protection. The overall risk is slightly greater than for AAA bonds
A	Bonds and obligations that are rated A exhibit many positive investment characteristics and are classed as upper to medium grade investment quality. Various factors giving protection to principal and interest are considered very sound, but certain components may be evident which indicate future potential impairment
BBB	Bonds and obligations that are rated BBB are regarded as medium grade. These securities are neither highly nor lowly protected. Both interest payments and principal security are currently adequate but certain protective elements may be missing or may be slightly more unreliable over the longer term. Bonds rated BBB do not display very strong investment characteristics. The bonds form the lowest level of investment grade and some may possibly possess speculative characteristics

Speculative grade

BB	Bonds and obligations that are rated BB are below investment grade and possess speculative characteristics. There is some uncertainty in the longer-term future of these bonds. The protection of interest and principal is likely to be very moderate, and thereby not well cushioned during both favourable and unfavourable conditions in the future
B	Bonds and obligations that are rated B generally do not possess attractive investment characteristics. The certainty of interest and principal payments, or of maintenance of other terms of the contract, over the long term, is limited
CCC	Bonds and obligations that are rated CCC are of poor standing. Such issues are highly vulnerable to default with a very high level of uncertainty with respect to principal or interest
CC	Bonds and obligations that are rated CC are highly speculative. Such issues are extremely vulnerable to default or have other substantial weaknesses
C	Bonds and obligations that are rated C are of low class. Such issues are regarded as possessing extremely poor prospects and may already be in default
D	The issue is in payment default. Interest or principal payments are not made on the due date

corporate financial contracts and bank obligations with an original maturity in excess of one year. Its short-term debt ratings (Table 2.20) assess the time period up to one year. Rating classifications for bonds and debt issued domestically in local currency are designated by attaching the country abbreviation to the rating. In such ratings, sovereign risk factors are not taken into account. In all other bond and debt ratings, sovereign risk factors are considered, hence the bond or debt rating will not pierce the CI sovereign ceiling for the country, unless the issue involves certain structured financing. CI uses + and − signs appended to an institution's long-term bond and debt ratings in the categories from AA to CCC to indicate that their relative position is, respectively, slightly higher or lower than that of similarly rated peers.

Seminar programme

As with any self-respecting rating agency, CI has extended its mandate to the 'public education and service' mission as evidenced by its provision of 'educational' services, which also provide a platform to increase the agency's worldwide visibility. Gleaned from the CI web site, this training seminar on analysing banks and Islamic financial institutions (see page 83) looks similar to the offerings of many rating agencies but its subject reveals CI's market specificity.

Table 2.20   CI definitions for short-term debt rating

Investment grade

A1	The highest short-term rating assigned. Issues are considered to have the highest capacity for timely repayment of short-term debt obligations. The issues in this category exhibit extremely strong protection factors. Interest payments and principal are safeguarded by a wide margin. Issues with a particularly strong profile have a + affixed to the rating
A2	The capacity for timely repayment of interest and principal is high. The issue and/or the issuer possess highly favourable characteristics and protection factors are good
A3	Satisfactory capacity for repayment of interest and principal. However, issues in this category are more vulnerable to adverse changes in business, economic and financial conditions. Protection factors are adequate but not as strong or certain as obligations in the higher short-term rating classifications

Speculative grade

B	Speculative capacity for timely repayment of interest and principal. The timely repayment of obligations is vulnerable to adverse changes and protection factors are not high
C	Doubtful capacity for timely repayment of interest and principal. Default risk is high
D	The issue is in payment default. Interest or principal payments are not made on the due date

PROGRAMME **Bank Analysis and Ratings in Emerging Markets and Rating of Islamic Financial Institutions, Bahrain Institute of Banking and Finance**	
D A Y 1 Monday, 17 May 1999	
Bank credit analysis	The need for analysis of banks Basic methodology Description of the techniques Assessing aspects of financial strength Balance sheet analysis Profit and loss statement
Ratio analysis	CI's spreadsheets and ratios Application of key ratios Advanced ratio analysis Peer group analysis Trend analysis Accounting disclosure and practices Transparency Window dressing
D A Y 2 Tuesday, 18 May 1999	
Looking behind the numbers	Asset quality, profitability, capital, and liquidity Specific analysis techniques Advanced numerical analysis Comparison, trends and anomalies What the numbers don't tell us What questions do the numbers prompt us to ask a bank's management? Non-financial factors Management quality Systems and controls Computerisation Economic and political considerations
The rating process	Theory and practice of rating Steps to a rating Key factors CI ratings Dynamics of a rating committee
D A Y 3 Wednesday, 19 May 1999	
Analysis and rating of Islamic financial institutions	Background and CI's history with Islamic banks Key variables Regulation and supervision Accounting issues Balance sheet and profit and loss statement for Islamic banks Legal issues Competitive issues
Challenges in analysing Islamic financial techniques	Key financial analysis techniques for Islamic institutions Performance CI's view of outlook Islamic banks Case studies

Source: Capital Intelligence, 1999

Japan Credit Rating Agency Ltd

Background

Japan Credit Rating Agency Ltd (JCR) was established in April 1985 by a group of prominent Japanese institutional investors. JCR is active in rating bond issuers and in issuing credit ratings. It was founded in part by the desire to have a domestic rating agency offering an alternative choice better in tune with local institutional investors and pension funds and their sensibilities than the service provided by the US duopoly. JCR sees its raison d'être not only as providing an information service for investors, but also as an institution which feels obligated to maintain and develop the Japanese pension markets. Indeed, the Japanese financial markets are some of the largest in the world, and JCR can see itself as providing a service within the context of Japanese deregulation and liberalisation measures with the credibility of being based in the Tokyo financial centre.

JCR is the largest rating agency in Japan and its standing in Japan's financial community ensures that its ratings play a central role for that country's institutional investors, in bond issues in both Japanese and overseas markets. In 1999 JCR claims to have assigned ratings to approximately 600 foreign and domestic issuers, covering almost 1200 issues. The main question affecting JCR is the extent to which it has been able to achieve credibility in the investor-creditor community outside of Japan. Certain critics outside of Japan dismiss JCR because it is perceived as kowtowing to Japanese interests by providing more favourable ratings to Japanese entities than those provided by foreign (non-Japanese) agencies.

JCR is in effect understood to be an item for the protection of the Japanese pension markets' reputation and the operability against the more unfettered competition (which has drawn local criticism as we shall see later on) of the US market leaders, Standard & Poor's and Moody's, who also have offices in Tokyo. JCR's shareholding structure includes numerous institutions: life insurers, hull insurers, banks, district banks, Sogo banks, the Bank of Tokyo, Norinchukin Bank as well as other institutes. The shareholders are at the same time JCR's most important subscribers. The dominance of any individual shareholder is prevented by placing an upper limit on share capital.

While the US agencies publish their analyses in English only, JCR publishes its reports in English and Japanese; this enables JCR's analysts to be more closely in contact and establish better trust with Japanese enterprises and institutional investors. JCR's work is also more carefully monitored and coordinated than with the US agencies; JCR's analysts aim to be able to represent Japanese enterprises more appropriately than foreigners. JCR's independence appears better secured not only by the broad working group, but also by the types of decision made regarding general principles and personnel; all members of JCR's rating committees, not just the reporting analyst, are well trusted to understand the particularities of the Japanese markets and conditions. JCR, however, is not the only entity to have identified the need to provide relevant information to Japanese institutional investors. Two other rating agencies have also sprung up in Tokyo: Nippon Investor Service and Japan Bond Research Institute. It remains to be seen whether the rating market has the necessary critical mass to support all three.

JCR has obtained legal acknowledgement by the Japanese Treasury as well as by the UK's Securities Association, but the Securities Association limits its recognition of JCT to the rating of Japanese-domiciled titles, issuers, and loans which are denominated in Japanese yen. In the USA, however, recognition is still pending, but an acknowledgement has yet to be sought since JCR focuses primarily on Asia and Europe. Based on JCR's modus operandi, the rating community's impression is that it is loosely inspired by the systems developed in the US by the duopoly. The rating does not always refer to specific issues but rather to the general ability of an issuer to fulfil its mandatory due liabilities and can be seen by some parties as a purchase or a sale recommendation for bonds. An issue can yield different ratings, depending upon the configuration of the security structure attached to the issue.

Marketing orientation

JCR has five divisions dedicated to rating, research, information services, marketing and planning, and general affairs. Here are its principal business areas:

- Rating long- and short-term debts of domestic and foreign issuers
- Research on domestic and foreign financial markets and industry trends
- Research on foreign political and economic conditions
- Dissemination of information through the publication of reports based on the findings of JCR's rating studies and other research

JCR rating fee schedule and revenue structure

JCR's income is primarily generated by the rating fees it charges its issuers. The regulation of charges reflects the three-stage rating procedure of JCR:

1. Preliminary rating fee
2. Initial bond rating fee
3. Subsequent ratings

The first stage analyses only the most important configuration features and end-of-year procedure information of the potential issuer.

The second stage is initiated when the issuer decides to obtain a rating; it typically takes a further two months before the issue of the debt. The issuer provides the detailed information required to enable JCR to undertake the rating, and JCR analysts meet with the management of the issuer to discuss and clarify aspects relating to the rating analysis. Finally, a rating presentation is made to the rating committee and a rating decision (provisional) is made by the rating committee. The rating is published with agreement of the issuer.

The third stage comes after the issue has been placed. After examination of various documents, e.g. a trust deed, the provisional rating is usually acknowledged; however, the rating procedure can be reinitiated if necessary.

JCR's user community is difficult to define. The agency supplies all publications free of charge; unlike some of the other agencies, there is no core of paying subscribers. In Japan about two thousand banks and other enterprises, in particular institutional investors, are provided regularly with JCR reports.

JCR publications and information services

JCR publishes its reports in English and Japanese. Here are two of its information services:

- JCR Ratings (English, by subscription)
- JCR Kakuzuke (Japanese, by subscription)

JCR Ratings covers all JCR ratings assigned to date to outstanding bonds, commercial paper, and other obligations, providing investors with a useful reference in their decision-making processes. In addition, it describes rationales for the ratings JCR gave on the individual issues during the previous month. JCR Kakuzuke mainly reports JCR's rationale for new and reviewed ratings with detailed rating lists. It also discusses perspectives of Japanese industries and financial issues. It is published monthly in Japanese only.

JCR provides rating information to the following organisations:

- Bloomberg
- Reuters
- Telekurs
- Telerate

JCR's three-tier rating process

Indication

Potential bond issuers may request that JCR conduct a preliminary study to determine an indication of the rating or range of ratings likely to be assigned before proceeding with a complete survey. If the request is accepted, a team of two or three analysts is formed to study information and materials provided by the issuer. In the case of a bond issue to be guaranteed by a third party, documents necessary to evaluate the guarantor's creditworthiness must also be supplied. In some cases the analysts will visit the issuer and conduct interviews at this stage in the rating process. Upon conclusion of their research, the analysts present a report to the rating committee, which then determines the indication. After notification of the indication, the issuer decides whether or not to continue with the rating process. The indication process requires approximately one month from receipt of documents to the actual notification.

Preliminary rating

A preliminary rating should be sought well in advance of a bond offering, before finalisation of exact terms and timing of the issue. If JCR accepts an issuer's application for a preliminary rating, it will appoint a team of analysts to thoroughly study materials provided by the issuer. Materials in addition to those supplied for the indication may be requested, and analysts customarily visit the issuer for discussions and on-site evaluations. Upon conclusion of their research, the analysts report to the rating committee, which determines the preliminary rating. The issuer is then notified of this rating. With the issuer's consent, the preliminary rating is made public and a JCR report is published in both English and Japanese. The preliminary rating process usually requires one to two months for issuers with a JCR indication and two to three months for those without.

Final rating

A final rating will be made after examination of the trust deed and other documents related to the issue. The final rating is usually the same as the preliminary rating, unless there is a special clause in the documents that adversely affects the rating. Changes are possible in extenuating circumstances, such as a substantial change in the conditions of the issuer or the guarantor. Determination of the final rating is usually made within one week of receiving the required documents. Notification is made verbally and is followed by written confirmation. The rating is released to the public after receiving the issuer's consent.

Review of ratings

To maintain the reliability of ratings throughout the life of an issued bond, JCR reviews ratings and ascertains the continued creditworthiness of the issuer. To assist in this review, the issuer is requested to provide such materials as quarterly and annual reports. Failure to provide up-to-date information can be grounds for withdrawal of the rating. JCR reserves the right to change, suspend, or withdraw a rating at any time, but will consult with the issuer before taking such action. Significant changes in the issuer's or guarantor's financial position are the typical reasons for rating changes.

JCR's rating committee and analyst methodology

JCR's rating committee typically consists of four experienced analysts, and in the true spirit of Japanese consensus they take rating decisions unanimously. If no agreement can be reached, JCR convenes its Credit Rating Council, which includes all the company's senior analysts. A rating criteria committee is responsible for coordinating the work of the various rating committees. In all other respects, JCR is divided into four departments: rating, research, news services, and administration.

Given the shareholding structure of JCR, the agency has implemented two mechanisms to try to ensure that it maintains its independence and objectivity. These mechanisms have no counterpart in the US agencies.

- JCR's Eligibility Advisory Board is determined by JCR's shareholders; it consists of important personalities in the Japanese economy. This board is consulted on principles of rating matters, and in the selection and qualification of candidates for leading positions within the agency.
- JCR's recruitment policy is to select its analysts from member shareholders. In the early phases of JCR, analysts of the shareholders participated in the creation of ratings; however, they were excluded from rating procedures, in order to avoid any possible conflict of interest.

JCR rating definitions (Tables 2.21 and 2.22)

Credit Monitor

When there is an outbreak of war; a serious accident, lawsuit, or administrative action; a substantial change in business performance; or a proposed merger that may necessitate a rating change, JCR will initiate, at any time, a review procedure for the rating and will announce publicly that the rating is placed under Credit Monitor. A rating under Credit Monitor is shown with # placed before the rating symbol.

Subscript p

A 'p' rating is based mainly on an analysis of public information and is given to entities that have not requested a rating. A 'p' rating is shown with a 'p' subscript. A 'p' rating is not modified by a plus (+) or minus (–) sign to indicate relative standing within a rating category.

Table 2.21 JCR long-term ratings

AAA	The highest level of capacity of the obligor to honour its financial commitment on the obligation
AA	A very high level of capacity to honour the financial commitment on the obligation
A	A high level of capacity to honour the financial commitment on the obligation
BBB	An adequate level of capacity to honour the financial commitment on the obligation. However, this capacity is more likely to diminish in the future than in the cases of the higher rating categories
BB	Although the level of capacity to honour the financial commitment on the obligation is not considered problematic at present, this capacity may not persist in the future
B	A low level of capacity to honour the financial commitment on the obligation, having cause for concern
CCC	There are factors of uncertainty that the financial commitment on the obligation will be honoured, and a possibility of default
CC	A high default risk
C	A very high default risk
D	In default
Notes	A plus (+) or minus (–) sign may be added to the rating symbols from AA to B, to indicate relative standing within each of those rating categories
	JCR's long-term ratings are gradings that enable comparisons to be made of obligors' capacity to honour the financial commitments on obligations of more than one year as contracted
	The subjects of JCR's long-term ratings include issuers' specific obligations such as bonds and financial programmes (e.g. medium-term note programmes). They also include obligors' capacity to honour the financial obligations such long-term senior obligations and ability to pay insurance claims
	The aforementioned symbols are also used for ratings of long-term securitised products, including asset-backed securities

Source: JCR 1999

Table 2.22   JCR short-term ratings

J-1	The highest level of capacity of the obligor to honour its financial commitment on the obligation. Within this rating category, obligations for which the capacity is particularly high are indicated by the symbol J-1+
J-2	A high level of capacity to honour the financial commitment on the obligation, but slightly less than for category J-1
J-3	An adequate level of capacity of the obligor to honour the financial commitment on the obligation, but susceptible to adverse changes in circumstances
NJ	Obligations unable to be included in any of the above three J (upper ranking) rating categories
Notes	JCR's short-term ratings are gradings that enable comparisons to be made of obligors' capacity to honour the financial commitments on obligations of no more than one year as contracted
	The subjects of JCR's short-term ratings include issuers' specific obligations such as commercial paper programmes, and obligors' capacity to honour short-term financial obligations such as short-term senior obligations
	The aforementioned symbols are also used for ratings of short-term securitised products, including asset-backed securities

Source: JCR 1999

Suspension and withdrawal

JCR may suspend or withdraw a rating when relevant information is lacking or if unfavourable circumstances develop. In the event that it becomes difficult or impossible to obtain information necessary for reviewing a rating, the existing rating will be suspended. In the event that JCR deems that, as a result of lack of cooperation with regard to the provision of information, it will be impossible to conduct rating reviews, the existing rating will be withdrawn.

Agencies in developing capital markets

As an example of the growth in 'domestic' agencies in the wake of global liberalisation, consider the following examples of rating agencies set up in various developing markets in the mid 1990s. The information was gleaned directly from their web sites and local press. What is particularly interesting is the fact that in most cases the founders are copying the models in use in the USA, with tacit encouragement, in the case of CERA, of US government agencies (such as USAID) or existing players. Despite all the focus on 'local credibility', their emulation (with its ideological agenda) of the methods pioneered by the duopoly is remarkable, as well as their methods of branching out into the rating of new products in the incessant quest for market share and profits.

Brazil: Atlantic Rating

Atlantic Rating is a Brazilian credit rating company. Atlantic Rating was founded in 1992 as an association with Thomson Financial BankWatch of New York to evaluate the risk of Brazilian banks (Table 2.23). The company has a team of 30 professionals, including financial consultants, credit, accounting and systems analysts, journalists and technicians. The technical team, the data bank, and the administrative, publishing and commercial areas are located in the Rio de Janeiro headquarters. The company analyses and classifies these risks:

- Brazilian banks
- Fixed-income securities of financial institutions
- Mutual funds

Atlantic Rating performs three types of classification: rating, score, and score with due diligence. Both rating and score with due diligence can be compared and provide an opinion. Score is a mathematical calculation and cannot be compared with other classifications. Risk classification was developed

Table 2.23   Subscribers to Atlantic Rating

Geographic distribution	
Brazil	70%
Abroad	30%
Profile	
Banks	45%
Companies	20%
Funds	25%
Others	10%

to advise creditors and investors regarding the risks. It is an independent evaluation prepared by specialised analysts. Each type of classification demands an appropriate methodology. Therefore, the symbols are different in each type of evaluation although the scales correspond.

The quarterly *Risk Analysis: Brazilian Banks* is published in Portuguese and English, based on the financial statements for March, June, September, and December of banks operating in Brazil. It is composed of the following parts:

- Analysis of the banking sector during the quarter, including trends and Atlantic Rating's view for the future months.
- Twenty-nine rankings of all the banks operating in Brazil; banks are classified best to worst according to transparency, size, liquidity, loan quality, leverage, and profitability.

Here are the criteria adopted by Atlantic Rating in financial statement analysis:

● Full account of the rating and score classifications.
● Analysis of all banks operating in Brazil with net worth of more than R$ 25 million. Each bank is in two pages, including the analysis, the consolidated financial statements, and the classifications (rating or score).
● In addition to the above information, subscribers have permanent access to Atlantic Rating analysts to clarify doubts or to request additional information on banks or the banking sector.

Bulgaria: Bulgarian Rating Agency

Activities

● Formation of ratings
● Fundamental financial analysis based on balances, reports, and own data
● Creation of a database with information for companies from all branches of industry and services

Achievements

The Bulgarian Rating Agency (BRA) has created, on the basis of its own research and in compliance with international standards, a system for estimation, analysis, and elaboration of the first national ratings of Bulgarian companies included in privatisation or listed on the stock exchange. BRA has formed a team of experts in the field of finance, accounting and investment analysis, database programming, and design of econometric models. It has developed detailed company records of Bulgarian companies included in mass and cash privatisation. It is in close contact with Bulgarian mass media, thus regularly informing the Bulgarian public and interested investors about the ratings of companies included in mass privatisation, as well as the ratings of privatisation funds taking part in the process.

Future activities

BRA will focus especially on situation analysis in these areas:

● New company entries in the capital market
● New issues of stocks and bonds of already existing companies

- Database and estimation related to the extension or obtaining of new credits

Symbols and definitions of the ratings

The methodology worked out by BRA enables the establishment of a unified letter-grade rating, which represents an option to evaluate the position of a particular company in an aggregation of 40 other companies by comparing it with a hypothetical company (sample) with optimal financial characteristics. On the basis of that evaluation, the companies are classified into four major groups (A, B, C, D). An in-depth analysis of the company characteristics gives a more precise evaluation of their remoteness from the characteristics of the sample company and helps to assign the rating.

Priorities

BRA long-term prospects are connected with the implementation of the rating system as generally adopted criteria for investment analysis and estimation of companies. BRA is an independent non-profit organisation which is not tied to any interested Bulgarian and foreign public or private institutions. Its efforts are focused especially in the field of financial analysis and the prospects of Bulgarian companies for cooperation with foreign investors.

India: ICRA Limited

ICRA Limited (formerly Investment Information and Credit Rating Agency of India Limited) was incorporated on 16 January 1991 and launched its services on 31 August 1991. ICRA is an independent and professional company providing investment information and credit rating services. Some milestones in its history are given in Table 2.24.

ICRA's major shareholders include leading Indian financial institutions and banks (Table 2.25). As the growth and globalisation of Indian capital markets have led to an exponential surge in demand for professional credit risk analysis, ICRA has actively responded to this need by executing assignments including credit ratings, equity gradings, and mandated studies spanning diverse industrial sectors.

In addition to being a leading credit rating agency with expertise in virtually every sector of the Indian economy, ICRA has broadened its services to the corporate and financial sectors, both in India and overseas, and presently offers its services under three banners:

- Rating services
- Information services
- Advisory services

Poland: Central European Rating Agency

The Central European Rating Agency was established by the Union of Polish Banks and the US Agency for International Development (USAID) in 1996, and it can be viewed as an initiative sponsored by the US government to graft US business ideology in Eastern Europe. Union of Polish Banks (ZBP) analysts say Poland badly needs a credit rating system serving banks, enterprises, and investors, and they think demand for the service will rise as the capital market develops. While the number of issuers needing credible ratings has been small, it is expected to grow rapidly. The commercial paper market, of increasing interest to life insurance companies and trust funds, is growing and in the near future pension funds should also begin operating.

The Polish rating agency will be based on US players such as Moody's and Standard & Poor's. However, in contrast to those agencies, it will not be fully independent of many of the businesses subject to assessment, primarily because of the lack of the required capital outside of those institutions. Banks, insurance companies, and enterprises will all invest in the agency. The founders plan to attract at least 20 shareholders, in order to guarantee the greatest possible independence by fragmenting ownership. Andrzej Wolski, deputy director of ZBP, says many institutions have already expressed their desire to participate in this venture.

The basic product offered by the Central European Rating Agency will be ratings of firms, but the agency will also want to carry out some data publishing. It plans to publish a weekly bulletin with complete information about new issues, as well as reports on the situation in particular sectors of the economy. Wolski believes the agency will start operations in the autumn. No doubt the agency will be potential acquisition material for the duopoly in the not too distant future.

Russian Federation: Skate

Some pre-1998 milestones are listed in Table 2.26. In 1998 Skate streamlined itself and actively expanded its coverage of the emerging markets of Central

Table 2.24 ICRA milestones

December 1999	ICRA launched its new corporate web site making all its research publications available through the internet in the electronic format. The new site offers many new and useful features, including a powerful on-site search engine, electronic subscription lists and customised e-mail update services
August 1999	Moody's Investors Service and ICRA Limited announced the final agreement for Moody's to make an equity investment and provide technical services to ICRA. The signing of the agreement follows the 8 December 1998 endorsement of a memorandum of understanding (MoU) between the two rating agencies
March 1999	Launched grading services for entities involved in construction projects, including contractors, consultants, project owners, and the project itself. The grading system, evolved in collaboration with CIDC, is an objective system designed to provide lenders and others with an independent opinion on the quality of the entity being examined
February 1999	Launched its rating services for the debt funds of Indian mutual funds. This extension of rating service to cover such funds is aimed at addressing the perceived need among investors countrywide to have an informed, reliable, and independent opinion on the risks associated with investing in individual mutual funds
February 1999	ICRA became the first Indian rating agency to rate all non-life insurance companies in the country. ICRA's latest feat follows its 1998 initiative in introducing a rating methodology for the claims-paying ability of general insurance companies in India
January 1999	Introduced the first edition of its corporate analysis report titled ICRA Corporate Review (ICR) which is a biannual publication by ICRA Information Services, a division of ICRA, tailored to meet the information needs of both the retail and wholesale investor. Specifically, ICR is conceived and designed to act as a 'first level' information resource for investors, asset managers, creditors, term lenders, bankers, merger and acquisition specialists, treasury managers, regulators, and academicians, among others
December 1998	The US-based international credit rating agency Moody's Investors Service and ICRA Limited announced their mutual agreement to Moody's, picking up a minority stake in the equity capital of ICRA. Significantly, this is a rare occasion where Moody's has agreed to a minority stake in a venture in a developing market
July 1998	Introduced a rating methodology for the claims-paying ability of general insurance companies in India. The rating of insurance companies enables purchasers of insurance policies and investors to access timely, authentic, and dependable information about the fundamental capacity of the insurance company to service claims and obligations. Simultaneously it helps the insurance company widen its market as name recognition is complemented by the objective opinion of ICRA
February 1997	Launched *Money & Finance*, a research programme (in the form of a quarterly publication) directed at analysis of contemporary developments that characterise Indian money and finance with the ultimate objective of developing analytical models which can explain the interrelated movements of the principal macrovariables defining the monetary and financial sector of the Indian economy
March 1996	Signed agreement with Financial Proformas Inc., a Moody's company, to provide credit education, risk management software, credit research, and consulting services to commercial banks, financial and investment institutions, financial services companies, and mutual funds in India
December 1995	Launched credit assessment for small and medium-scale industry (under CII cluster approach)
April 1995	Launched EPRA (earnings prospects and risk analysis) range of services; launched an information service for the equity investor
March 1993	Launched its investment information service and research publications

Table 2.25   ICRA: major shareholders

Industrial Finance Corporation of India Limited	United Bank of India
State Bank of India	Indian Bank
Moody's Investment Co. India Private Limited	Canara Bank
Life Insurance Corporation of India	UCO Bank
Unit Trust of India	Andhra Bank
Punjab National Bank	Export-Import Bank of India
GIC	20th Century Finance Corporation Limited
Union Bank of India	Housing Development Finance Corp. Limited
Central Bank of India	Infrastructure Leasing & Financial Services Limited
Allahabad Bank	The Vysya Bank Limited
Indian Overseas Bank	Oriental Bank of Commerce

Source: ICRA, 1999

and Eastern Europe. It offered a comprehensive set of data products covering the financial markets of Turkey, Poland, Hungary, the Czech Republic, Russia, other CIS states, the three Baltic States, Cyprus, Croatia, Bulgaria, Romania, Slovenia, and Slovakia. In line with its new strategy, Skate developed and introduced many composite indicators which are registered under the Skate Global Benchmarks brand name and make up a harmonious system to monitor the dynamics of fixed-income and equity markets of the region's 15 major countries (Table 2.27). In October, Skate announced the launch of a

Table 2.26   Skate milestones up to 1998

1992	Sergey Skaterschikov, a young Russian entrepreneur, recognises the need for financial data on the Russian securities market, and creates Skate. Launch of the first ever Russian equity index, ASP 12. Development of MIBOR and MIBID rates, fixed-income indices, and other statistical benchmarks to guide investors
1994	Skate becomes the official data contributor to the IFC Russian Index and other financial information vendors such as Reuters, Bloomberg, and Datastream. Skate and the *Moscow Times*, the daily newspaper published by Independent Media, form a joint venture to supply the marketplace with a reliable Russian equity market benchmark, the MT-Index
1995	Launch of *Capital Markets Russia*, a weekly newsletter on Russia's financial markets; it becomes a standard-bearer and expands to 16 pages. Launch of Skate's third-party service on Bloomberg (SKAT GO) and internet service at http://www.skate.ru/. With more than 150 000 hits a week, Skate is the most visited business web site in Russia
1996	Launch of *Skate Blue Chips*, a quarterly handbook on Russian companies, providing key financial data on the top enterprises, lists of major shareholders, etc. Launch of *Russia XTension*, a fortnightly newsletter on the Russian telecommunications industry
1997	Reuters launches Securities 3000 in Russia, taking Skate financial data feed as an important component of Russian financial coverage. Skate launches Skate Investor Services and becomes the first Russian classic rating agency. Monthly the ratings will be published in three publications: funds ratings, equity ratings, and fixed-income ratings

Table 2.27   Skate rating scale

SR-5.0	Highest safety. Company performance is largely independent of short-term adverse business, financial, and macroeconomic conditions (conditions). Share price less linked to market movements. Frequent or large fluctuations are low
SR-4.0	Above average safety. Changing conditions moderately affect company strength and investor perception. Share price fluctuations likely to be more frequent and/or larger
SR-3.0	Average safety. Adverse conditions may prevent the company from meeting business targets and financial obligations. Sensitive to investor perception. Share price fluctuation higher
SR-2.0	Below average safety. Company is heavily dependent upon favourable conditions. Adverse conditions more likely to prevent company from meeting business targets and financial obligations. Frequent and large fluctuations are not atypical
SR-1.0	Lowest safety. Corporate and/or operational shortcomings retard company's performance even in favourable market conditions. Business targets and financial obligations will not likely be met. Share price fluctuation is likely the highest

Source: Skate, 2000 (www.skatefn.com)

new benchmark for Central and Eastern European equity markets, the Euroskate 15 equity index, soon followed by Euroskate 100 and the related sectorial indices. Skate's activities have been dampened considerably since the collapse of the Russian ruble in late 1998. It remains to be seen how the business or rating agencies develop in this large and problematical market.

Switzerland: Swiss Community Financial Rating

In order to assess the creditworthiness of all public law entities (communities, cities, cantons, public corporations) by an independent body (i.e. an institution without any lender or borrower as a shareholder), ComRating (Swiss Community Financial Rating SA) was founded in Zollikon (near Zurich) in August 1998. By the end of 1996 the debts of the federal government, cantons, and communities had amounted to CHF 180 billion. These debts have largely to be covered by borrowings in the financial and money market. In the past, loans granted to public law corporations used to be safe and were therefore considered good business dealings.

However, along with the arrival of new credit risk models in commercial banking, and with some public households partly getting out of control, a new era began. Increasingly, there will be a correlation between the quality of the debtor and the margins, and therefore the interest to be paid. Implementing credit conditions by considering the lending risks involved is not a must in the private sector only, and public authorities can and will not be spared.

The rating methodology of the first independent Swiss rating agency is based on the latest findings of public law corporations. Various quantifiable, so-called hard, and qualitative, so-called soft, criteria are the basis for a sound assessment. The final result clearly shows a public household's credit-worthiness. The rating scale consists of five levels, AAA representing the highest and C representing the lowest creditworthiness.

In the long term, debtors as well as creditors will benefit from a reliable rating offered at a fair and reasonable price. The market will become more transparent and the conditions in net terms will clearly improve for all parti-cipants. Moreover, no institution will be able to do without a reliable rating given the rapidly increasing level of asset security.

Benefit for all market participants

Borrowers assessed by ComRating will at any time be able to access financial and money markets at valid market conditions. Corporations that received a high rating will of course be offered the best conditions. Apart from that, they can inform taxpayers and other interested parties about the results of the independent assessments. On the other hand, communities that received low ratings benefit from the rating evaluation as follows. In a short additional report, ComRating outlines the areas in need of improvement so that the community will be able to benefit from excellent conditions in the future, too. Since every client can decide whether or not they want the rating to be published, corporations are not branded as inferior by ComRating; there is still time left to improve, ideally until the next capital raising. Creditors profit from corporations assessed by ComRating due to the independent and trans-parent rating performed by a competent body. This cost-saving risk assess-ment allows all market participants (banks, insurance companies, pension funds, etc.) to offer fair market conditions at lowest costs.

Thailand: Thai Rating and Information Services

Thai Rating and Information Services (TRIS), Thailand's first credit rating agency, was established in 1993 with sponsorship from Thai financial institu-tions. TRIS originally received three years of technical assistance from Standard & Poor's Rating Group (S&P) in developing its credit rating methodology and administrative matters. TRIS is a founding member of AFCRA (ASEAN Forum of Credit Rating Agencies), an association of regional credit rating agencies established to provide additional training and facilitate the exchange of infor-mation and ideas concerning credit rating and the bond markets throughout Asia. By incorporating global quality credit rating skills with significant knowledge and insight on the Thai economy and debt market, TRIS is fully committed to providing the best credit rating service available.

TRIS's primary mission is to provide a credit rating service and to disseminate the rating results and other related information in the Thai bond market for the benefit of investors both local and international. It draws on support from various organisations in both the government and business sectors to achieve a broad-based shareholding structure. To ensure freedom from outside interference, no single shareholder is allowed to own more than 5% of the company. TRIS has a ten-member board of directors that oversee the company's policy; it consists of five shareholder representative directors, four expert directors, and the agency's president, Dr Warapatr Todhanakasem. The board is chared by Dr Panas Simasathien, former permanent secretary and minister of finance. TRIS shareholders include commercial banks and finance companies, life insurance companies, Thai government institutions, the Asian Development Bank and the Thai stock exchange.

Some rating agencies on the web

A. M. Best	http://www.ambest.com
Atlantic Rating	http://www.atlanticrating.com/
Bulgarian Rating Agency	http://www.bgra.com
Canadian Bond Rating Service (CBRS)	http://www.cbrs.com
Capital Intelligence	http://www.ciratings.com
ComRating (Swiss Community Financial Rating SA)	http://www.comrating.ch
Czech Rating Agency	http://www.czechrating.cz
Dominion Bond Rating Service (DBRS)	http://www.dbrs.com
Equilibrium Clasificadora de Riesgo	http://www.cosapidata.com.pe/empresa/eqbwper/eqbwper.htm
Fitch	http://www.fitch.com
Investment Information and Credit Rating Agency (ICRA)	http://www.icraindia.com
Japan Rating and Investment Information, Inc. (R&I)	http://www.r-i.co.jp/eng
Moody's Investors Service, Inc.	http://www.moodys.com
Skate	http://www.skatefn.com
Standard & Poor's Corporation (S&P)	http://www.standardpoor.com
Thai Rating and Information Services (TRIS)	http://www.tris.tnet.co.th
Thomson Bank Watch (TBW)	http://www.bankwatch.com
Unternehmens Ratingagentur	http://www.ura.de
Weiss Ratings, Inc.	http://www.weissratings.com
Cantwell & Company	http://www.askcantwell.com
Everling Advisory Services	http://www.everling.de

3 Methodologies and characteristics

Rating agencies' methodologies

In the previous chapter we looked at the historical background, development, and modus operandi of various rating agencies, as well as their business and commercial strategies and use of rating scales to communicate their opinions on creditworthiness to the investor-creditor community. However, this process of identifying the players and their market behaviour in terms of their strategy and market positioning does not address the essential underlying questions: How do the rating agencies go about analysing the issuers seeking a rating? How to they situate this within the context of the overall economy? And what are the actual methodologies used?

Much commentary has been given to evaluating markets, assessing creditworthiness and situating the borrower within peer group analyses, etc., but what does this actually mean? For example, some rating agencies may list as desirable factors the state of the country's educational or economic infrastructure and later down in the same list include the country's pro-business attitude or favourable/unfavourable tax system. Are good scores in all three areas consistent or contradictory? How are these contradictions assessed? What do they mean? Are they factual, economic, or ideological in nature?

This chapter will look at a typical rating process as well as some of the methodological 'tools' or frameworks used by the rating agencies in assessing borrowers in specialised categories. There are many specialised sectors in the ratings business, but we shall look at the three traditional areas of rating entities: sovereigns, banks, and corporates. It is not an exhaustive treatment but it does introduce some of the methodologies and tools used by the rating agencies and it should help to explain their modi operandi and assess their appropriateness.

Many of the methodologies or checklists in this chapter are extracted from materials distributed by the agencies for self-promotion. They are designed to reassure ratings users about the scope and thoroughness of their work. But bear in mind that we are not looking at a tried and true mathematical formula as in thermodynamics or stress analysis; these documents are designed to reassure and impress the investor-creditor community and related parties that everything has been looked at without actually defining the specifics underlying the assessment process.

What become striking when looking at the rating industry as a whole are the similarities in the checklists, the similarities in the disqualifying statements, and the similarities in the subjectivity of their opinions and conclusions, which are translated into a supposedly rigid and defined rating scale terminology. Rating scales can sometimes be compared to default rates; this is true in the case of bonds, commercial paper, or US corporates, which provide a large sample population and time frame to work with. But banks or corporations in foreign countries, or sovereign states, have a much smaller population size and it is more difficult to establish a clear-cut link between the rating and any default rates that exist. Yet the rating agencies issue these ratings across the board without necessarily making the distinction between the two; indeed Moody's admits that it applies the exact same US-developed yardsticks across the board. We shall now consider some of the key methodologies in further detail.

A typical credit rating procedure

The typical credit rating procedure may be familiar to some readers, others may wonder how these rating reviews are conducted behind the scenes. This section therefore provides a generalised illustration of the process; the methodologies, procedure, quorums, credit committee deliberations, and issuance of the rating to the public naturally vary from agency to agency. Still, there are only so many permutations possible in the game and we can therefore generalise to some extent.

A credit rating may be solicited or unsolicited. The main difference is that solicited rating is a cooperative process (cooperative in that the issuer provides information of a public and confidential nature), whereas unsolicited rating relies almost exclusively on information which the agency is able to compile on its own, information typically in the public domain. The procedures and methodologies are largely similar for solicited and unsolicited rating, with the proviso that solicited rating relies on interviews and contacts but unsolicited rating does not. In some cases, entities will be presented with an unsolicited rating with the unspoken understanding that if they pay a rating fee, the agency will do more thorough work and produce a better rating.

Analysing the issuer's environment

To begin with, the issuer's environment can vary considerably, depending on the nature of the entity. Sovereigns are countries; banks operate within a regulatory framework and risk flows from capitalisation and asset quality; corporates are characterised by issues such as cash flow and industry sector positioning. The obvious starting point in a rating process is therefore to collect and analyse data relating to the background environment in which the issuer operates. For a bank, a good place to start would be the banking system in which it operates and its place within that system. For a corporate, one might start with the positioning of the issuer vis-à-vis its competitors in the economic marketplace.

Banks typically offer the most detailed background assessment since this means analysing the national banking market and its various subsectors, and degree of banking concentration, as well as the role and functions of the country's banking supervisory authorities, the degree of state control of the banking system, the public reporting requirements of banks, and the accounting practices in use. This process may be extended to other aspects such as EU directives on the single banking market, accounting, and consolidated supervision as well as the requirements of the Basle Agreement on international convergence of capital measurement and capital standards, and subsequent interpretative statements from the Basle Committee.

The analysis typically compares the issuer's financial statements to other players in its peer group (a group of comparable entities within the country or, if necessary, of similar entities in different countries).

The checklist

After laying the groundwork of background research and peer group analysis, the agency will typically have a list of questions needing further clarification. These may be highlighted against a standardised checklist, and a questionnaire then prepared for presentation to the management of the bank to be rated. The checklist is a guide to help orient the review and will rarely be answered in its entirety. For example, a bank may not be significantly involved in derivatives trading, thereby obviating that particular line of inquiry.

The checklists are typically organised by section; Moody's uses the acronym CAMEL (capital, assets, management, earnings, and liquidity) to analyse banks, although for unsolicited ratings the M has a tendency to get lost. Corporates in turn may be organised by industry issues, cash flow forecasts, debt servicing, and management strategy. Detailed checklists for sovereigns, banks, and corporates appear later in this chapter.

The issuer may respond to a checklist or prefer to take control of the operation by hosting a presentation and trying to answer the questions in its own fashion. Alternatively, the questions may be answered in a face-to-face meeting. The questionnaire may include requests for data which are considered by the bank in question to be confidential, and the agency may in turn be required to sign a confidentiality agreement.

Meeting with the issuer

Meetings typically form part of the rating process. They usually include discussions to assess the data provided and seek further clarification. This will typically be with the issuer's chief financial officer, although more sophisticated entities will use rating agency liaison officers for better PR. The length and number of meetings with management depend on the complexity of the entity being rated. Visit length is reported in the rating agency survey carried out by Cantwell & Company; the meetings typically last between half a day and a whole day.

Meetings are typically followed up with telephone contact and further meetings, perhaps to review interim figures or to discuss a major development in the issuer's business such as the acquisition or disposal of a subsidiary or lawsuit. Annual meetings will be scheduled for review of annual figures.

Focusing the analysis

The main areas the rating agencies will focus on, as reflected in their questionnaire, will obviously be defined by the nature of the entity in question. For banks, typical areas of inquiry are risk, funding, capital, performance/ earnings, market environment and planning, prospects, ownership, audit and contingent liabilities. Sovereigns and corporates will also have their areas of inquiry, organised in the questionnaire along thematic lines.

Approach to differing structures

The rating agency will typically consider consolidated as well as stand-alone accounts, particularly in the case of banks with large diffuse holding structures. However, this does not necessarily mean that only the consolidated figures of the holding company of a banking group are of interest, because much will depend on the purpose behind the rating. For example, if it is an entity rating of a banking group then it is preferable to analyse the consolidated figures of that group, but if it is an entity rating of a group holding company then it may be desirable to analyse both its consolidated and unconsolidated figures. If it is a rating of a particular security issue, the agency may then want to focus on analysing the results of the issuing entity, which may be a subsidiary or a sub-subsidiary of a group holding company. The approaches therefore vary according to the nature of the issuer's structure.

The analytical process

The rating process will typically include two analysts: a senior analyst, typically from the head office, and a junior analyst, who may be the local contact point and who chases down the documentation and does the grunt work. The analysts will focus on pertinent areas of risk.

In the case of a bank, this will be in areas such as lending, investments (holding, dealing, trading), fund management, off-balance sheet transactions (particularly derivatives), interest rate and currency risk. In non-G8 countries the analysis will probably focus on the loan portfolio composition, as well as the bank's funding and liquidity in terms of volatility. This will be summarised in terms of adequate capital, measured in the agency's terms as well as those imposed by regulatory authorities.

The analysis will also look at the bank's prospects and the relationship with and likely support from its owners as well as bailout by regulatory authorities. It will also check on the bank's relationship with its independent auditors (if any) and with its national regulatory authority—adverse reports from either are potentially disturbing. Furthermore, it will check whether there are contingent liabilities looming over the bank, such as court cases or legal suits.

Corporate analysis will focus on market positioning, cash flow, steady profitability, sustainable earnings, and adequate cushion to ensure debt servicing in the case of adversity. Rating analysts look favourably on consistency and diversity of earnings and profitability. They also examine the markets in which the issuer is operating along with past and future management actions to maximise their exploitation. Sovereigns will be assessed on factors such as the fiscal, monetary, and inflation outcomes of government policies that support or erode incentives for timely debt service.

The draft report

Following the meeting with its management and subsequent analysis of the data obtained, the analysts will draft a rating report. Depending on the rating agreement and the particular circumstances, this may be a short-form report (one page of text forming the rating report, plus spreadsheets) or a long-form report (one page of text forming the rating report, plus five pages of text detailing the rating analysis, plus spreadsheets, spreadsheet annex, and explanatory notes to the spreadsheets).

It is not unusual to occasionally see memoranda penned by senior managers complaining about the length of rating reports and stating that reports over five pages will not be considered suitable for submission. These measures are typically short-lived and reports up to 30 pages in length with spreadsheets, annexes, photocopies of various letters, and last-minute press cuttings often get produced.

Presentation of a draft report to the issuer

Some agencies send the draft report (with provisional rating pending formal issuance) to the issuer, justifying this with two arguments:

- Its accuracy can be checked
- Confidential items can be removed

These two points seem to suggest that, in dealing with the issuer, the agency is not very rigorous in its control of facts or not very clear in its communications. A cynic might suggest that the agency does not wish to jeopardise its relationship with the issuer, who is seen as a source of repeat business in paying rating fees, and hence wants to ensure no feathers have been ruffled before releasing the report.

Indeed, it is not unheard of for an issuer to threaten to cancel the rating and repeat business if a rating agency does not cancel a rating downgrade it is about to issue, a decision which then gravitates from the rating committee to more senior marketing concerns. One agency notes, 'We are always ready to correct factual errors and to exclude genuinely confidential items, but we are not, of course, prepared to have our rating assessments and opinions dictated to us by the bank being rated'. Can such absolute statements, one wonders, weather the vicissitudes of the market and the quest for ever increasing profits and bonuses?

Amendments and circulation to the rating committee

Following the submission of the draft to the issuer for 'pre-approval', the next step is to transmit the report to the agency's rating committee. The documentation supporting the analysts' presentation to the rating committee is typically provided to its members in advance of its meeting. During the credit committee meeting, the analysts may also present relevant confidential data, omitted from the report to preserve confidentiality. Extra information such as peer group analyses comparing the entity with its domestic and foreign peers, or last-minute press cuttings, may also be in the presenting analyst's dossier; this may come in useful for question and answer sessions.

Composition of the rating committee

The composition of rating committees varies from one agency to another but the mechanics are largely similar. The committee may be governed by a quorum, and for the sake of impartiality, it may include a member covering a peer group of banks in another country, the two analysts who visited the bank and prepared the analysis, and one or more senior analysts who may cover banks in other countries. On the other hand, the committee may consist solely of US-based members to ensure adherence to US methodologies and ideological concerns and hence avoid specialist analysts becoming too intimate with the banks or countries they cover (e.g. going native or having a particular axe to grind).

After submission the proposed rating is held to a vote; the quorums and the required majorities vary from agency to agency. The votes are typically not secret, so less powerful members or members seeking to demonstrate their ideological enthusiasm may be voting to secure their own position instead of concentrating on the rating decision itself. After all, the time frame for getting fired is less than for the agency to go bust.

Dissemination (or non-dissemination) of the ratings

The process varies but some agencies note that 'while the issuer has no recourse to an appeal, it does have the right to decide whether it wishes our ratings to be made public and the rating report to be sent to our subscribers'. In the event that the issuer accepts the rating, the rating report and the ratings will then be publicly released via various publications and communications media such as the internet, wire services, and press releases. Some agencies will respect the confidentiality of the client; if the issuer does not want the ratings published and the report disseminated, then the project will be terminated, and regular subscribers will not be informed that rating work was done on the bank in question. One may wonder how this fits into 'investor service'.

Sovereign credit ratings

The financial community has travelled a long way since Walter Wriston, then head of Citibank, asserted that countries do not go bankrupt because they always own more than they owe. Many debtor countries caught up in the 1982 crisis made considerable attempts to maintain their borrower credibility, and this shows that most governments remain extremely reluctant to dishonour their debts.

With the implosion of the USSR/COMECON bloc, the world is presently in a period where there is, at least in the world of power elites, ostensibly more international consensus about the broad policies that are required for 'encouraging economic activity' than has existed for several decades. To that extent, the world's present situation bears some comparison to the situation existing before the First World War. Coincidentally, the pre-war period was also a time of enormous international capital flows by the standards of the post-war period. This era of increased capital flows means that the rating of sovereign governments has burgeoned in recent years.

Sovereign rating criteria

Sovereign credit ratings represent an attempt to assess a government's capacity and willingness to repay debt. Sovereign ratings address the credit risks of national governments, but not the specific default risks of other issuers such as state-owned entities (airlines, railways). Ratings assigned to other public and private sector entities in each country can therefore vary, and frequently they do. Sovereign ratings, however, set the benchmark for the ratings assigned to other issuers under the sovereign's jurisdiction. For example, a corporate cannot have a better rating than the sovereign entity in which it is domiciled.

Defaults by sovereign issuers of bank and bond debt have declined in recent years, at least until 1998. However, based on the volume of bond issuance by emerging market sovereigns in the 1990s, many with ratings in the speculative grade (BB+ ratings or lower) category, it seems that default rates for sovereign issuers, over time, may parallel the default rates for similarly rated corporate issuers (Table 3.1).

Past sovereign defaults were due to various factors, including wars, revolutions, lax fiscal and monetary polices, and external economic shocks. This, however, has shifted in the wake of deregulation and globalisation; as the 1990s drew to a close, fiscal discipline, debt management, and the contingent liabilities arising from weak banking systems in particular, were significantly impacting the financial well-being of sovereign entities. While the associated credit risks may for a time seem manageable, they can mushroom quickly, as events in Asia have shown.

How then do rating agencies assess the creditworthiness of a sovereign? After all, they cannot refer to an audited set of financial statements and cash

Table 3.1 Total number of sovereign debt defaults, 1956–94

Albania	1	Jordan	4
Algeria	2	Liberia	7
Angola	1	Madagascar	8
Argentina	12	Malawi	3
Bangladesh	1	Mali	4
Benin	3	Mauritania	5
Bolivia	8	Mexico	9
Brazil	12	Morocco	7
Bulgaria	3	Mozambique Rep.	5
Burkina Faso	2	Nicaragua	5
Cambodia	1	Niger	8
Cameroon	3	Nigeria	5
Central African Rep.	6	Pakistan	5
Chad	1	Panama	3
Chile	10	Peru	11
Columbia	3	Philippines	9
Congo	3	Poland	12
Costa Rica	8	Romania	4
Côte d'Ivoire	7	Russian Federation	3
Cuba	4	Sao Tome and Principe	1
Dominican Rep.	5	Senegal	11
Ecuador	7	Sierra Leone	7
Egypt	4	Somalia	2
El Salvador	1	South Africa	5
Equatorial Guinea	3	Sudan	6
Ethiopia	1	Tanzania	4
Gabon	6	Togo	10
Gambia	2	Trinidad and Tobago	2
Ghana	7	Turkey	10
Guatemala	1	Uganda	6
Guinea	4	Uruguay	8
Guinea-Bissau	2	Venezuela	4
Guyana	9	Vietnam	1
Honduras	4	Yugoslavia	7
India	9	Zaire	11
Indonesia	6	Zambia	6
Jamaica	9	**TOTAL**	**389**

Source: *Euromoney*

flow forecasts based on projected levels of sales and financing or operating costs. The following checklist, or sovereign ratings methodology profile, is typical of those produced by ratings agencies. At first glance it looks exhaustive and complete. Indeed, the literate observer can even be tempted to add an item or two to one of the categories in the checklist. Where these checklists seem vague, however, is in how the various elements are assessed, quantified, and incorporated into the assessment of creditworthiness. Moreover, many of the items are mutually contradictory yet none of the agencies explain how they are reconciled.

The descriptions are replete with terms such as 'carefully monitored' and 'analysed' or 'assessed' but this begs the question as to what these terms mean. Take the items 'extent of popular participation', 'tax competitiveness' and 'orderliness of leadership succession'. How does one define these terms and incorporate them into a systematic mode of evaluation?

These terms appear precise but how does one draw the distinction of popular participation in a country such as China, Indonesia, or Chile and compare this to the tax regimes in Iran or Saudi Arabia (which has none)? Does a democracy such as Ireland receive a better political score than China? At one time the USSR had excellent credit ratings, yet much of the current indebtedness of Russia stems from debts incurred by the Soviet government. These may be rhetorical questions but when one examines the documentation or 'research' produced by the rating agencies, their approach may be characterised as serious-sounding opinions resting on a logical framework best described as opaque.

Such research is often couched in approximate terminology which leaves the writer space to alter or modify the conclusions in light of subsequent events, as the East Asian crisis well demonstrated. This often puts the agencies in the awkward position of having to go through amusing contortions in the media to extricate themselves from past pronouncements and issue corrective statements—a rather imprecise situation for entities anointed as a mandatory rite of passage for access to the financial markets by the SEC and other regulatory bodies.

Sovereign ratings checklist

The following checklist is an amalgam of items noted by various rating agencies, arranged in thematic categories which a rating agency may look at. These lists obviously include many factors which may not be applicable in all cases. Since each country is different, the checklists will obviously be tailored to the particular circumstances relating to that country (e.g. an oil exporter).

While these checklists appear to be thorough, remember that the method of weighting or calculating the elements and categories is a procedure which can most charitably be described as nebulous; moreover, the methods in which mutually contradictory elements such as income distribution and the presence or lack of labour movements are assessed is not clear. Finally, one may wonder whether the agency actually compiles and analyses all this information. Clearly, the checklists are designed to impress with their thoroughness; however, the mechanisms, techniques, weightings, and assessment procedures receive little explanation from any of the rating agencies, most likely because this supposedly detailed process is in reality a highly subjective exercise in guesswork and the less said about specificities, the better.

Demographics, education and structural factors

These include elements such as growth rate of the population, percentage of urban population, scholarisation rates, measures of educational output, particularly if internationally benchmarked, living standards as measured by gross domestic product (GDP) per head, consumer spending per head and both measures at purchasing power parity, income distrubution, and measures of landholding and infrastructure in transport and telecommunications together with principal plans.

Labour market

These include size, historical development and projection of total labour force, sector breakdowns, unemployment, unionisation, collective bargaining agreements, unionisation, and income policies as well as incomes policy affecting the growth of pay, social security, the degree of trade union density and days lost through industrial action, and description of the key influences on wage determination.

Output and trade

These include nominal and real gross domestic product (GDP), gross national product (GNP), composition of GDP by sector, the ratio of oil consumption to GDP, share of imports and exports in GDP and trend over time, and exports and imports by commodity type; and by geographical area.

Private sector characteristics

Rate of business creation and failure and its trend, self-employment and its trend, rate of return on capital employed in the business sector, estimate of the capital stock and trend in the business sector, framework for ensuring competition and lack of concentration, R&D and patents activity, estimate of the size of the publicly owned marketed sector and any plans for privatisation with expected proceeds, and description of the method of privatisation.

Supply and demand

This includes aggregate supply and demand as a percentage of GDP, including exports of goods and non-factor services, gross domestic expenditure as a percentage of GDP, external balance on goods and non-factor services as a percentage of GDP, gross domestic savings as a percentage of GDP, annual percentage changes in consumer spending, government spending (current and capital); gross fixed capital formation; exports and imports of goods and non-factor services, breakdown of gross domestic saving into personal, business and public sector as percentage of GDP, breakdown of gross domestic investment between public and private as a percentage of GDP.

Balance of payments

This includes description and analysis of the level and growth of the export of goods and services, the split between convertible and non-convertible currencies, merchandise trade balances, growth rates of exports and imports of services (split by major categories), export and import unit values as indices, and the terms of trade. Current account balance in local currency, dollars and as a percentage of GDP, short- and long-term capital flows, and analysis of comparative advantage in trade are also supposedly undertaken.

Growth constraints

The agency will look at statistics such as the non-accelerating inflation rate of unemployment (NAIRU), estimates of GDP growth, the difference between GDP and potential GDP, calculation of GDP growth, and assessment of the growth trend and whether it is improving or deteriorating.

Macroeconomic policy

This comprises elements such as the objectives and setting of monetary policy; the commitment to achieving and maintaining price stability, and degree of independence of the central bank. Trends such as inflation indicators (including the consumer price index and measures of intermediate prices, public sector charges and details of any direct price controls), pressures on the currency, exchange rate policy objectives, and conflicts between exchange rate objectives and domestic price stability are looked at. Interest rate and exchange rate trends, as well as monetary growth trends and velocity trends will also be looked at. The setting of fiscal policy objectives, and evaluation of the public sector borrowing requirement (PSBR) as a percentage of GDP are also areas of inquiry. Taxation and social security regimes as well as sources of financing of the PSBR are also looked at. Finally, a breakdown of the PSBR and stock of national debt by borrower (general government, central government, local authorities, public enterprises) in nominal terms and as percentage of GDP will be made.

Trade and foreign investment policy

The agency will look at the principal measures taken to control imports (quotas, tariffs, non-tariff barriers), tariffs applied to manufactures and the degree of effective protection, description of the agricultural import regime, export subsidies and export promotional measures, and policy towards trade liberalisation. The agency will also consider the country's policy towards foreign investment and note any prohibited sectors or regions and limits on foreign ownership. This naturally carries through to controls on repatriation of interest, profits, dividends and proceeds from disinvestment, and positive or negative differences in the tax or legal regime applied to foreign investors, including portfolio investors.

Banking and finance

The agency will look at the banking system and analyse bank lending by type of institution and sectorial destination, forecasting borrowing requirements of private and state-owned corporations. The overview will focus on description of credit policies, open-market operations, reserve requirements, credit controls, interest rate regulations and rediscount facilities. The banking system and prudential regulations will be looked at (including the level of non-performing assets). Overviews of the domestic capital markets, including liquidity and scope, will be made and market capitalisation in relation to GDP will be assessed.

External assets

This comprises elements such as the central bank's foreign exchange reserves, the ratio of reserves to imports (expressed in months), foreign assets of the banking system, public sector external assets such as loans and export credits, and non-bank private sector assets such as bonds, and shares.

External liabilities

The agency will look at the authorities' debt strategy, use of interest rate swaps and other off-balance-sheet obligations, and legal restrictions on government and other borrowing. The agency will want to know how the central government monitors other state sector borrowings, and will want a breakdown of external debt by borrower (private, public, etc.) and by creditor (multilateral, bilateral, banks, bonds, suppliers' credits, etc.), as well as net maturity schedules. The proportion of debt at floating interest rates and spreads over LIBOR will be looked at as well as recent bond issues. The external debt and debt servicing will be assessed against exports and GDP.

Political framework

The political framework assessment will look at factors such as the constitution, principal institutions including the courts, political parties, bases of support, share of the vote, stability of support, and election timetables. The assessment will look at the degree of consensus on macro- and microeconomic policy of main parties, and durability of the policy directions on which the government is embarked. Leadership succession is obviously a factor to be considered. The underlying rationale for economic and financial reforms will be assessed as well as a description of alternative policies put forward by other political parties. Descriptions of the legal framework for private property and contract settlement, and the effectiveness of the tax collection system will be analysed.

International position

The assessment will look at foreign policy objectives and strategy, membership of international, multinational and supranational organisations and trading blocs, relationship with the International Monetary Fund, relationships with neighbouring countries, the European Union, USA and Japan, plus external and internal security questions.

Behind the ratings

Table 3.2, from S&P, illustrates the typical views and clarifications given by a rating agency. The entries are for 25 August 2000; they are updated weekly. The quantitative aspects incorporate a number of measures of economic and financial performance such as ratios. The analysis is subjective, however, because S&P ratings rely on subjective data and indicate an opinion as to future debt service capacity. One agency similarly concedes that the sovereign risk rating exercise is

> far less certain than our ability to analyse either bank or corporate risks of default. The essential problem is that the world of sovereign borrowers is far smaller than the world of large banks or corporations, and that the number of instances of default in the modern period when we have reasonable national accounts is tinier still. . . . So the rating of sovereigns depends more on the art of political economy than on the science of econometrics. The assessment of sovereign risk inevitably requires more judgement because we have fewer examples of success and failure.

None of the agencies, however, will admit that the exercise in guesswork should be treated as such in their promotional literature. Some agencies use

Table 3.2 Sovereign ratings from S&P

Sovereign	Local currency			Foreign currency		
	Long-term rating	Outlook	Short-term rating	Long-term rating	Outlook	Short-term rating
Argentina	BBB–	stable	A-3	BB	stable	B
Australia	AAA	stable	A-1+	AA+	stable	A-1+
Austria	AAA	stable	A-1+	AAA	stable	A-1+
Barbados	AA–	stable	A-1+	A–	stable	A-2
Belgium	AA+	stable	A-1+	AA+	stable	A-1+
Belize	BB+	stable	B	BB	stable	B
Bermuda	AA	stable	A-1+	AA	stable	A-1+
Bolivia	BB+	stable	B	BB–	stable	B
Brazil	BB	positive	B	B+	positive	B
Bulgaria	BB–	positive	B	B+	positive	B
Canada	AAA	stable	A-1+	AA+	stable	A-1+
Chile	AA	stable	A-1+	A–	stable	A-1
China				BBB	stable	A-3
Columbia	BBB	negative	A-3	BB	negative	B
Cook Islands	B	stable	B	B	stable	B
Costa Rica	BB+	positive	B	BB	positive	B
Croatia	BBB+	negative	A-2	BBB–	negative	A-3
Cyprus	AA–	stable	A-1+	A	stable	A-1
Czech Republic	AA–	stable	A-1+	A–	stable	A-2
Denmark	AAA	stable	A-1+	AA+	positive	A-1+
Dominican Republic	SD		SD	B+	stable	C
Ecuador	SD			SD		
Egypt	A–	negative	A-1	BBB–	negative	A-3
El Salvador	BBB+	stable	A-2	BB+	stable	B
Estonia	A–	stable	A-2	BBB+	stable	A-2
Finland	AA+	stable	A-1+	AA+	stable	A-1+
France	AAA	stable	A-1+	AAA	stable	A-1+
Germany	AAA	stable	A-1+	AAA	stable	A-1+
Hellenic Republic	A–	positive	A-1	A–	positive	A-1
Hong Kong	A+	stable	A-1	A	stable	A-1
Hungary	A	positive	A-1	BBB+	positive	A-2
Iceland	AA+	stable	A-1+	A+	positive	A-1+
India	BBB	stable	A-3	BB	positive	B
Indonesia	B–	stable	C	SD		SD
Ireland	AA+	stable	A-1+	AA+	stable	A-1+
Isle of Man	AAA	stable	A-1+	AAA	stable	A-1+
Israel	AA–	positive	A-1+	A–	positive	A-1
Italy	AA	stable	A-1+	AA	stable	A-1+
Jamaica	B+	stable		B	stable	
Japan	AAA	stable	A-1+	AAA	stable	A-1+
Jordan	BBB–	stable	A-3	BB–	stable	B
Kazakhstan	BB	stable	B	BB–	stable	B
Korea	A	positive	A-1	BBB	positive	A-3
Kuwait	A+	stable	A-1+	A	stable	A-1

(*continued over*)

Table 3.2 (*cont.*)

Sovereign	Local currency			Foreign currency		
	Long-term rating	Outlook	Short-term rating	Long-term rating	Outlook	Short-term rating
Latvia	A−	stable	A-2	BBB	stable	A-3
Lebanon	BB	watch neg	B	BB−	watch neg	B
Liechenstein	AAA	stable	A-1+	AAA	stable	A-1+
Lithuania	BBB+	stable	A-2	BBB−	stable	A-3
Luxembourg	AAA	stable	A-1+	AAA	stable	A-1+
Malaysia	A	stable	A-1	BBB	stable	A-3
Malta	AA−	stable	A-1+	A	stable	A-1
Mexico	BBB+	positive	A-2	BB+	positive	B
Mongolia	B	stable		B	stable	
Morocco	BBB	stable	A-3	BB	stable	B
Netherlands	AAA	stable	A-1+	AAA	stable	A-1+
New Zealand	AAA	stable	A-1+	AA+	negative	A-1+
Norway	AAA	stable	A-1+	AAA	stable	A-1+
Oman	BBB	stable	A-3	BBB−	stable	A-3
Pakistan	B+	stable	B	B−	stable	B
Panama	BB+	stable		BB+	stable	B
Papua New Guinea	BB	stable	B	B+	stable	B
Paraguay	BB−	negative	B	B	negative	C
Peru	BBB−	stable	A-3	BB	stable	B
Philippines	BBB+	stable	A-2	BB+	stable	B
Poland	A+	stable	A-1	BBB+	stable	A-2
Portugal	AA	stable	A-1+	AA	stable	A-1+
Qatar	BBB+	stable	A-2	BBB	stable	A-3
Romania	B	stable	C	B−	stable	C
Russia	B−	stable	C	SD		SD
Singapore	AAA	stable	A-1+	AAA	stable	A-1+
Slovak Republic	BBB+	stable	A-2	BB+	stable	B
Slovenia	AA	stable	A-1+	A	stable	A-1
South Africa	A−	stable	A-2	BBB−	stable	A-3
Spain	AA+	stable	A-1+	AA+	stable	A-1+
Suriname	B	stable		B−	stable	
Sweden	AAA	stable	A-1+	AA+	positive	A-1+
Switzerland	AAA	stable	A-1+	AAA	stable	A-1+
Taiwan	AA+	stable	A-1+	AA+	stable	A-1+
Thailand	A−	stable	A-2	BBB−	stable	A-3
Trinidad and Tobago	BBB+	stable	A-2	BBB−	stable	A-3
Tunisia	A	stable	A-1	BBB	stable	A-3
Turkey	B+	positive	B	B+	positive	B
United Kingdom	AAA	stable	A-1+	AAA	stable	A-1+
United States	AAA	stable	A-1+	AAA	stable	A-1+
Uruguay	BBB+	stable	A-2	BBB−	stable	A-3
Venezuela				B	stable	B

Source: Standard & Poor's, 2000

top-down analysis as well as bottom-up analysis to determine sovereign ratings:

- Top-down analyses consider global systemic factors—past experience suggests they influence both the timing and magnitude of sovereign defaults—using quarterly analysis of default trends throughout the sector and examination of global financial sector risks.
- Bottom-up analyses focus on the credit fundamentals affecting each government. S&P divides its analytical framework into eight categories. Each category relates to economic risk and political risk, the two key determinants of credit risk. Economic risk addresses the government's ability to repay its obligations on time; it is a function of both quantitative and qualitative factors. Political risk addresses the sovereign's willingness to repay debt.

Although this appears clear enough, the specifics of these techniques are never clearly described, reminding one of the old adage that it does not pay a prophet to be too specific. Yet the rationales and justifications of the agencies' business are expected to be considered as immutable as those of a regulatory body such as the Federal Aviation Agency.

An example of a qualitative issue is assessing a sovereign's willingness to pay. This issue is one that distinguishes sovereigns from most other types of issuer. Because creditors have only limited legal redress, governments can (and sometimes do) default selectively on their obligations, even when they possesses the financial capacity for timely debt service. A rating agency would be hard-pressed to come up with an exact formula to assess the likelihood of such selective defaults, meaning that the process is highly subjective.

Moreover, while political, social, and economic factors affect a government's ability and willingness to honour local and foreign currency debt, they do so in varying degrees. A government's ability and willingness to service local currency debt is supported by its taxation power and ability to control the domestic financial system by printing money. To service foreign currency debt, however, the sovereign must obtain foreign exchange, usually by purchasing it in the currency markets. This can be a binding constraint, as reflected in the higher frequency of foreign as opposed to local currency debt defaults.

While rating agencies look at the fiscal, monetary, and inflation outcomes of government policies that support or erode incentives for timely debt service, the specific methodologies and formulae in use (if any) remain arcane and little understood. Standard & Poor's, for example, states that its foreign currency debt analysis 'places more weight on the interaction between fiscal and monetary policies, the balance of payments and its impact on the growth of external debt, and the degree of each country's integration in the global financial system' without exactly stipulating what this means or how it is quantified. Indeed, the value attached to such pronouncements is largely an act of faith in the rating agency—a dangerous position to be in during events like the East Asian meltdown.

Local and foreign currency ratings

Local currency ratings

Stability of political institutions

How does an agency assess stability of political institutions, and is this stability considered positive (as in an OECD democracy) or negative (as in an authoritarian pressure cooker like Indonesia)? S&P, for example, justifies its evaluation of France's AAA credit standing in part due to the country's democratic political framework and stability which has been achieved over time. Ukraine's evolving political institutions, by contrast, are considered to hamper its foreign currency and local currency ratings since its future direction of economic policy is less predictable. Such statements, however, are mere generalisations which any reader of the press could make. S&P's statement that 'a country's economic structure also factors into the analytical process' sounds authoritative but can lead one to wonder how this structure 'factors' into an 'analytical process', and to ask how objective or subjective such analytical processes are.

Indeed, S&P ventures forth into territory which is almost ideological (and hence confining) when it asserts that 'a decentralised decision making process and market economy, with legally enforceable property rights, is less prone to policy error and more respectful of the interests of creditors, than one where the state dominates'. One wonders how true this statement is when comparing the People's Republic of China with Korea, Israel, or Brazil.

Such statements are indeed ideological and the resulting rating is therefore based on the ideological opinions or Weltanschauungen held by S&P. By such yardsticks, S&P obviously favours the implementation of market-based economies in areas such as Central and Eastern Europe, and indeed has produced various studies supporting these beliefs. One may wish to consider how objective such corporate-sponsored studies are when compared to academic studies which are not subordinated to the profit motive.

Income and economic structure

The conventional wisdom with rating agencies postulates that a government in a country with a growing standard of living and income distribution can support relatively higher levels of public debt than a government with a poor or stagnant economy. Still, efforts to achieve 'broadly equitable' levels of income distribution may result in policies which the rating agencies, in their Weltanschauungen, may consider as 'unfriendly to business'. The agencies, in their various and voluminous documentation, do list all these factors in one permutation or another but they do not clearly explain how they reconcile the contradictions inherent in the two sets (or various sets) of policies within a checklist.

Fiscal policy and budgetary flexibility

Fiscal policy is within the preserve of economics and is hence somewhat more quantitative in nature. When evaluating fiscal policy, a rating agency will typically consider three related issues:

- The purpose of public sector borrowing
- Its impact on the growth of public debt
- Its implications for inflation

Deficit financing can be an appropriate policy tool for any government. Public sector infrastructure projects, for example, can be prudently financed through borrowing when they generate revenues sufficient to cover future debt service. Singapore, for example, has transformed itself into a prosperous manufacturing and service-based economy partly by astute investment in its public infrastructure.

Governments, however, also borrow to finance combinations of consumption and investment that increase public debt. Depending on their political support, policy-makers can raise taxes to meet their obligations. But a growing tax burden can also act as a drag on economic growth. Moreover, proposals to raise taxes can be politically unpopular. Efforts to cut spending can be thwarted by special interest groups that benefit from government programmes. Sovereigns moreover, in control of the money supply, can succumb to the temptation to print money, thereby debasing the currency. It is therefore important to distinguish between the two in the rating process, and this assessment more easily lends itself to the quantitative line of reasoning.

Fiscal policy, budgetary flexibility, and monetary policy

Monetary policy can also yield clues to the underlying creditworthiness of a sovereign. Significant increases in the money supply to cover budget deficits fuel price inflation, and price inflation can undermine popular support for governments. Left unaddressed, it can lead to serious economic damage and an erosion of public trust in political institutions. Assessing these pressures typically relies on evaluating the level and maturity structure of the public debt burden—total borrowing of central, regional, and local governments in relation to GDP—together with the likely extent of future borrowing. Other items included in the analysis are off-balance-sheet items, public sector pensions, and contingent liability items, such as banks and other enterprises, in order to try to predict their possible impact on inflation.

What the agencies typically do not disclose is how these items are factored into their analyses, or how these data (in their varying levels of completeness) are statistically compiled and related to a specific rating scale. There is a difference after all in compiling data and establishing a clear-cut link of cause and effect. S&P states in its documentation that it 'looks at institutional factors affecting inflation. For instance, an autonomous central bank with a public mandate to ensure price stability can be a stronger check on fiscal imbalances than a central bank tied closely to the government'. But it does not say whether the existence of one or another generates a necessarily positive or negative score in the ratings process, and whether or not there are uniformly applicable yardsticks in such cases.

Foreign currency rating factors

The economic and political factors influencing a sovereign's local currency credit standing can also impact its ability and willingness to honour foreign currency debt, often to a greater degree because of the binding constraints the balance of payments can impose. Rating agencies therefore typically look at foreign currency debt and how government economic policies impact trends in public and private external debt. The extent of each country's integration or isolation from the global trade and financial system is considered. Integration is seen as providing strong incentives to play by the international financial community's rules of the game.

Likewise, relations with neighbouring countries are examined with an eye for potential security risks as in the case of countries such as Kuwait/Iraq, Lebanon/Syria, and Taiwan/China, all adjacent to geographical hotspots. While one can appreciate these scenarios, once again, rating agencies do little to explain how these factors or threats are assessed and quantified into the ratings process. Here are some other factors considered in the assessment of foreign currency.

Balance of payments flexibility

The typical approach works on the premise that macro- and microeconomic policies affect balance of payments behaviour (S&P). For this reason the size of a country's current account deficit, even when very large, may not by itself be an important rating consideration. The tendency for some countries to run current account surpluses and others to run current account deficits is well documented. It is the product of many factors, not all of them negative, and not all related to government policies.

External financial position

External balances are typically compared to balance of payments flows, using macroeconomic data provided by agencies such as the OECD (Organisation for Economic Cooperation and Development). The main focus is on trends in the public external debt position, the magnitude of contingent liabilities of the government, and the adequacy of foreign exchange reserves to service its foreign currency debt and (especially in a crisis) the private sector's foreign currency debt.

International liquidity

Central bank reserves are also another indicator looked at by the agencies. Reserves usually act as a financial buffer for the government during balance of payments stress. Reserve adequacy is measured in relation to imports, and to projected current account deficits and total debt service. A related factor is access to funding from the IMF and other multilateral and bilateral official sources. Reserve levels deserve particular scrutiny during periods of global financial volatility, as in the latter part of 1998, when bond markets effectively closed their doors to emerging market issuers.

Rating distinctions

Any divergence between a sovereign's local and foreign currency ratings reflects the distinctive credit risks of each type of debt. For example, longstanding political stability, fiscal and monetary policies resulting in relatively low inflation, and a high degree of international economic integration are characteristics of sovereign issuers of AAA-rated local currency debt. The manageable public external debt burdens of these issuers, in turn, result in foreign currency debt ratings at the upper end of the investment grade spectrum.

Differences between local and foreign currency debt ratings can widen to some degree with sovereigns that are further down the ratings scale. These sovereigns typically fall into one of two categories:

- *Category 1*: these sovereigns have long records of timely service on both local currency and foreign currency debt. Inflationary pressures are moderate and public finances are relatively sound, but foreign currency indebtedness may be relatively high or is likely to become so over time.

- *Category 2*: these sovereigns also have unblemished local currency debt servicing track records, but relatively recent histories of foreign currency default. The local and foreign currency debt ratings assigned to them often balance substantial improvements in inflation and public finances with the risks inherent to still heavy foreign currency debt burdens.

A number of factors must be examined when considering whether distinctions between local and foreign currency ratings are appropriate. The default frequency for sovereign local currency debt is generally much lower than for foreign currency debt, but local currency defaults do occur.

Sovereign rating changes

Until recently, rated sovereigns formed an exclusive club of the world's most creditworthy governments. Standard & Poor's, for example, only rated a dozen sovereign issuers in 1980—all at the AAA level. Today the sovereign sector is far more numerous and heterogeneous. Rating changes occur more frequently, typically whenever new information (perhaps a newspaper headline) significantly alters the agency's view of likely future developments. For example, significant changes in the inflation outlook figure in local currency terms may result in a rating change.

A typical sovereign rating process

Once a sovereign issuer has agreed to a rating, rating agencies typically send a questionnaire to the relevant officials asking for information, not in the public domain, about indebtedness and the sovereign's view of its debt servicing ability. These questionnaires are largely standardised, but may include sections tailored to a particular sovereign if its economic and political circumstances are unusual or special. The answers to this questionnaire form the basis of the rating interviews subsequently conducted. These interviews seek to clarify aspects such as the debt burden of the country and its ability to service it, as well as other external liabilities of the economy such as foreign holdings of direct and portfolio investment.

Other indicators such as debt to exports and debt to GDP ratios are considered, providing a measure of the current and prospective ability to service debt. This can be extended to other areas such as debt service and interest payments relative to exports; the fiscal balance and the growth of the monetary aggregates; the size and nature of the official foreign exchange reserves, and so on. Other macroeconomic indicators may also be looked at, such as growth and the level of living standards. High incomes give countries a cushion in times of adversity, and the distribution of income can also be important as an indicator of social stability.

Assessment of policy

Assessment of policy involves relatively conventional economic exercises based on models which may be established by entities such as the IMF to assess the trends of gross national savings and investment and their implications for the current account of the balance of payments. Rating agencies look favourably on a coherent policy; an articulate defence of policy by policy-makers is reassuring when compared to policy-makers that are failing to recognise or tackle problems. Policy initiatives that have been announced but never implemented suggest inconsistency.

Rating agencies will also look at other key indicators such as growth, inflation, external balance, and unemployment. Some agencies also look at other elements such as the growth rate of the population; the age distribution of the population; the scale of differences in productivity levels between different sectors of the economy such as agriculture and industry; the degree of urbanisation of the economy; and the effectiveness of the educational system.

Authoritative as this sounds, however, it is not exactly clear how these elements are measured, evaluated and scored; for example, are these elements factored into some sort of mathematical matrix or scoring system, or are they incorporated into an educated guess? Again, assessing matters such as the competence of the country's administrative machinery, the skill of policy managers in dealing with external debt in a manner that demonstrates understanding of the nature of world markets, these are largely subjective exercises.

Rating agencies, as apostles of the globalised economy, naturally look favourably upon the openness of the economy to international influences and innovations, and openness to foreign investment. More specifically, the level of investment as a share of GDP is an important indicator of economic health and vitality, and ability to earn or save foreign exchange.

Can the sovereign withstand economic shocks?

Some rating agencies claim to run sensitivity or stress analysis to better understand the ability of a given economy to weather economic shocks. These analyses obviously relate to the nature of the sovereign in question—an oil producer will be assessed in terms of increased or decreased oil production or prices. More diversified economies pose a more challenging model for sensitivity analyses, and it is not clear whether these analyses are run on simple or complex econometric computer models or a summary ratio checklist.

Rating agencies also take a dim view of other potential threats to the economic status quo such as labour market institutions and 'inflexibility', caused in the words of one agency by 'fragmented and militant trade union movements' apparently failing to link unions to more equitable income distribution patterns, ensuring social tranquillity.

The assessment of political risk

The prime criterion is political stability, whether a liberal democracy or a military government. Rating agencies try to assess whether national leaders are able to mobilise support among the population even for unpopular measures. Some agencies claim to examine the existence of political and social tensions of economic, social, ethnic, and religious nature, although it is understandable to wonder how exactly rating analysts go about assessing ethnic and religious questions using Western European or US business school yardsticks.

The presence of internal or external challengers to the status quo, military spending patterns of the country and its neighbours, and the attitude of neighbours and great powers towards any potential conflict form another natural area of inquiry, although once again we may ask how effective a business school graduate can be in assessing geopolitical power struggles, a subject quite removed from business or economics.

As part of placing things into the status quo, rating agencies naturally look favourably on membership of transnational organisations or institutions such as the IMF, OECD, G8, EU, NAFTA, or other similar groupings. Where there are closer understandings about support, e.g. credit lines or a healthy relationship with the IMF, this will obviously impact the assessment favourably.

Confidentiality

Much of the information provided by the sovereign entity to the rating agency will be confidential in nature, so the agency will usually provide a written undertaking of confidentiality; this will typically cover all views, policy advice, assessment, and data that are not publicly available. The existence of these materials will also not be disclosed externally or in the rating report without permission of the authorities involved.

Assigning the rating

Once the rating visit is complete, a report is typically drafted and transmitted to the concerned officials of the sovereign government. The report may include comparisons between the rated country and its peer group. When the two parties reach consensus on the conclusions in the report, it is then submitted to the rating committee and a rating is assigned.

Bank credit ratings

Introduction

The rating of banks is diverse as there are a wide variety of countries with differing social and historical traditions, political systems, and economic systems. Rating banks on an international basis therefore necessitates a flexible approach but not so flexible as to lack coherence.

A basic rating framework will seek to understand the business of the bank in question, the objectives of its management, the environment it operates in, and the most likely future development of its business. This enables the formulation of a rating judgement rooted in an international perspective, but which accommodates the particular circumstances of the bank (national, regional, or sectoral).

Rating agencies, as marketing-driven organisations, will often back off in demanding requests for data which can be justified as irrelevant or inapplicable to the rating assessment. There are, however, certain universally applicable attributes of banks—asset quality is a good example—where full disclosure and uniform quality of information are necessary.

The particular nature of banks

Banks operating in free market economies are in most ways like other business entities, but there are significant differences; the most important is the role of banks in the supply of, the demand for, and the price of money (in most cases the national currency). This peculiarity distinguishes the most anodyne bank from, say, the largest retail store business or a major real estate developer.

Even the most liberalised administrations in the least regulated market economies may on occasion hesitate before standing aside to allow the failure of a bank, particularly if it is a constituent of the national payments system. When the chips are finally down, the authorities usually cave in and rescue the bank, rationalising the action afterwards with suitable *post hoc, ergo prompter hoc* arguments.

Most national bank regulators have two goals:

- They want confidence in their banking system to be maintained
- They want market participants to behave in a prudent and professional manner

Sometimes the two goals may be in conflict. One of the best ways to ensure prudence is to allow a degree of risk, i.e. occasionally to allow bank depositors or creditors to lose money. However, if this were to become a regular occurrence, it would undoubtedly impinge on the maintenance of confidence in the whole system. It is therefore in the interests of the bank regulator or the central bank to be deliberately vague about which banks it would support and when, or in the words of Gerald Corrigan, former president of the New York Federal Reserve Bank, to create an undercurrent of 'constructive ambiguity'.

Thus, a particularly important factor to be taken into account when rating banks is the presence (or possibly absence) of a lender/rescuer of last resort, and a very important part of the analytical work is an attempt to assess whether, and under what circumstances, a bank would be supported, and by whom. Although regulators may be cryptic, by making regular calls, by reading between the lines—look at all their pronouncements, for what seems unrelated may well prove quite revealing—and by studying their actions during past bank crises, it is possible to build up a fair understanding of their current views.

Bank rating criteria

The classic approach to bank analysis can be greatly facilitated by placing it within a framework which Moody's rating agency has summarised with the acronym CAMEL (Table 3.3) but whose presentations can vary. The CAMEL approach basically emphasises the principal aspects of concern in assessing a bank's stability. Although there is a tendency of viewing the CAMEL elements as independent (e.g. a bank may be described as having strong capital but poor asset quality), these elements are viewed as interrelated variables in assessing a bank's overall safety and soundness. If a banking institution has significant subsidiaries (brokers, leasing, etc.), the consolidated statements of the group are also an important analytical tool.

Capital

Capital, capital adequacy, or solvency is the measure to which a financial institution's portfolio and business risks are adequately offset with risk capital (i.e. equity) available to absorb potential losses. A high level of capital can help an institution ride out a protracted downside cycle, adopt more aggressive strategies, and take larger risks with the possibility of larger returns, whereas a lower level of capital reduces management's

Table 3.3   The CAMEL framework

Capital	Strong capital base High capital adequacy ratio High-quality shareholders
Asset quality	Diversification of loan portfolio No excessive loan growth Return on loan (product) appropriate to risk Good, clearly stated credit policy Low/adequate provisions (but realistic) Country risk spread well
Management	Management experienced Honesty and integrity Well-regulated environment Good spread of technical and management skills Clear and logical strategy Size and market reputation Well-trained staff Good internal/external communication Long-term relationships Competitive rates High-quality service
Earnings	High ROA and ROE Stable income stream; little exceptional items Good trend and track record of profits Controlled expense/income ratio High dividend payout potential
Liquidity	Stable customer base Loans and funding well matched Good liquidity

decisional flexibility. Capital adequacy is also important because it is the primary measure by which regulatory authorities gauge an institution's financial health.

Asset quality

Asset quality is the most important and the most difficult element of bank analysis, as it is highly subjective or opaque, as various studies have suggested. The majority of bank failures are due to poor quality of risk assets. The greatest risk in having exposure to a bank is that it can have substantial unrecognised asset quality problems which are not apparent in its accounts and which could eventually crystallise and cause it to fail. Asset quality problems can stem from a variety of causes

The main difficulty in assessing a bank's asset quality is due to the fact that accounting is by nature an activity whose assessments are subjective; this is especially true when assessing the quality of loans which may not be experiencing difficulties *at the time of the audit*. Furthermore, management's allocations of provisions for potential loan losses, based on 'experience' is inherently subjective and therefore difficult to assess. Therefore, the analyst's ability to assess a bank's stability based on financial statements is equally subjective.

Management

One of the most important and yet most subjective areas of bank analysis is the evaluation of management. While one can make certain generalisations about management behaviour, it is important to realise that banks often emerge from different cultures or sectors of the economy, hence they are unique entities with their own individual qualities, characteristics, and problems.

Management, although highly subjective, is often considered a key issue in understanding the creditworthiness of a bank. This is typically manifest in the area of problem loans, where poor management usually proves a main factor in the demise of any bank. Assessing management is extremely subjective as well as 'political'; there are no quantitative ratios or yardsticks to use in rationalising one's opinion. But there are four basic questions:

- Who are they?
- Where are they now and where do they plan to go?
- Do they have a credible plan to get to where they want to go?
- Are they capable of executing the plan?

Earnings

Earnings, or profitability, is the ultimate measure, the bottom line in assessing the financial performance of an institution. It measures an institution's ability to create shareholder value and, by adding to its storehouse of resources, maintain or improve capital soundness. It is also a quantitative measure of management's ability to achieve success in the critical areas of asset quality, overhead control, and revenue generation.

In analysing profitability, it does not suffice to compare it to historical performance indices, the quality of the earnings stream should also be assessed. Does the bank have a diversified earnings stream or does it have particular dependence on a specific activity? Which areas of the bank have historically generated the bulk of profits: merchant banking fees, foreign exchange trading, or loan fees? These all represent sources of revenue besides those of the loan portfolio's interest income, and they should be included in the assessment.

Liquidity (liability management)

Liability management, also known as asset liability management or liquidity, is an important element of the overall assessment of the bank's soundness. This involves analysing liquidity and interest rate sensitivity. Illiquidity is often the primary factor in a bank's failure, whereas high liquidity can help an otherwise weak institution to remain funded during a period of difficulty. Liquidity is therefore important, especially in assessing smaller banks, or banks which may not have a large retail depositor base and are obliged to fund themselves on the interbank markets. This is best measured by the degree to which core assets are funded by core liabilities, or to state the inverse, the extent to which the bank is reliant on 'confidence-sensitive' funds to finance illiquid assets—and viewed in light of the bank's asset structure.

Evaluating bank risk: how are banks different?

Banks and corporates are rated using very different sets of criteria. While corporates provide fodder for the managerial press and entertain the public with the epic goings-on of senior corporate managers or charismatic mavericks, banks by contrast form a dull and boring lot; at least until a major bank goes bust and the repercussions have an electrifying panic effect or there is a major merger on the scale of Chase–Chemical–Manufacturers Hanover or Deutsche–Dresdner bank. Why do bank failures catch people by surprise? As in the case of the Asian crisis or Continental Illinois, BCCI or Barings, why aren't the warning signals more evident? One reason is the nature of the banking business.

This uniqueness of banking is one of the reasons why rating agencies have developed special methodologies to assess banks. Banks, as providers of funds rather than borrowers, are typically lesser known than corporates; moreover, the nature of the business makes assessing bank risk a more difficult proposition. The assessment of bank risk is a topic warranting further consideration and is treated in extremely thorough and fascinating detail in *Analysing Bank and Country Risk* by A. Fight and K. I'Anson, two ex-bankers (Euromoney Plc, 1999). From our perspective, it is useful to consider the nature of the banking business before we look at the agencies' methodologies.

Characteristics of bank risk

In a study dated 1997, Donald P. Morgan argued that the risk of banks is hard for outsiders to judge because the risk of their mostly financial assets is either hard to measure (opaque) or easy to change (volatile). This is borne out by various studies reporting evidence that rating agencies seem to disagree more (or have split ratings) over banks than over other types of firm. Rating agencies disagree over opaque assets like loans, and easily substitutable assets like cash and trading assets. Fixed assets, like premises, are relatively easier to assess. Capital also reduces disagreement, but only at trading banks, where the risk of asset shifting may be most severe.

The rationale for much of the regulation and protection of banks hinges on the premise that the risk of banks is hard for outsiders to judge—it is opaque. If depositors could determine whether their bank was safe, they would not panic or need deposit insurance. Banks are relatively opaque because they hold few fixed assets. Their primary assets, loans, are made to borrowers who require substantial screening and monitoring, and are hence opaque. Large trading banks who have shifted from lending into trading liquid securities and derivatives may actually be more opaque.

Various industry studies suggest that Moody's and Standard & Poor's tend to have split ratings more often over bank holding companies and insurance firms than over other firms of comparable size and risk because banks often substitute loans for securities, rendering the lending activity opaque. Splits are also increasing in trading assets, while premises and other fixed assets decrease the probability of a split. Increased capital reduces the probability of a split but, paradoxically, increased capital seems to mitigate problems where the problems may be most severe, e.g. at trading banks.

Banks may fail to fully diversify because of regulatory distortions. The restriction on interstate branching may have limited their ability to diversify geographically. Deposit insurance, which is based only loosely on risk, may also lead banks to take inefficient risks. Because loans are riskier, regulators now require banks to hold more capital (weighted capitalisation ratios) against loans than against cash and securities. To increase their risk without raising more capital, banks may therefore substitute one type of loan for another, even if doing so reduces their diversification. Banks may also fail to eliminate risk because they cannot observe it themselves.

What are banks' unique characteristics?

Loans

Banks are opaque because of the loans they hold. Banks screen and monitor borrowers. Banks therefore theoretically know more about the risk of their loans than depositors or other outside investors. Assessing delinquent and non-performing loans is a largely subjective exercise; moreover, loans can conceal conditions of interior rot until the last moment, unlike more obvious indicators in the corporate world such as cash flow. It is therefore understandable that rating agencies disagree more often over banks with large loan portfolios since assessing those portfolios is a largely subjective and difficult exercise.

Trading

Increased trading also makes banks more opaque. Much bank trading now involves complex derivative instruments whose risk may be hard to measure. Trading in general, even in plain vanilla securities, also leads to the classic agency problem of asset substitution since traders can change their position unbeknownst even to their own managers, much less outsiders like creditors and regulators. A series of spectacular losses has highlighted the risk associated with trading by banks. Barings Bank, a British institution, was brought down by losses resulting from trading in currency derivatives by a single trader, while at Daiwa Bank a senior bond trader managed to lose over USD 1 billion while maintaining secret accounts for eleven years. Rating agencies are obviously powerless to assess such direct matters and must therefore satisfy themselves with more circuitous analyses such as assessing the management control measures in place.

Fixed assets

If more liquid trading assets increase uncertainty about risk, fixed assets like premises should reduce it. Fixed assets fluctuate in value but these fluctuations are more likely due to market changes than the actions of the owners and managers.

Leverage

The easily substitutable nature of banks' assets gives them opportunities for risk shifting and their high leverage gives them an incentive to do so. Leverage increases risk because such firms have smaller capital cushions against the risks inherent in the firm, or against market risk. Risk shifting not only increases risk, it will also make the banks' risk harder to judge, to the extent banks have incentive to conceal their risk taking.

Why do credit rating agencies split over banks?

Rating agencies are in the business of measuring risk. So if the duopoly disagree over the risk of a firm, it seems reasonable to infer there is something about the firm, or bank, that makes its risk hard to judge. In a 1994 study of the credit rating industry, Cantor and Packer compared the ratings of eight different bond rating agencies to Moody's. Six of the eight agencies split more often over banks than over other types of firm, usually by a substantial margin. Banks, however, are better rated on average and control substantially more assets than other firms. But the probability of a split is closely linked to the opaqueness and shifting structure of the bank, on both risk and assets. Those differences are at the heart of why rating agencies split more over banks—the opaqueness results in subjectivity.

Conclusion

The existence of bank regulation and protection presumes that the risk of banks is hard for outsiders to judge. Studies by Morgan suggest that bond raters serve to confirm the degree of difficulty in judging the risks in banks, as they seem to disagree more over banks and insurance companies than over other types of firm. Among banks, disagreement between the raters increases as banks substitute loans for securities, suggesting that the risk of a bank's loan portfolio is hard for outsiders to observe. The raters also disagree more over banks with more cash and trading assets, whose risk is easy change.

Taken together, the results suggest that the business of banks makes them opaque: banks are highly leveraged firms with few fixed assets, engaged in the business of lending and trading. These results provide some basis for the regulation and protection of banks, particularly the recent initiative requiring increased capital at trading banks; the uncertainty about the risk of such banks seems to reflect the combination of their trading activity and low capital.

Sample bank rating questionnaire

Every rating agency has its questionnaire to frame the ratings process. The following questionnaire is an offering from one of the rating agencies, obtained from their web site, with a few modifications. It is organised under thematic headings intended to reduce overlapping of topics to a minimum; nevertheless, since the activities of a bank may intermesh, there is bound to be some overlap. On questions that require financial data, agencies typically like to see a minimum of three years' financial statements but ideally five. Rating agencies are loath to inconvenience their clients, the issuer. If the data requested are available as internal management information but in a different form from that actually asked for, then they will often accept this management information.

Bank ratings checklist

Lending and other counterparties risk

Rating agencies will typically want to look at asset quality and will ask for a breakdown of the bank's loan portfolio, in terms of economic sector, country risk, and currency. Areas of interest will focus on real-estate-related lending exposure. Further information relating to the breakdown between secured and unsecured lending, with the nature of the security and its valuation techniques will also be investigated. Particular concentrations of exposure to single entities (including groups of related entities) as well as off-balance-sheet exposures will be required. Particular exposures to major shareholders, associates or affiliates will also be noted. For example, a list of the twenty largest risk exposures may be requested.

Agencies are naturally interested in seeing formalised procedures for defining credit/exposure approvals and defining exposure limits. These credit policy inquiries will assume more detailed inquiry in areas such as whether the bank uses credit scoring techniques for evaluating consumer or mortgage lending, or other credit grading systems for other types of lending.

Rating agencies will want to see control mechanisms such as formalised country or geographic limits, understand how industry or economic sector limits are defined, and see what industry or economic sector definitions the bank uses. Distinctions will be drawn between the borrower's industry classification and the nature of the collateral offered by the borrower. Agencies will also want to understand how the bank imposes limits on loans to individual borrowers, and whether these limits tie in with limits set by the law or by the regulatory authorities. Finally, regarding the establishment and management of limits, the rating agency will want to understand who sets the limits, who can alter them, and for what reasons.

Queries will be made regarding how the bank defines and assesses doubtful and/or non-performing credits, with detailed exposure statistics specifying whether they are domestic or foreign. This naturally leads to inquiries on how much, if at all, the bank has allocated loan loss provisions.

Finally, the rating agency will want to understand how the bank manages its problem loan management process, and understand how the bank ensures maximum recovery on loans that have gone bad. For example, does the bank have a separate 'recoveries' section? If so, how is it organised and how does it operate? How successful has it been?

Investment and securities risk

The agency will want to look at a breakdown of trading and investment securities portfolios, distinguishing between types of securities, in particular interest, and any portfolios managed separately at the discretion of senior management. Explanations regarding portfolio valuation policies and policies for managing investment risk will be looked at.

Fund management and administration of fiduciary funds risk

The agency will want to see details of the portfolios managed, e.g. a breakdown by type of instrument (equity or fixed interest) and further breakdowns by issuer, currency and maturity. The rating agency will also want to identify particular concentrations of clients for the bank's fund management business. These concentrations can be identified by breakdowns along lines such as type of investor (institutional or private), nationality, size of portfolio managed or any other characteristic which may be relevant.

Rating agencies will also be interested in knowing whether the bank ever reimburses clients for losses incurred as a result of changes in market values: if not, whether they would ever consider reimbursing clients; if so, under what circumstances (with any examples).

If the bank administers fiduciary funds or deposits, the rating agency will want to see details such as their totals, by country of origin and by currency, and to know how they are invested (i.e. country, currency and nature of investment). Although these funds are legally at the client's risk, the rating agency will want to know whether the bank ever reimburses clients for losses incurred on them (with any examples).

Interest rate and currency risk

Regarding interest rate and currency rate risk management, the rating agency will want to be able to assess the bank's interest rate and currency sensitivity. In particular, attention will focus on the degree to which mismatches are allowed, how the policy is implemented, and how successful it has been.

Derivatives risk

For banks active in derivatives, rating agencies may have specific assessment questionnaires. The rating agency will want to assess the following items:

- *Consolidated derivatives*: the portfolio of the entire bank, including the trading portfolio and any similar exposures (e.g. resulting from partial hedging strategies), the main derivative products, and a breakdown of these exposures by notional principal, and earnings (including the earnings for the year and the largest daily profit or loss), plus the bank's explanation of any differences which may exist in accounting treatment for public reporting and management reporting.

- *Credit risk*: inquiry will focus on current exposure, gross and net (of the effect of netting agreements) for the most recent year end, as well as the high, low and average figures for the year. Details will be requested on potential future exposure and how this is measured, as well as a breakdown of counterparties by credit quality.
- *Market risk*: the rating agency will want to understand how the bank assesses market risk and distinguishes between derivatives used for trading and hedging purposes. The bank will be queried on whether it uses concepts such as value at risk (VAR) or a similar measure plus the models used to calculate value, and statistical elements such as observation periods, confidence intervals, holding periods, high, low and average VAR in the most recent reporting period. The rating agency will also want to know if the bank uses stress testing for managing this exposure.
- *Legal risk*: the rating agency will want to understand how well derivatives are managed and whether the bank has a legal department specialising in the derivatives area, how the bank defines its netting policy in regard to netting in various legal jurisdictions, and whether all transactions are covered by industry standard agreements such as ISDA master agreements. Finally, the agency will want to understand whether the bank has adopted any measures to reduce risk of client litigation.
- *Operational risk*: the rating agency will want to know how the bank's board of directors manages this risk area as evidenced by presentations made to the board on the group's approach to derivative business, as well as board submission on derivatives exposure. The agency will want to understand how position limits are set, at what level of seniority they are set and how they are enforced. As a follow-up, management and internal audit controls in respect of trading operations will be queried.

Funding risk

The rating agency will want to understand the principal sources and likely volatility of a bank's funding. They will be particularly interested in knowing how dependent the bank is on any major shareholders. For bank borrowing, they will want a breakdown of the concentrations of such borrowing, the currencies involved and the countries of origin of the lenders. They will also be interested in potential liquidity crunches and want to know about any significant long-term borrowings which will mature in the year.

Capital and hidden reserves, loan loss and risk reserves

Rating agencies will seek information on hidden or inner reserves and establish whether these reserves are officially recognised and qualify as eligible capital or not. They will also calculate the bank's capital weighted risk ratio (as per the Basle G10 Committee or the EC capital requirements). Other ratios such as the bank's capital adequacy ratio in accordance with the national requirements will be required if these differ from the Basle G10 agreement (or the EC capital requirements).

Rating agencies will be particularly interested in detailed breakdowns of movements in loan loss, risk reserves, allowances and accumulated provisions, i.e. opening balance, the transfer (provision) from income for the year, adjustments for exchange rate variations, write-offs (charge-offs) against reserves, recoveries of past write-offs and write-backs of past provisions, and the closing balance of the reserves, allowances and accumulated provisions. Breakdowns of the closing balance of the above reserves in terms of economic sector, ultimate country risk and currency.

Other areas of inquiry will concern valuation reserves (i.e. market value higher than carrying value) on securities, foreign exchange and precious metals, and information about any real estate undervaluations or overvaluations.

Performance and earnings risk

Rating agencies will focus on the nature and characteristics of the bank's revenue stream and expenses:

- If published annual earnings figures differ substantially from the unpublished, management account figures, then information explaining the difference and reconciling the two will be required.
- Information on the development of the bank's net interest revenue and net interest margins will be required. The bank's policy on recognition of interest on problem loans as well as any recent changes will also be required. Other information such as breakdowns of fees and commissions by type, and breakdowns of other income.
- Breakdown of operating expenses with a commentary on significant changes up or down and an explanation of the tax charge.
- Explanatory breakdown of extraordinary income and expenses.
- Details of any appropriations to equity or quasi-equity reserves made as deductions from income and/or of transfers from equity or quasi-equity reported as income in the bank's published figures.
- Management's assessment of earnings and other prospects for the current year and beyond.

Market environment and planning

Rating agencies will also focus on other less quantitative aspects relating to the bank's position in the economic landscape. The starting point will be to have an organisation chart of the bank or group. A more broad assessment of the bank's domestic and international position will focus on these items:

- How dependent the bank is on the state of the domestic and international economies, and how it assesses this; what the bank's targets are for future market share, asset growth, return on assets and return on equity, as well as how these are prioritised.
- Assessments of capital expenditure on technology and automation over the past three years, and the plans for further technological development.
- The state of labour relations, the operational mechanics of any fully funded pension schemes or what other pension arrangements currently exist, and whether there is a national requirement or consensus that pensions should be fully funded in the foreseeable future.
- The bank's plans for expansion or diversification into sectors other than the ones currently conducted.

Ownership

Areas of inquiry will focus on details specifying beneficial as well as nominal ownership. And most importantly, the substance of potential support from shareholders of the bank.

Audit and control by supervisory authority

Rating agencies will want to see the latest report by the independent auditors, and the latest report on the bank by the national supervisory authority's own examiners.

Contingent liabilities

Information will be required on court cases, legal suits or adverse moves by regulatory bodies, domestic or foreign, current or pending, likely to involve the bank.

Corporate credit ratings

Introduction

Corporate ratings are aimed at providing investors with a relative indication of the ability of an issuer of a fixed-interest security to repay interest and capital on the security on time and in full. Ratings are intended to be comparable across different industry groupings and across issuers from differing countries, although the underlying assessments vary from industry sector to sector. The rating process reflects a review of the key underlying strengths and weaknesses of the company being rated and is typically based on five years' past financial data, plus sector information, management forecasts, and discussion of future performance and strategic direction.

The rating methodology for industrial companies may be segmented into two broad areas: business risk and financial risk. Business risk is a qualitative risk whereas financial risk is a quantitative risk. Ratings on credit quality are looking into future ability to repay debt. A short-term rating in particular considers those factors affecting the immediate financial outlook, such as liquidity, the asset conversion cycle, and assurance of near-term performance; a longer-term view looks at qualitative industry factors:

- Industry environment
- Volatility and outlook
- The entity's market position
- Competitive strengths and weaknesses
- Management's ability and aims
- Accounting quality
- Historical and forecast financial results
- Revenue structure and earnings protection
- Operating efficiency
- Cash flows and financial flexibility
- Capital structure
- Other relevant matters

Corporate rating criteria

Industry risk

The rating analysis typically starts off with an industry overview—the type of industry often sets the broad parameters and risk profile of the rating assessment. The sovereign rating of the country of domicile of an entity normally represents the upper ceiling on the rating for that entity's debt obligations. A government's powers generally make its credit standing higher than other debtors in the country. For issuers whose operations are centred on OECD countries, country risk will not adversely impact the rating level. It may be a factor for companies with major operations in territories of higher risk, such as Brazil or Indonesia.

The geographic and national importance of a particular industry in a country, perhaps in terms of employment, contribution to GDP or exports, or providing work to subsidiary industries, is a factor considered in the rating process. The relationship with government is also examined in an attempt to arrive at a view on the government's attitude to the industry and its constituents.

The rating analysts will seek to understand the nature and structure of the industry. Certain industries are more risky and volatile, and ratings need to reflect this. An industry in decline may adversely affect a corporation's long-term rating, as may a particularly volatile or competitive industry. Food retailing would clearly be regarded as a generally more stable industry with less risk of revenue volatility than, say, steelmaking. Food retailing may be characterised by oligopoly market positions, competition that is national rather than international, and demand levels that are stable and predictable. But steelmaking may have high capital intensity, worldwide competition, and limited or no product differentiation.

Other factors such as expensive entry barriers, competitive structure of the industry, scope for competitive changes, cyclical behaviour, research and development needs, and capital spending cycles are covered in the rating process. Important industry developments and trends are discussed with companies to assess their likely effect on future performance, and management's view is sought on the consequences of unfavourable business scenarios.

Market position and operating environment

The rating agency will want to get a feel for the relative importance (as measured by sales and share in key markets) of a company's ability to influence price, achieve product dominance, maintain reputation, and resist competitive pressures. Size may give an entity major advantages in terms of nationwide supply, distribution, advertising, and competitive position. The structural analysis will encompass aspects such as product diversity, geographic spread of sales and production, significance of major customers, reliance on particular suppliers, availability of alternatives, control over distribution, industrial relations record, trade union activity, and potential for external events to influence the business. The analysis will also attempt to appreciate variables such as productivity, comparative cost position, external influences such as environmental issues and employee relations, with the aim of assessing the potential long-term impact of these variables on market position.

Management

Assessing management is a highly subjective exercise; it can be based on the close monitoring of press cuttings as well as the agency's experience in having made previous assessments. Management risk will become evident in the company's operational and financial history, trend and record, and is an integral part of the assessment of business and financial risk; it is therefore rarely a factor in its own right. Although evaluation of a firm's management is necessarily subjective and may properly be carried out only over a period of time as results against planned goals are considered, past financial performance provides an element of objective assessment of past management performance.

Management's corporate aims are considered, alongside those of peers, to better appreciate their strategic motivation, attitude towards risk, and awareness of the industry environment. A rapidly growing company focusing on earnings per share may be primarily concerned with maximisation of near-term published earnings, whereas a more established entity may be more interested in optimising cash flow and longer-term performance. Past expansion and financing methods may provide some objective underpinning to subjective judgements.

Financial risk

Analysing financial statements and projections forms an integral part of the credit review. We will not delve into the specificities of corporate financial analysis and cash flow forecasting; suffice it to say that the rating analysis will typically not assign any formal weighting or ratio crunching to yield a score. Sometimes the rating decision may be heavily influenced by financial measures, sometimes business risks and other subjective influences may determine the rating level.

Accounting quality

To dispel a popular misconception, in no way does the rating process involve an audit of a corporation's financial statements, but it does involve consideration of their composition. Accounting quality is covered by looking at the accounting policies, including consolidation principles, valuation policies, depreciation methods, income recognition, reserving policies, pension provisions, goodwill treatment, changes in group structure, and off-balance-sheet items such as leasing and borrowings in unconsolidated entities.

Management are often able to provide further breakdown and information on the composition of published financial data, to give further insight into underlying economic figures. The aim is to arrive at a conclusion on the overall conservatism or creativity of the accounting presentation (as in the valuation of intangibles such as trademarks) and to decide what adjustments may be necessary in order to restate the figures using a basis comparable with other corporations in the same industry. Accepted accounting policies in the particular industry should normally be identified and any deviation from GAAP (generally accepted accounting principles) should be investigated.

Earnings and cash flow

Earnings are the key element in the overall financial health of an entity. Rating agencies are typically interested in stability and diversity of the cash flow stream, usually obtained from the company's annual report breakdown of the company's activity by sector. Companies often provide their own management-prepared cash flow forecasts; they are typically impossible to reconcile with the company's audited statements and are exercises in hopeful 'what if' scenarios. Some agencies, for purposes of expedience, work off these forecasts instead of actually spreading the company's audited statements and subsequently calculating their own cash flow forecasts.

It is not unheard of for some agencies seeking to expand their market share to issue ratings based on brief two-page company-prepared cash flow forecasts which are impossible to fathom or understand. The ratings are then issued with a poker-faced solemnity asserting how these analyses are on a par with ratings issued by competitor agencies or research undertaken by investment banks. In any case, some effort is made to focus on continuing flows from the company's major business activities and understanding to what extent they can be expected to be sustainable over time. The task, however, can be difficult if the company is less than transparent in providing information.

Changes in group composition, consolidation policy, inventory valuation methods, depreciation and amortisation policies, the effects of exchange rate movements, equity accounting and timing of recognition of revenues, costs and provisions all make trend analysis and valid comparisons difficult, and define the characteristics of hide and seek played between issuers and analysts. To draw meaningful opinions and comparisons between issuers, these items need to be assessed and appropriately adjusted, an often thankless task.

The point of analysing cash flow is to assess the company's ability to finance its present and projected business from internally generated cash flow. If the analysis is done properly, the cash flow forecasts will be adjusted to arrive at funds available for operations, by amending for non-cash provisions and contingency reserves, asset write-downs which do not affect cash, equity accounting to the extent this cannot be relied on as a cash source, blocked-funds overseas subsidiaries not accessible by the parent, and one-off items.

The company's capital structure and ownership will influence dividend payments and will be accordingly assessed in light of historical levels of dividend payments. Obviously, the company's position either as a quoted entity, subsidiary, or private company will have a significant effect on its dividend policy.

Capital and debt structure

The rating agency will assess leverage (total liabilities/equity) in order to appreciate the relative risk profiles of different companies as regards their reliance on external finance. Capital structures may differ due to the characteristics of local capital markets, the relationship between banks and industrial corporations, taxation treatment of dividends, interest, and so on. Capital structure similarly differs across industries; a supermarket will not have the same capital structure and financial position as an aircraft manufacturer.

The company's equity base relative to its ongoing operations and off-balance-sheet borrowings will be assessed, especially where partly-owned entities or non-consolidated subsidiaries exist, since these may at times involve claims on the parent company. The rating analysis will also examine the structure of debt, including its type, maturity schedule, currency (fixed or floating), and relationship with providers. Seasonal factors may also distort year-end figures for borrowings and therefore affect the leverage and gearing measures. The analysis should ideally address these seasonal variations. It should also look at how swaps, caps, and hedges are used as tools to manage risk (not for specualation).

Funding and liquidity

Rating agencies look favourably on low leverage. The financial flexibility of a firm is its ability to carry out its planned activities even in times of difficulty without hindering credit quality. The more conservative its capitalisation, the greater its leeway. The agency may also look to see if the issuer maintains adequate banking relationships, other financing options, or the ability to access equity markets, as well as any restrictive covenants on existing financing facilities that may limit its field of action.

The agency may also look at the structure of the company's share capital and attempt to identify major concentrations of shareholdings by individual shareholders. Such concentrations, particularly if hostile, could potentially inhibit the raising of additional equity capital, since the shareholders themselves may not have ready financial resources to meet rights issues without diluting their shareholding. By contrast, major holdings from long-standing, supportive, and financially strong shareholders could represent a positive feature.

Group structure

The situation of the corporation may have either positive or negative implications for the rating. The strength, status, and financial position of the owners of the entity, their relationship with it, the autonomy or degree of control exercised, any benefits or disadvantages associated with the ownership, all are reviewed. Structure of ownership is clearly important. A group with a pyramid structure of partly owned associates invariably gives the impression of being financially stronger than it is in reality. Equity invested down through the pyramid suggests that each company is adequately capitalised, but on a consolidated basis it becomes clear that 'group' equity is often inadequate for the level of debt.

Backup policies

An important consideration in a commercial paper rating is adequate alternative liquidity. Insufficient committed facilities unnecessarily expose a company to the vagaries of the market. Sources of such liquidity include cash and equivalents which are immediately realisable and accessible, unused committed bank lines, or other available facilities. The necessary composition of backup liquidity will vary from one issuer to another; important determinants will be the company's overall risk profile, debt structure, fluctuation in borrowings, and planned short-term financing levels.

Confidentiality

Much of the information provided by the issuer to the rating agency will be confidential in nature (e.g. strategies and financial policies). The company may therefore want the rating agency to provide a written undertaking of confidentiality; this will typically cover all views, policy advice, assessment, and data that are not publicly available. The existence of these materials will also not be disclosed externally or in the rating report without permission of the authorities involved.

Corporate ratings checklist

Industry

The agency will want to look at the importance of the industry to the country as well as the potential for support. Particular focus will be targeted to assessing employment characteristics such as the industrial relations record. Significance of legislation, protective and harmful, and relations with government. General characteristics of the operational environment enabling the situation of the company will also be assessed. These include factors such as the maturity of the industry, the nature of international competition, entry barriers, competitive domestic situation (monopoly, oligopoly, fragmentation), nature of the industry, capital intensity, product lifespans, marketing requirements, and cyclicality (demand, supply, implications for price volatility). Important developments and trends in the industry, and characteristics such as industry cost and revenue structure: susceptibility to energy prices, interest rate levels, government policies.

Market position

Classic risk analysis elements will be undertaken, such as SWOT analyses evaluating the company's competitive position within the industry (size, market share and trend, price-setting ability). Rating agencies also try to assess major product importance, factoring in elements such as product life cycles, competition, degree of product diversification, significance of R&D expenditure and new product development. To avoid excessive dependence, the agencies will also assess the geographic diversity of sales and production, and any particular dependence or concentrations of major customers, suppliers and access to alternatives. Finally, importance will be attached to the company's marketing and distribution network, with special attention to control and susceptibility to external factors.

Ownership and support

The ownership of the entity will be assessed plus its size, status, and relationship with owners, as well as the degree of autonomy of the company management. The rating agency will also want to evaluate the potential for the company to receive support or make funds withdrawals, as well as other aspects such as access to technology, products, and capital markets.

Management

Classic focus on management competence will target areas such as the management's record to date in financial terms, as well as ability to articulate corporate goals. Whilst not favouring adventurism, the agency will look favourably on an aggressive stance and outlook, coupled with a prudent attitude to risk. Ths combination will obviously be in function of management's experience, background, and credibility, and can be assessed by evaluating the depth of management (key individuals, succession, track record compared with peers).

Accounting quality

The agency will focus on the quality of accounting information and look into details such as reporting and disclosure requirements, auditors and audit opinions, consolidation methods (merger accounting, accounting for disposals, unusual treatments), revenue recognition policies: long-term projects, inventory (stock) valuation policies, fixed-asset valuation methods. The agency will also examine the treatment of goodwill and intangibles, undervalued assets (such as freehold property), debt/equity hybrid instruments, depreciation methods and rates, foreign currency treatment, deferred taxation policy, accounting for pension obligations, treatment of finance costs, and contingent liabilities. The overall assessment will focus on the overall aggressiveness or prudence of accounting presentation, and use of unusual accounting policies, movements on reserves, changes in accounting policies, and changes in group composition.

Earnings

The analysis of earnings will focus on the consistency and trend of core earnings, and earnings mix by activity and geography, the occurrence of exceptional and extraordinary items and their impact on past earnings levels, the true earnings levels available for cash flow, the use of equity accounting, restrictions on profit repatriation, and the relationship between internal growth versus acquisition-driven growth.

Profitability and protection measures

Profitability analysis will focus on assessing the quality of earnings by looking at profit margins, interest and pre-tax coverage measures, dividend cover, payment levels and future policy, taxation situation (effective tax rate, specific reliefs, unutilised losses), and the sufficiency of retained earnings to finance growth internally.

Cash flow

Analysis will focus on the company's ability to finance ongoing operations and service debt by looking at the adequacy of cash flow to maintain the operating capacity of the business, the working capital levels, and the replacement of fixed assets. Future possibilities will be assessed by looking at the contribution from cash flow towards expansion (major capital spending projects, acquisitions) as well as discretionary spending (advertising, exploration, R&D expenditure). Cash flow will also be evaluated for volatility and the relationship between cash flow and total debt. The analysis will also seek to identify any restrictions on cash flow (limits on repatriation, potential taxation effects, access to dividends from subsidiaries) which may exist or constrain the group's operational flexibility.

Capital and debt structure

This assessment is a mix of quantitative and qualitative measures. It includes analysis (historic and projected) of classic financial ratios such as gearing (debt/equity), leverage (total liabilities/equity), interest and leasing coverage ratios, sensitivity analysis on projected levels and seasonal variations. The assessment will also look at adjustments to balance sheet items: leased plant and buildings, non-consolidated subsidiaries, guaranteed associates or joint ventures, and the appropriateness of capital structure for the business given the country concerned (e.g. overreliance on short-term funding, sensitivity to interest rate changes). Asset shrinkage in a liquidation scenario will also be assessed (nature of underlying assets, ability to realise without loss, attraction to buyers in a forced sale, valuation methods and potential for moderation of gearing or leverage measures). Finally, the nature and distribution of the company's debt structure will be assessed (type, maturity, currency, service schedule, covenants, security, default clauses).

Funding and financial flexibility

The company needs a cushion or flexibility; assessment will therefore focus on the flexibility of planned financial needs (capital spending, dividend lends, acquisitions), the company's ability to raise additional financing under duress, and the existence of backup and standby lines of credit (including periods and covenants of underwritten facilities and committed lines, and the nature of overall bank relationships). The company's ability to attract additional capital (shareholder make-up, access to equity markets) will be assessed. Existing capital commitments, and the margin of safety in present and planned gearing or leverage levels will be assessed. In the event of difficulties or restructuring, the nature of assets and the potential for their reduction or disposal under stress, and the existence of saleable units will be looked at. Finally, off-balance-sheet assets and liabilities will be noted: goodwill or other intangibles written off, undervalued assets, pension underfunding.

Some terminology

The ratings business uses certain terms and ratios in assessing corporate financial statements, usually recast into a standardised spreadsheet. Tables 3.4 and 3.5 show some of the terms and ratios used by the rating agencies in their assessments. As we are not concerned with elements of financial analysis, we do not enter into detailed explanations.

Table 3.4 General definitions and policies

Finance lease commitments	Due to the nature of the commitment we consider finance lease commitments to be debt rather than creditors. Finance lease liabilities are therefore classified as current or non-current accordingly
Secured debt	Includes mortgages, debentures and lease liabilities (except where lease liabilities are shown separately)
Unsecured debt	Includes bills payable
Redeemable preference shares	Redeemable preference shares are normally classified as debt. Classification depends on the holder of the shares, the maturity date and/or the rights of redemption
Equity	Includes minority interests
Gearing	Total debt/equity
Leverage	Total liabilities/equity or in some cases equity/total assets. If the latter is being used, it will be stated in the text
Interest expensed	Interest payable less interest capitalised. Interest includes dividend payments on redeemable preference shares classified as debt
Cash flow	Net profit after tax but before minorities plus depreciation and other significant non-cash charges, less interest capitalised and ordinary dividends paid and payable. The figure excludes extraordinary items and includes only the dividends received from related companies. (Pre-dividend cash flow does not subtract ordinary dividends paid and payable)
Fixed charges coverages	These measure coverage of the company's interest, finance, operating lease, and rental costs taken together. Given the nature of these commitments, this measure is often considered to be more important than pure interest cover
Minority interests	Net income includes the earnings attributable to minority interests; and the value of minority shareholder interests are included in the calculation of equity

Table 3.5 Selected ratio calculations

Gross profit margin (%)	Sales less cost of sales and admin and distribution expenses (including depreciation and hire, lease and rent costs)/sales
Gross fared charges cover	Profit before interest and hire, lease and rent costs excluding the retained earnings of associated and related companies/interest payable, plus hire, lease and rent costs
Net fixed charges cover	Profit before net interest and hire, lease and rent costs excluding the retained earnings of associated and related companies/net interest payable, plus hire, lease and rent costs
Net interest cover	NPBIT (excluding the retained earnings of associated and related companies) net interest payable
Dividend cover	Net income (excluding the retained earnings of associated and related companies) after tax and minorities but before extraordinaries/dividend paid and proposed
Current debt payback period	Debt repayable within 12 months/post-dividend cash flow
Total debt payback period	Total debt/post-dividend cash flow
Net debt payback period	Total debt less cash/post-dividend cash flow
Quick ratio	Trade debtors, other debtors, liquid investments, cash and deposits/current liabilities
Average inventory held	Average inventory for the year/cost of sales (including overheads)
Average trade debtors held	Average trade debtors for the year/sales
Average trade creditors held	Average trade creditors for the year/cost of sales (including overheads)
Gross cash cycle	Average inventory held plus average trade debtors held. This approximates the average length of time that a company needs to fund the manufacturing, warehousing, and sale chain from the purchase of the raw materials to the receipt of sale proceeds
Net cash cycle	Gross cash cycle less the average trade creditors held. This approximates the tenets average length of time to fund the working capital cycle
Secured debt/total debt	Finance lease liabilities are included as secured debt and also within total debt

Appendix: Sample confidentiality letter

To Gosbank Durakistan

We are writing to confirm our undertaking that Weratum
Limited will not publish or otherwise disclose to
third parties any information given to it by Gosbank
Durakistan on a confidential basis. We also undertake to
restrict access to such confidential information
exclusively to officers or employees of Weratum
Limited.

This undertaking applies to all data which you
designate as confidential and which is not available to
us from other sources. After each rating meeting you
will be sent a draft copy of our rating and report.

If this draft contains any information which you
consider to be confidential and do not wish to be
published, we shall amend the text accordingly,
albeit maintaining the right to express our own
judgements of Gosbank Durakistan's performance and
creditworthiness.

Yours sincerely

Wolfsbane Troweltool
Senior Analyst
Weratum Limited

4 Rating agencies in the economic environment

Introduction

We have looked at the world of rating agencies, what it is they purport to do, how they do it, and some of their underlying motives. The evidence suggests that these matters warrant consideration and debate. But what do the users think? And why should we be interested? For two simple reasons:

- To establish how much the rating agencies actually succeed in providing the service they claim satisfies the needs of their users as measured by their users.
- To solicit feedback from other interest groups in the investor-creditor community.

This chapter therefore examines how the rating agencies are perceived by the economic community at large. The bulk of the market research in this chapter was kindly provided by the consultants Cantwell & Company and by the Japan Center for International Finance (JCIF). The interest here is soliciting market feedback from a US source and a Japanese source. Unfortunately, the author was not able to find similar research in the European market, probably because the culture underlying communication and market feedback is more confidential in nature.

The author is grateful that Cantwell and JCIF willingly provided their input for this chapter; and the author acknowledges it is the fruit of their work and that the author was unable to marshal the time or resources to undertake similar studies. Nevertheless, the author believes their results might reach a broader audience by inclusion in this book, which brings together information from disparate sources. And there emerge several interesting findings that shift my comments from the realm of speculation to the realm of serious belief.

A US perspective: Cantwell's survey

Introduction

Cantwell & Company is a specialised consultancy advising issuers on how to manage the ratings process. Every year it conducts an international survey of credit ratings. The surveys reveal that the active management of credit ratings has become an increasingly higher priority for senior-level executives, as they increasingly realise it has a direct impact on financing costs and hence the bottom line. The Cantwell survey is based on questionnaires that are typically sent to some 2000–3000 entities which have published debt ratings from one or more of the major international credit rating agencies. The survey questionnaires are typically completed by some 300–400 issuers from the United States and 32 other countries (see the end of the chapter for a list of participants).

Cantwell's annual survey is unique in the business and sheds important light on the relationship between rating agencies and issuers; it also dispels certain myths about the importance attached to the research and 'investor service' provided by the agencies. Here are some key findings in a recent Cantwell survey:

- The survey confirmed the widespread existence of initially unsolicited ratings

    Critics of unsolicited ratings argue that unsolicited ratings are compromised because analysts do not have full access to company data, while proponents insist investors need to have as much information as possible from independent third-party observers. The controversy surrounding unsolicited ratings stems from the concentration of power in the hands of a relatively small number of rating institutions, and the possibility of using unsolicited ratings as a strong-arm sales technique.

- Corporate treasurers complained that many rating agency analysts were unprepared

    More than 18% said the preparation by the lead analysts from Moody's was either poor or just fair. Roughly 10% of the lead analysts from Standard & Poor's were similarly rated. The question about the knowledge of the primary analysts received similar responses.

- Survey respondents complained about a high turnover rate among analysts

    More than 30% said that with Moody's they did not deal with the same primary analyst from year to year, and roughly 17% said they saw significant turnover at Standard & Poor's.

- Providing financial projections facilitates the rating process

    Aside from banks, most respondents furnish projections over three to five years. Issuers which are reluctant to supply projections may quickly find themselves at a comparative disadvantage.

Poll results: methodology

Cantwell has maintained the same general methodology in conducting its international survey of credit ratings since its inception in 1996. The survey draws upon publicly available lists of rated companies. Surveys were initially sent to some 2000–3000 issuers. Entities approached included corporations, banks, and sovereign issuers. Tax-exempt issues and structured financing vehicles were not approached. All survey responses were initially screened for authenticity by requesting that the respondent attach their business card to facilitate their receipt of the survey results. Further checks were conducted if no business card or cover letter was included with the survey response. Respondents were also contacted directly in the relatively few instances where the survey responses were not clear (or where answers to questions were omitted).

Overall participation

A recent Cantwell survey received 309 responses, which represented a 13% overall response rate as compared to 12% the previous year. Slightly less than half of the respondents were in the industrial sector, followed by the financial and utilities sectors. The remaining respondents included the transportation sector, the sovereign issuer sector, and the non-financial services sector.

Over the four years of the survey, the breakdown of respondents by sector has been fairly consistent. A recent survey broke down as follows:

- The industrial sector represented 48% of the respondents. The energy, consumer products, chemicals, and telecommunications segments were the most heavily represented.
- The utility sector represented 13% of the total respondents, including 39 issuers in electricity, gas, and water businesses. The majority of companies classified as utilities were based in the USA. Several other countries were represented. Of those, the UK had the most participants.
- The financial sector represented 32% of the total respondents, representing a significant increase in financial services sector respondents in this year's survey. These included banks, insurance companies, leasing companies, and other financial institutions. Among the other financial institutions were securities brokers, mortgage institutions, and captive auto finance companies. Half the respondents in this sector were banks (14 US banks and 36 non-US banks). Overall the majority of companies classified within the financial sector (55%) were non-US institutions.

Geographic breakdown of non-US respondents

Thirty percent of the issuers approached were located outside the USA. The response rate among US issuers was slightly over 11% compared to a response rate of nearly 16% from non-US issuers. Responses were received from 32 countries outside the USA. While 35% of the respondents were non-US entities, certain geographical areas showed higher response rates. Above average participation rates were seen in the UK, Canada, Australia, and Sweden. Below average participation continues to be seen in those countries where ratings are a relatively recent phenomenon.

Distribution of respondents by number of rating agencies

While many issuers surveyed had ratings from just two rating agencies, 55% of respondents were rated by three or more agencies. Most issuers with ratings from three or more agencies were US issuers. Two-thirds of all the financial sector respondents were rated by at least three rating agencies, and two-thirds of the issuers with four or more ratings were banks. Over 95% of respondents had at least two long-term ratings (Standard & Poor's and Moody's). There is clearly a growing trend toward more than two ratings, but this is not yet the 'standard' in the market. On the whole, US issuers tended to be rated by more agencies than non-US issuers, although many of the non-US issuers in the survey had ratings by more than two agencies.

Distribution of respondents by number of ratings

Ninety-two percent of all respondents with long-term ratings had at least two ratings. For the most part these were duopoly ratings. The survey notes a growing trend toward obtaining additional ratings beyond the usual Moody's and Standard & Poor's combination, as evidenced by the 49% of issuers surveyed with more than two long-term ratings. Thirty-eight percent of the respondents did not have short-term ratings. Sixty percent of those without short-term ratings were industrial companies rated BBB and below. Fifty-two percent of those issuers with short-term ratings had three or more ratings, substantially higher than in the previous year's survey. This supports the trend toward additional ratings. This group was not dominated by any specific geographic region but financial sector respondents had the most short-term ratings.

Distribution of respondents by rating level

The survey respondents ranged in rating from AAA to CC. Where an issuer was rated by more than one rating agency and where the S&P and Moody's ratings differed, a split rating was assigned for comparison.

Questionnaire findings

Was your initial rating requested or was it unsolicited?

	S&P	Moody's	Fitch-IBCA	DCR	TBW
Number of responses	284	271	79	110	41
Percent requested	94.01	90.41	73.42	94.55	63.41
Percent unsolicited	5.99	9.59	26.58	5.45	36.59

In 1996 S&P ended its long-standing policy of only assigning ratings upon request and began the practice of assigning unsolicited ratings with a 'pi' notation (for public information) to indicate that the rating was unsolicited. Last year there was a significant increase in the number of unsolicited ratings from S&P. This year that number seems to have levelled off a bit, dropping from 9% to 6%.

Slightly less than 10% of the respondents with Moody's ratings reported that their initial rating was unsolicited. Duff & Phelps (DCR) had the lowest incidence of unsolicited initial rating at 5%, but Duff & Phelps maintains a stated policy of not issuing unsolicited ratings.

Twenty-seven percent of the organisations rated by Fitch-IBCA reported that their initial rating was unsolicited; this number was lower than the 40% claiming their Fitch-IBCA rating was unsolicited in last year's survey. Thirty-eight percent of the issuers rated by Thomson Bank Watch (TBW) reported that their initial rating was unsolicited, representing a 26% increase over last year's results. Note that many ratings which were initially unsolicited eventually became requested ratings.

If your initial rating was not requested, was your most recent rating requested or unsolicited?

	S&P	Moody's	Fitch-IBCA	DCR	TBW
Number of responses	292	275	79	120	34
Percent requested	73.63	73.45	72.15	80.00	67.65
Percent unsolicited					
Regular agency meetings	25.00	26.18	25.32	19.17	29.41
No regular agency meetings	1.37	0.36	2.53	0.83	2.94

On average, about 90% of respondents whose initial ratings were not requested are now paying for their rating. The only notable exceptions are TBW ratings, which are only being paid for by 50% of the respondents claiming their initial rating was unrequested from that agency.

Approximately how many years has it been since your initial rating was obtained?

	S&P	Moody's	Fitch-IBCA	DCR	TBW
Number of responses	303	287	78	117	37
Less than one year (%)	5.28	3.83	6.41	5.13	2.70
One or two years (%)	6.93	6.62	11.54	10.26	0.00
Three to five years (%)	14.85	17.07	26.92	27.35	29.73
Six to ten years (%)	23.76	22.30	28.21	23.93	32.43
Eleven to fifteen years (%)	13.53	13.59	15.38	10.26	18.92
More than fifteen years (%)	35.64	36.59	11.54	23.08	16.22

Differences were noted in the length of time an issuer was rated by each rating agency. Moody's and S&P had the longest-standing ratings, with nearly 40% of participants reporting that their ratings were more than 15 years old. Duff & Phelps and Fitch-IBCA had the greatest percentage of new ratings, with roughly 17% of their ratings obtained in the past two years. In general, US respondents had longer-running ratings than non-US respondents, which is not surprising since ratings were invented in the USA.

What is extremely interesting is the number of newly rated issuers each year. When Cantwell initiated the survey in 1996, some 1600 issuers (defined as a parent company and affiliates with similar credit characteristics) were identified. This rose to 1950 for 1997 and 2400 for 1998. It is expected there will be well over 3000 rated issuers by end 1999.

Which rating did you obtain first?

	S&P	Moody's	Fitch-IBCA	DCR	TBW
Number of responses	289	273	75	112	34
Long-term rating (%)	55.71	57.14	40.00	61.61	17.65
Short term rating (%)	15.22	12.09	13.33	4.46	20.59
Obtained both at the same time (%)	29.07	30.77	46.67	33.93	61.76

Years ago, a common practice was to 'test' the ratings waters by initially seeking just a short-term rating. Non-US issuers tended to obtain a short-term rating first, particularly in their approach to S&P. The survey found that the current trend is for most new issuers to obtain both ratings at the same time or to obtain a long-term rating first. This trend is accentuated by the fact that many of the newest first-time issuers are below investment grade and do not even consider obtaining a short-term rating.

The survey also noted a 29% increase in the percentage of respondents that felt their long-term rating was most important. There was also a decrease in the percentage stating that their short- and long-term ratings were equally important, from 50% in 1997 to 42% in 1998.

What is your opinion of the accuracy of your current credit ratings?

	S&P	Moody's	Fitch-IBCA	DCR	TBW
Number of responses	304	289	81	122	38
Much too high (%)	0.00	0.69	0.00	0.82	0.00
Too high (%)	0.00	0.00	2.47	2.46	2.63
About right (%)	66.78	54.67	81.48	86.07	86.84
Too low (%)	28.95	38.06	14.81	9.84	10.53
Much too low (%)	4.28	6.57	1.23	0.82	0.00

Most respondents continue to feel that their ratings are about right and this year's respondents appeared more satisfied overall with their ratings. Moody's continued to have the highest percentage of respondents (44%) who felt that their rating was either too low or much too low, with the comparable figure for S&P at 33% (slightly lower than last year's 36%). With under 11% of the respondents making similar comments, TBW again received the highest level of issuer satisfaction with the accuracy of their current rating. A very small number of issuers thought that their ratings were too high. In fact, two Moody's issuers and one Duff & Phelps issuer even stated that they felt their current rating was much too high.

What criteria do you use when assessing the accuracy of your rating?

Criteria (multiple responses permitted)	$N = 309$	
Competitors' ratings	227	74%
Your rating from other agencies	218	71%
Publicly available ratings criteria	185	60%

Credit ratings can be considered a competitive business; the vast majority of respondents considered their competitors' ratings when assessing the accuracy of their own credit rating. Since competitors do not necessarily have similar financial profiles, this reinforces the need for issuers to understand how competitors are managing their ratings and agency relationships and to benchmark your organisation's procedures accordingly.

Would you like to cancel any of your current ratings?

	S&P	Moody's	Fitch-IBCA	DCR	TBW
Number of responses	7	20	5	6	1
Long-term rating (%)	1.32	4.15	1.23	4.10	0.00
Short-term rating (%)	0.33	0.69	0.00	0.00	0.00
Both ratings (%)	0.66	2.08	4.94	0.82	2.63

Responses to this question reflect the percentage of issuers with ratings from the rating agency indicated. Moody's had the highest percentage of issuers with a desire to cancel their current credit rating. Interestingly, this number was nearly twice the number who had reported that their rating was much too low.

The number who wanted to cancel their S&P rating approximated the number who felt that that rating was too low. S&P didn't have many respondents who thought that their rating was much too low. Issuers seem resigned to the fact that even unpopular ratings cannot simply be cancelled. With results just behind Moody's, Fitch-IBCA also had a significant percentage of issuers with the desire to cancel their current credit ratings.

What factors would cause you to pursue additional credit ratings?

N = 309		
121	39%	Discontent with current rating
116	38%	Investor or banker recommendation
98	32%	Split rating
62	20%	Large acquisition or major restructuring
49	16%	New or increased CP programme
46	15%	Rating change

Multiple responses are permitted.

Issuers seek additional credit ratings for a number of reasons. Among the respondents in the survey, discontent with their current rating level was the primary reason for seeking an additional rating. Following closely, investor or banker recommendation was also a popular reason for seeking an additional rating.

How would you rate the overall level of service provided by each rating agency?

	S&P	Moody's	Fitch-IBCA	DCR	TBW
Number of responses	301	287	80	122	35
Excellent (%)	15.28	11.15	15.00	25.41	14.29
Very good (%)	40.20	29.27	36.25	49.18	40.00
Good (%)	30.23	33.10	37.50	22.95	34.29
Fair (%)	12.96	19.86	11.25	2.46	11.43
Poor (%)	1.33	6.62	0.00	0.00	0.00

Duff & Phelps scored the highest in this category. S&P and TBW also fared rather well on this question. At the other end of the spectrum, more than a quarter of the companies rated by Moody's reported that the service they received was fair or poor. The most notable change here is in the increased satisfaction (40% increase) with the service provided by TBW. By industry, companies in the financial sector were less likely to feel they received an excellent level of service than those in the industrial and utilities sectors. US issuers tended to rate the agencies higher than non-US issuers in terms of level of service.

Do you feel that the rating agencies understand your concerns regarding your ratings?

	S&P	Moody's	Fitch-IBCA	DCR	TBW
Number of responses	298	285	77	122	36
Yes (%)	80.20	66.67	79.22	93.44	86.11
No (%)	8.05	16.14	5.19	0.00	2.78
Uncertain (%)	11.74	17.19	15.58	6.56	11.11

Ninety-three percent of respondents stated that Duff & Phelps understood their ratings-related concerns. One-third of the Moody's respondents felt that Moody's did not understand their concerns or were uncertain as to its understanding. There was an improvement in the case of S&P, with more respondents stating their ratings-related concerns were understood. TBW, which scored the best on this question in last year's survey, suffered a noticeable decline in issuer satisfaction. No significant differences were observed based on industrial sector, geographic region, or rating level. Note that the majority of issuers with unsolicited ratings did feel the agencies understood their concerns about ratings.

How often does each agency publish a full analytical report on your company?

	S&P	Moody's	Fitch-IBCA	DCR	TBW
Number of responses	276	260	74	116	34
More than once per year (%)	3.99	4.23	9.46	14.66	8.82
Once per year (%)	73.19	71.54	81.08	79.31	85.29
Every two years (%)	22.83	24.23	9.46	6.03	5.88

For the most part, full analytical reports continue to be published on a yearly basis. An average of 13% of the respondents reported that the interval between 'annual' analytical updates by the rating agencies was actually more than one year. S&P-rated issuers and Moody's-rated issuers stated they received full analytical reports most often. Banks tended to receive their analytical reports most frequently.

How would you rate the quality of each agency's published research or analysis on your company?

	S&P	Moody's	Fitch-IBCA	DCR	TBW
Number of responses (%)	300	282	80	122	36
Excellent (%)	8.33	4.96	5.00	17.21	5.56
Very good (%)	36.00	28.37	33.75	44.26	30.56
Good (%)	34.67	34.04	41.25	26.23	50.00
Fair (%)	18.33	25.18	17.50	11.48	13.89
Poor (%)	2.67	7.45	2.50	0.82	0.00

Duff & Phelps scored highest in this category with under 13% of its rated companies reporting that its research was fair or poor. TBW came in second with a 14% dissatisfaction rate, followed by Fitch-IBCA and S&P at 20%. At 32% Moody's had the highest level of dissatisfaction with its published research. The utility sector presented the highest overall satisfaction with the rating agencies' published research, followed by the financial sector. The industrial sector was most dissatisfied with the research.

What factors cause the agencies to publish updated analytical reports on your company?

	S&P	Moody's	Fitch-IBCA	DCR	TBW
New issue (%)	42.91	40.99	28.92	54.31	15.00
Rating change (%)	65.88	66.78	53.01	73.28	55.00
Major development/acquisition (%)	66.55	62.90	61.45	68.97	45.00
Release of interim results (%)	10.81	10.25	13.25	12.93	20.00

Multiple responses permitted.

Rating changes and merger-related developments were the commonest reasons for agencies to publish updated analytical reports on issuers. Another important reason was new issues.

Do you have an opportunity to review rating agency write-ups on your company before they are published?

	S&P	Moody's	Fitch-IBCA	DCR	TBW
Number of responses	295	282	77	123	36
For factual information only (%)	31.86	35.82	32.47	27.64	27.78
For factual and analytical information (%)	59.32	50.71	66.23	69.92	66.67
Unable to review write-ups (%)	8.81	13.48	1.30	2.44	5.56

Fourteen percent of the respondents with Moody's ratings and 9% of the respondents with S&P ratings reported no such opportunity for review. Respondents rated by Fitch-IBCA reported the greatest opportunity to review write-ups before they were published, followed very closely by Duff & Phelps and TBW.

Do you subscribe to research published and sold by the rating agencies?

	S&P	Moody's	Fitch-IBCA	DCR	TBW
Number of responses	302	286	88	132	50
Yes, a wide range (%)	7.95	6.29	9.09	3.79	6.00
Yes, selected publications (%)	46.03	46.15	25.00	33.33	26.00
No subscription (%)	46.03	47.55	65.91	62.88	68.00

Less than half the respondents subscribed to any materials published by the rating agencies for which a fee was charged.

How frequently do you normally meet with each rating agency?

	S&P	Moody's	Fitch-IBCA	DCR	TBW
Number of responses	304	290	80	123	37
Less than once per year (%)	4.61	4.83	2.50	1.63	5.41
Once per year (%)	65.79	64.83	56.25	60.16	64.86
Twice per year (%)	22.04	23.10	33.75	28.46	24.32
Three or more times per year (%)	7.57	7.24	7.50	9.76	5.41

While annual meetings with the rating agencies are still the norm, more than 35% of the respondents report that they meet with the agencies two or more times per year. These more frequent meetings seem to involve the most active issuer and those issuers experiencing credit difficulties. Financial institutions continue to meet with the agencies more frequently than other types of issuers probably because of the level of issuing activity common to banks.

Where do your annual ratings review meetings usually take place?

	S&P	Moody's	Fitch-IBCA	DCR	TBW
Number of responses	297	283	77	123	36
At the rating agency (%)	43.10	44.52	27.27	34.96	11.11
At our office (%)	39.73	38.52	55.84	40.65	69.44
Evenly divided (%)	17.17	16.96	16.88	24.39	19.44

Overall the location of the meetings continues to be fairly evenly divided. Slightly more than half the meetings with Moody's and S&P take place in the offices of the rating agencies. Fitch-IBCA, Duff & Phelps, and TBW are more likely to go to an issuer's offices for the annual update. Higher-rated issuers generally tended to host the meetings at their offices whereas lower-rated issuers more frequently had their meetings at the rating agencies. By sector, banks hosted the annual review meetings twice as often as industrials and utilities. Non-US issuers were much more likely to be the meeting hosts than their US counterparts.

Do you initiate the annual ratings meetings or do the rating agencies initiate the process?

	S&P	Moody's	Fitch-IBCA	DCR	TBW
Number of responses	297	282	79	122	36
We initiate the meetings (%)	66.67	70.92	54.43	72.95	19.44
The rating agency initiates the meetings (%)	28.62	25.18	39.24	23.77	63.89
Evenly divided (%)	4.71	3.90	6.33	3.28	16.67

Most issuers reported that they initiate the annual meetings. There were some clear variations by industrial category and geography. Specifically, both the industrial group and the utility group tended to initiate the annual meetings more than 75% of the time. However, within the financial sector there was a roughly even split between the issuers initiating the meetings and the agencies initiating the meetings. Non-US issuers were significantly more likely than US issuers to wait for the agencies to initiate the annual meetings.

Aside from the actual ratings meetings, how often do you receive questions from the rating agency analysts regarding industry developments?

	S&P	Moody's	Fitch-IBCA	DCR	TBW
Number of responses	301	287	78	123	36
Frequently (%)	13.29	12.20	19.23	15.45	13.89
Sometimes (%)	53.16	52.96	53.85	60.98	47.22
Rarely (%)	28.90	26.48	21.79	21.95	33.33
Never (%)	4.65	8.36	5.13	1.63	5.56

Thirty-one percent of the respondents stated they rarely or never received questions from the rating agencies about industry developments.

What is the average length of your annual update meeting?

	S&P	Moody's	Fitch-IBCA	DCR	TBW
Number of responses	298	284	78	123	37
Less than two hours (%)	24.16	24.30	20.51	26.02	27.03
Two to three hours (%)	47.65	47.18	43.59	46.34	37.84
Four to five hours (%)	13.42	14.08	16.67	13.01	16.22
Six to eight hours (%)	12.42	11.97	17.95	11.38	18.92
More than one full day (%)	2.35	2.46	1.28	3.25	0.00

The typical annual update meeting lasts three hours or less. Higher-rated companies reported holding longer meetings. While these meetings may be longer simply because there are more good things to talk about, it has not been conclusively demonstrated that longer meetings result in higher ratings. By industry, banks held the longest meetings of all the sectors. Non-US issuers tended to have slightly longer meetings than their US counterparts.

Who is the highest-ranking officer who routinely attends the rating agency meetings?

	S&P	Moody's	Fitch-IBCA	DCR	TBW
Number of responses	299	285	77	124	36
CEO/president (%)	39.46	39.65	35.06	37.10	44.44
CFO (%)	52.17	50.53	49.35	52.42	44.44
VP, finance (%)	2.68	3.16	3.90	3.23	5.56
VP, investor relations (%)	0.33	0.35	1.30	0.81	2.78
Treasurer (%)	5.35	6.32	10.39	6.45	2.78
Assistant treasurer (%)	0.00	0.00	0.00	0.00	0.00

The CEO or the CFO was most often in attendance at the rating agency meetings. However, there was a trend in a number of issuers bringing their CEO to the meetings with S&P, Moody's, and Duff & Phelps. For banks it is the CEO who routinely chairs the rating agency meetings; for utilities and industrial companies it is the CFO. There was no particular distinction by geographic region or rating level for this question.

Who is the officer responsible for the day-to-day contact with the rating agency?

	S&P	Moody's	Fitch-IBCA	DCR	TBW
Number of responses	301	286	79	123	38
CEO/president (%)	0.66	1.05	0.00	1.63	0.00
CFO (%)	15.95	14.69	17.72	16.26	13.16
VP, finance (%)	11.63	11.89	13.92	13.82	15.79
VP, investor relations (%)	16.94	16.08	24.05	16.26	44.74
Treasurer (%)	40.20	41.96	26.58	37.40	15.79
Assistant treasurer (%)	14.62	14.34	17.72	14.63	10.53

On a daily basis, contact with the rating agencies is regarded as a treasury function. Among the respondents, treasurers and assistant treasurers, followed by investor relations personnel, most often handle the day-to-day ratings issues. There is a discernible trend toward greater involvement of investor relations personnel in the day-to-day dealings with the agencies. The most noteworthy differentiation from this is seen in the financial sector. There the day-to-day ratings issues are more typically handled by the finance vice president or the investor relations vice president. The industrials and utilities maintain ratings issues primarily as a treasury function.

Aside from the face-to-face meetings, how frequently do you communicate with the rating agencies?

	S&P	Moody's	Fitch-IBCA	DCR	TBW
Number of responses	301	287	81	122	37
Prior to all announcements (%)	14.29	13.24	8.64	16.39	13.51
Prior to major announcements only (%)	60.47	62.02	50.62	60.66	35.14
After all announcements (%)	4.32	3.83	3.70	1.64	8.11
After major announcements only (%)	14.62	15.33	22.22	11.48	27.03
Only when they call us (%)	6.31	5.57	14.81	9.84	16.22

Most issuers continue to try to be proactive in attempting to contact the rating agencies in advance of all significant announcements. However, 10% of respondents only communicate with the agencies when the agencies call them.

What level of financial disclosure do you routinely provide to each rating agency?

	S&P	Moody's	Fitch-IBCA	DCR	TBW
Number of responses	301	286	78	124	38
Publicly available info only (%)	6.64	5.59	7.69	2.42	10.53
Selected non-public info (%)	52.49	54.20	51.28	48.39	52.63
Substantial non-public info (%)	40.86	40.21	41.03	49.19	36.84

The majority of issuers reported that they provided selected non-public information. Over 40% of participants this year reported that they provide substantial non-public information to the rating agencies. On average, utilities generally provided the most non-public information to the rating agencies. Non-US issuers were about 20% less likely to give the agencies substantial non-public information than US issuers.

What type of financial projections do you normally provide to each rating agency?

	S&P	Moody's	Fitch-IBCA	DCR	TBW
Number of responses	303	287	81	124	36
None (%)	10.23	8.71	16.05	8.06	22.22
Budget or one year (%)	28.05	28.57	40.74	24.19	61.11
Two years (%)	6.27	5.92	6.17	6.45	5.56
Three years (%)	25.41	26.83	14.81	25.00	8.33
Four or five years (%)	27.72	27.87	20.99	33.06	2.78
Six to nine years (%)	0.99	1.05	0.00	0.81	0.00
Ten years or more (%)	1.32	1.05	1.23	2.42	0.00

Nearly half of respondents provide financial projections in the three to five year range. Over 35% of the respondents said they only provide budget or one-year projections and 12% claim they do not provide any projections to the agencies. The study noted some variation in response to this question based on rating agency. TBW had the largest percentage of issuers not providing projections (20%) or providing one-year projections (63%) while Duff & Phelps had the largest percentage of issuers providing projections of ten years or more. Responses for Moody's and S&P appeared roughly parallel, with the majority of issuers providing projections of between three and five years. Ninety-five percent of US issuers provide some form of projection to the agencies compared with 82% of non-US issuers.

How do you present your financial projections?

	S&P	Moody's	Fitch-IBCA	DCR	TBW
Number of responses	273	263	67	113	31
On a consolidated basis only (%)	41.76	41.83	46.27	34.51	67.74
By business segment (%)	37.36	36.88	40.30	33.63	22.58
By subsidiary (%)	9.89	9.89	4.48	15.93	0.00
By both business segment and subsidiary (%)	10.99	11.41	8.96	15.93	9.68

Over half of respondents presented their financial projections in greater detail than simply consolidated. This seems to be the case for all agencies except TBW. This is probably explained by the fact that, by industry, the financial sector was more likely to present its financial projections only on a consolidated basis. Issuers in the industrial sector generally tended to present their financial projections by business segment. Among respondents, the majority of non-US issuers presented their financial projections on a consolidated basis only (55%) whereas their US counterparts tended most often to present theirs by business segment (36%) or on a consolidated basis (31%).

How would you rate the explanation by each rating agency of its methodology and its ratings process?

	S&P	Moody's	Fitch-IBCA	DCR	TBW
Number of responses	301	288	82	123	36
Excellent (%)	12.62	3.47	6.10	15.45	8.33
Very good (%)	34.22	24.65	34.15	39.84	30.56
Good (%)	33.89	31.60	36.59	34.96	38.89
Fair (%)	13.62	27.43	18.29	8.13	16.67
Poor (%)	5.65	12.85	4.88	1.63	5.56

In general, the rating agencies still have some work to do in better communicating their methodologies and rating processes to the issuers. Duff & Phelps received the highest marks again this year for the explanation of its methodology, with 90% of respondents judging it good or above. S&P followed closely with 81% judging it good or above. Fitch-IBCA and TBW were just slightly behind S&P, at approximately 71% satisfaction. Moody's lagged behind a bit with approximately 60% of issuers judging its explanation as good or above. US issuers gave the explanations higher scores than the non-US issuers.

How consistent do you feel the rating agencies are in terms of their approach to the ratings process?

	S&P	Moody's	Fitch-IBCA	DCR	TBW
Number of responses	300	288	82	124	36
Very consistent (%)	37.33	26.04	43.90	57.26	50.00
Generally consistent (%)	55.00	59.03	56.10	42.74	50.00
Inconsistent (%)	7.67	14.93	0.00	0.00	0.00

Duff & Phelps received the highest marks this year for being very consistent by nearly 60% of issuers. TBW and Fitch-IBCA also had excellent marks. The improvement shown by Duff & Phelps, TBW, and Fitch-IBCA enabled them to surpass S&P. Moody's was considered the least consistent of the rating agencies. The 14% of respondents citing Moody's for an inconsistent approach were mostly US issuers in the financial and industrial sectors. Of those issuers who felt the agencies were inconsistent in their approach to the ratings process, the majority had ratings more than six years old and therefore had a lengthy history of dealing with the rating agencies.

How would you rate the primary analyst in terms of their preparation for the rating meetings?

	S&P	Moody's	Fitch-IBCA	DCR	TBW
Number of responses	301	287	79	123	37
Excellent (%)	21.26	16.72	17.72	30.08	16.22
Very good (%)	41.20	32.40	41.77	43.09	40.54
Good (%)	27.91	32.40	32.91	24.39	35.14
Fair (%)	7.31	15.33	6.33	2.44	8.11
Poor (%)	2.33	3.14	1.27	0.00	0.00

Duff & Phelps was the clear leader in this category three years running with nearly 73%. Compared with last year, both S&P and Moody's showed slight improvement in the number of respondents judging the preparation by their primary analyst as either excellent or very good. US respondents judged analyst preparation as excellent or very good more often than the non-US respondents. Non-US respondents tended to judge analyst preparation as very good or good.

How would you rate the primary analyst in terms of their knowledge of your company and its industry?

	S&P	Moody's	Fitch-IBCA	DCR	TBW
Number of responses	301	288	81	123	37
Excellent (%)	22.59	16.67	22.22	28.46	32.43
Very good (%)	39.20	35.07	40.74	44.72	24.32
Good (%)	26.25	27.08	25.93	21.95	32.43
Fair (%)	8.64	14.58	9.88	4.88	10.81
Poor (%)	3.32	6.60	1.23	0.00	0.00

Respondents felt Duff & Phelps had the most knowledgeable primary analysts, with two-thirds of the respondents rating the knowledge of the primary analyst as either excellent or very good. Fitch-IBCA posted a 50% rise in satisfaction of the primary analyst's level of knowledge, compared to the previous year's 27% percent decline. An average of 58% of the utilities judged the primary analyst's level of knowledge as either excellent or very good. This was followed by the financial sector at an average of 54%. Industrial companies placed the lowest judgement on the primary analyst's level of knowledge, with an average of 37% selecting excellent or very good. US respondents gave higher marks than non-US respondents although overall both judged the analyst as generally good.

How would you rate other members of the rating team in terms of their level of knowledge about your company and its industry?

	S&P	Moody's	Fitch-IBCA	DCR	TBW
Number of responses	295	283	75	120	35
Excellent (%)	9.49	7.42	9.33	19.17	8.57
Very good (%)	37.29	30.04	38.67	45.83	25.71
Good (%)	35.59	35.69	37.33	28.33	42.86
Fair (%)	14.92	21.20	14.67	6.67	22.86
Poor (%)	2.71	5.65	0.00	0.00	0.00

Duff & Phelps again ranked highest in this category, with 65% of respondents judging the other members of the rating team as very good or excellent. Fitch-IBCA showed improvement in this area over last year, with just under 50% of respondents judging the other team members as very good or excellent. Moody's team members also had slightly higher marks than in last year's survey. Supporting team members were perceived as slightly less knowledgeable than the primary analyst.

Do you typically deal with the same primary analyst or do you feel there is a high level of analyst turnover?

	S&P	Moody's	Fitch-IBCA	DCR	TBW
Number of responses	297	285	77	124	36
Same primary analyst (%)	82.83	68.77	83.12	90.32	94.44
Significant analyst turnover (%)	17.17	31.23	16.88	9.68	5.56

The perception that Moody's has the highest analyst turnover seems to remain intact. The turnover rate was almost double that of the other agencies. All the other agencies experienced fairly similar rates of turnover.

Approximately how much do you pay in total fees to each rating agency on an annual basis (USD equivalent)?

	S&P	Moody's	Fitch-IBCA	DCR	TBW
Number of responses	278	263	68	107	37
Do not pay for ratings (%)	3.96	6.46	7.35	0.00	21.62
Less than $25 000 (%)	11.51	9.51	19.12	14.95	32.43
$25 000 to $50 000 (%)	32.01	31.56	33.82	49.53	37.84
$51 000 to $100 000	26.98	23.19	23.53	19.63	5.41
$101 000 to $200 000 (%)	16.19	20.15	14.71	10.28	2.70
More than $200 000 (%)	9.35	9.13	1.47	5.61	0.00

Banks tended to pay the highest fees, often up to four times the amount paid by industrials and utilities. On average, banks tended to pay more than USD

100 000 per year, partly due to the amount of debt being issued. Utilities and industrials tended to pay on average between USD 25 000 and USD 75 000 per year. There is a clear correlation between rating level and non-payers. A significant percentage of issuers rated BB and B claimed they do not pay for ratings.

Assuming that issuers will continue to be charged for credit ratings, how do you feel ratings fees should be structured?

The majority of issuers preferred ratings fees to be based on a fixed annual fee plus service charge for each issue. About a quarter of the respondents felt fees should be based solely on the amount of debt issued. Not surprisingly, there were very few banks or other large issuers represented in this group.

How important is your credit rating in terms of your company's advertising and marketing?

Sixty percent (57% in 1997) of respondents felt that their credit rating was an important part of their company's advertising and marketing. This group was more heavily weighted toward non-US issuers. Forty percent did not consider their credit rating to be an important part of their company's advertising and marketing. Three-quarters of these were US companies ranging across all business sectors.

Where do you go for advice regarding the management of your credit ratings?

Source	$N = 309$	
Internal sources	168	54%
Investment bankers	162	52%
Rating agency personnel	125	40%
Commercial bankers	37	12%
Independent advisors	5	16%

Multiple responses are permitted.

Most of the issuers surveyed rely on their internal management as the primary source of advice on credit ratings.

How do you identify and present your debt ratings in your company's annual report?

Twenty-one percent of those surveyed presented their debt ratings prominently in their company's annual report. Not surprisingly, all issuers presenting their ratings prominently had ratings of BBB and above. On the other hand, a full 42% of respondents said they do not identify or present their debt ratings in their annual report. This group is comprised of issuers at all rating levels.

Conclusion

Some salient points

- There is a considerable divergence in opinion between the market feedback provided by the survey participants and the self-promoting documentation provided by the agencies. The agencies' emphasis on the thoroughness of their research, their quest to provide investor service, and the importance attached to the research disseminated, which in reality is subordinate to the main business of generating fees, does not seem to meet with universal acceptance.
- The market respondents' view of unsolicited ratings suggests that this practice is more motivated by a desire to proactively manage the sales process of generating ratings fees rather than providing quality research, especially in the case of agencies not distinguishing between solicited and unsolicited ratings.
- The survey respondents' feedback regarding the qualifications and preparedness of rating analysts suggests that the product of their work is not as cast in stone as the rating scales and the incremental changes would suggest.
- Considerable questions arose as to the transparency of the methodologies used by the rating agencies in defining a rating.
- Considerable questions arose as to the rationale underlying the scales used in calculating rating fees.

Overall findings

Overall the survey suggests there is not the unanimity of opinion lauding the agencies' role and modus operandi, a unaminity they would have us believe. Nevertheless, as active players in the communications media, the agencies manage to hammer home their message with more frequency and consistency than the dispersed and dissipated entities which buy ratings, consume their offerings, and offer only haphazard and uncoordinated feedback. Hence it is hardly surprising that a message hammered home incessantly and repetitiously is soon regarded as fact.

It is clear that issuers will benefit more if they understand these developments and if they more actively manage their rating agency relationships. Likewise, investors will benefit if they broaden their sources of information.

And it is clear that entities consuming the offerings presented by the agencies as research have a few questions about the consistency, completeness, and accuracy of these offerings.

Finally, Cantwell's survey illustrates how hundreds of issuers worldwide deal with the reality of rating agencies in terms of financial disclosure and senior management involvement. The survey also chronicles the general attitudes of issuers toward the rating agencies and the research and publications they produce.

Poll respondents

AAF-McQuay, Inc.	Bowater, Inc.	Development Finance Ltd
Advanced Micro Devices	Boyd Gaming Corporation	Devon Energy Corporation
Advanta Corporation	Bradford & Bingley Building Society	Dexter Corp.
AES Corporation	BRE Properties, Inc.	Diageo Plc
African Development Bank	Bristol-Myers Squibb Co.	Dimon Incorporated
Aljba Alliance	British Petroleum Co. Plc	Doral Financial Corporation
Alpharma Inc.	British Sky Broadcasting Ltd	Duke Energy Corp.
Allegheny Ludlum Corporation	Brunswick Corp.	Duke Realty Investments, Inc.
Allgemeine Hypothekenbank	Brush Wellman Inc.	Eastern Edison
Allergan, Inc.	Caisse Centrale Desjardins	Eastman Chemical Co.
Amcor Ltd	Caisse Francaise de Development	Elan Corporation
Amerco	Caja de Madrid	Electrolux AB
Ameren Corporation	CalEnergy Company, Inc.	El Paso Electric Company
American Annuity Group	Canada Life Assurance Co.	Embotelladora Andia SA
American Color Graphics	Canadian National Railway Co.	Enterprise Oil
American Express Company	Capex SA	Ericsson AB
American Financial Group	Carlton Communications Plc	Executive Risk Inc.
American General Finance Corp.	Carolina Power & Light Co.	Farmland Industries
AmeriCredit Corp.	Central and South West Corp.	Fiat SpA
Amerin Guaranty Corp.	Charles Schwab Corporation	First Tennessee National
AmerUs Life	Chase Manhattan Corporation	FirstEnergy Corporation
Amresco, Inc.	Chevron Corporation	Fletcher Challenge Ltd
AMVESCAP	Christiania Bank Og	Florida Power & Light Group
Anadarko Petroleum Corp.	Kreditkasse	Foster's Brewing Group
Anheuser-Busch Co.	Chrysler Financial Corp.	Furon Company
Anthem Insurance Companies	CIGNA Corporation	GenAmerica Corporation
ANZ Banking Group	CINERGY	GenCorp Inc.
Applied Materials Inc.	Clear Channel Communications, Inc.	Gener SA
Aramark Corp.	CLECO Corporation	General Mills, Inc.
ARCO	CMS Energy Corp.	General Motors Acceptance Corp.
Associates First Capital Corp.	Coles Myer Ltd	Georgia-Pacific Corp.
ASLK-CGER	Columbia Energy Group	GPU Inc.
Atlantic Mutual Insurance Co.	Comerica Incorporated	GTE Corporation
Banca Commerciale Italiana	Comforce Corporation	Guidant Corporation
Banco do Nordeste do Brasil	Cominco Inc.	Harleysville Group Inc.
Banco General SA	Commercial Federal Corporation	Harsco Corporation
Banco Santander SA	Compania de Telecomunicaciones	Hasbro, Inc.
Bancomer SA	Computer Associates International	Hercules Inc.
Bank Austria	Computer Sciences Corporation	Hewlett Packard Corp.
Bank Gesellschaft Berlin	Consolidated Natural Gas Company	Hoechst AG
Bank of America	Cooper Industries	Homeside Incorporated
Bank of Greece	Credit Lyonnais	Host Marriott Services Corp
Bayerische Landesbank	Crown Central Petroleum Corp.	Household International
Beckley Water Co.	Crown Life Insurance Company	Hydro-Quebec
Bell Atlantic Corporation	Cytec Industries Inc.	IDEX Corporation
Bell South Corporation	Daimler-Benz AG	ING North America
Blount International, Ltd	Danmarks Nationalbank	Ingersoll Rand Co.
Borden, Inc.	Den Danske Bank	Instituto de Fomento Industrial
Borg-Warner Security Corp.	Den Norske Bank	Interim Services Inc.
Boston Gas Company	Deutsche Bank AG	International Business Machines

(continued over)

International Lease Financing Corp.
International Multifoods Corp.
International Technology Corp.
J.B. Hunt Transport Services
J.P. Morgan & Co., Inc.
Kansas City Power & Light
Kellogg Co.
Kimberly-Clark
Lincoln National Corp.
Litton Industries
Madison Gas & Electric Co.
Manulife Financial
Marsh & McLennan Companies
MascoTech, Inc.
Matson Navigation Company
McKesson Corporation
MCN Energy Group Inc.
Mead Corp.
Mellon Bank Corp.
Mercantile Safe Deposit & Trust
Metropolitan Bank and Trust Co.
Middlesex Water Company
Midland Enterprises Inc.
Midlands Electricity
MKB Rt. (Hungarian Foreign Trade)
Mo och Domsjo AB
MONY Life Insurance Co.
Morton International Inc.
Mutual Group, The
Nash Finch Company
National Australia Bank
National City Corp.
National Cooperative Bank
NatWest Group
NetSat Servicos Ltd
Nestle SA
New York Life Insurance Company
Newfield Exploration
Newpark Resources, Inc.
Nippon Oil Co., Ltd
Nokia Group
Normandy Mining Ltd
Northeast Utilities
Northern Trust Corp.
Northwest Airlines
Northwest Natural
Nova Chemicals Ltd
Oklahoma Gas & Electric Co.
OmniCom Group
Otter Tail Power Company
Pacific Life Insurance Company
PacifiCare Health Systems, Inc.

PacifiCorp
Paine Webber Group Inc.
PDV America, Inc.
Pearson Plc
Pennsylvania-American Water Co.
Pennzoil-Quaker State Co.
People's Energy Corporation
PetroFina SA.
Phelps Dodge Corporation
Polaroid Corporation
Powergen Plc
Praxair Inc.
Procter & Gamble Co.
Providence Gas Co.
Province of Alberta
Province of Prince Edward Island
Province of Quebec
Public Service Co. of New Mexico
Quantas Airways Ltd
Questar Corporation
Raytheon Co.
Reebok International Ltd
Reliance Standard Life Insurance Co.
Republic of Austria
Rexam Plc
Rio Algom Ltd
Rio Tinto Plc
Rizal Commercial Banking Corp.
Rockwell International Corp.
Rouse Co.
Royal Caribbean Cruises Ltd
Royal Philips Electronics
Ryder System Inc.
Sandvik AB
SBAB
SBC Communications Inc.
Schering-Plough Corp.
Scottish Power
Seacor Smit Inc.
Security Bank Corporation
Sequa Corp.
Skandia Insurance Co. Ltd
Skandinaviska Enskilda Banken
Solidbank Corporation
Solutia, Inc.
Sony Corporation
Southcorp Finance Ltd
Southern Company
Southern Indiana Gas & Electric
Southwest Airlines
Southwest Gas Corp.

Spintab AB
Sprint Corporation
Staples, Inc.
St George Bank Ltd
Sumitomo Chemical Co., Ltd
Sunkist Growers Inc.
Svensk Exportkredit AB
Svenska Cellulosa Aktiebolaget
Tandy Corporation
TCI Communications Inc.
Teco Energy Inc.
Tektronix Inc.
Telecom Corp. of New Zealand Ltd
Telephone and Data Systems Inc.
Tembec Inc.
Terra Nova Holdings Ltd
Texas Utilities Australia
TI Group, Inc.
TJX Companies, Inc.
Toronto-Dominion Bank
Transamerica Corporation
Triton Energy Limited
TRW Inc.
Unibank A/S
Unigate Plc
Union BanCal Corporation
Union Carbide Corp.
Union Oil Company of California
United States Cellular
Universal Corporation
Universal Health Services Inc.
Universal Hospital Services Inc.
USG Corporation
Valmet Corporation
Vastar Resources, Inc.
Vattenfall Treasury AB
VEBA AG
Viad Corporation
Volvo AB
Warner-Lambert Co.
Wells Fargo
Western and Southern Life
Western Resources Inc.
Westpac Banking Corporation
Wickes Inc.
Wisconsin Public Service
  Corporation
WMC Finance Ltd
Xtra, Inc.
Yellow Corporation
Yorkshire Water Plc

A Japanese perspective: JCIF's appraisal

Introduction

The influence of credit rating companies in the international financial and
capital markets has been growing rapidly in recent years due to the increasing trend to a globalised economy characterised by cross-border flows of
money looking for investment opportunities.

Under such circumstances, enterprises using rating companies when they raise funds or make investment decisions have started to claim the necessity of conducting objective comparative analysis of the characteristics and rating performance of the rating companies. Certain practices of some rating agencies, moreover, have courted hostility in various circles in Asia and Europe.

The Japan Center for International Finance (JCIF) accordingly began research into rating companies in the summer of 1997. Its report, *The Recent Debate Concerning Rating Companies* (October 1997, available only in Japanese), identified various issues about the rating industry as a whole. In August 1998, JCIF prepared outlines of each of the rating companies designated by the Japanese Ministry of Finance (MOF).

Following these previous researches, JCIF issued a 1999 report, *Focusing on Ratings in Japan and Asia*, which conducted a comparative analysis of six of the seven rating companies designated by MOF. These six rating companies have track records of ratings in Japan and Asia, namely Japan Credit Rating Agency (JCR), Japan Rating and Investment Information (R&I), Fitch-IBCA, Moody's Investors Service, Standard & Poor's (S&P), and Thomson Bank Watch (TBW). The analysis includes evaluations of each rating company by Japanese market participants and evaluations of their rating performances.

- To ascertain the assessments of the performances of rating companies by parties involved in the Japanese markets, JCIF conducted a questionnaire survey covering 264 leading financial institutions and industrial corporations, and analysed the results of the survey. In this survey each of the respondents was requested to evaluate rating companies from (1) the standpoint of obtaining a rating as an entity raising funds, and (2) the standpoint of an investor using rating information. In addition to these evaluations of individual rating companies, the survey sought out market views on core issues of the rating industry. These issues include unsolicited ratings and the relationship between the administrative authorities and the rating companies.

- JCIF analysed the characteristics and the performance of the ratings carried out by the major rating companies. For the purposes of this survey, the analysis focused on the ratings in Japan and elsewhere in Asia, bearing in mind that the credibility of ratings in the Japanese, Asian, and other markets outside the USA, the home of credit rating, is being called into question.

Credit rating traces its history back for nearly a century in the USA, and is well established as an important source of information for investment decisions. But the history of rating is still short in markets outside the USA, and it cannot yet be said to have found acceptance and credibility. This report accordingly deals with two major subjects:

- How rating companies have responded to the new type of sovereign crisis in emerging markets that has been manifested in the Asian currency crisis.
- How to strike a balance between the uniformity of global rating criteria and factors unique to individual countries whose corporate systems differ from those of the English-speaking world.

Outside the USA, the differences between the ratings of US rating companies and those of local rating companies are frequent subjects of debate. This phenomenon is sharply illustrated by the ratings of Japanese companies.

In the USA there is vigorous controversy about the desirable form of the credit rating industry in the public and private sectors. In addition, numerous surveys of individual rating companies are being made public and are being used as reference materials for the choice of rating companies by investors and issuers of bonds. In Japan, by contrast, there was a tendency in the past to regard ratings as being handed down unilaterally from some authoritative body.

Since rating companies themselves are also commercially driven entities and a rating is only an opinion, it is important to study the ratings with a critical eye.

Results of the questionnaire survey concerning rating companies

Issues concerning the rating industry as a whole

Multiple-choice questions were asked on what the researchers considered to be the most important of recent issues in the rating industry. Approximately two-thirds of all respondents agreed with this statement: The influence of the two major US rating companies, Moody's Investors Service and Standard & Poor's, is too strong, and the principle of healthy competition among rating companies is not functioning. About 60% of the respondents also agreed with this statement: When ratings are announced, the explanations are inadequate or inappropriate, causing confusion to investors. This percentage can be interpreted as reflecting the requirement among investors for a greater degree of accountability on the part of rating companies than at present.

From a different angle, nearly 60% of the respondents agreed with this view: Investors place excessive reliance on information provided by rating companies and tend to abandon their own investment judgement. And with respect to unsolicited ratings, over 60% of the respondents agreed with the following two opinions: (1) Rating companies should disclose in greater detail the grounds for their unsolicited ratings. (2) Rating companies should clearly distinguish which are unsolicited ratings and which are solicited ratings. Some 30% of the respondents agreed that 'unsolicited ratings are used by rating companies in their marketing strategies to solicit ratings, and this creates problems regarding the reliability of the ratings'. This reveals deep-rooted suspicion among Japanese market participants of unsolicited ratings.

Among the questions concerning the relationship between the rating industry and the regulators in Japan, there was extensive support for this view: Regulations should not be imposed directly on the activities of rating companies, but from the standpoint of the protection of investors and clients, the administrative authorities should play a more active role than at present, including requesting reports from rating companies, setting disclosure standards, and monitoring for inappropriate sales activities.

Evaluation of major rating companies

Evaluation from the standpoint of issuers

Some questions regarding the rating process were asked in the first place. On the points of whether 'the rating company gives issuers sufficient opportunity to explain before deciding or changing ratings', and whether 'the rating company provides the issuer with convincing explanations of its reasons for deciding or changing ratings', the two Japanese rating companies (JCR and R&I) were given high marks but the international rating companies were generally assessed as poor. These results suggest Japanese issuers believe that whereas international rating companies attach importance to the uniformity of global rating standards, they place relatively little importance on factors relating to systems that are peculiar to Japan. The overall evaluation was that no particularly large differences were seen among the four rating companies which conduct larger numbers of ratings on Japanese companies (JCR, R&I, Moody's, and S&P).

Evaluation from the standpoint of investors

S&P and Moody's surpass other rating companies in the categories of breadth of rating coverage and extent of influence on markets. They received universally high regard with respect to the high quality of their ratings and analytical reporting in all rating fields: sovereigns, industrial corporations, financial institutions, and structured financing. JCR and R&I received a slightly higher grading than the non-Japanese rating companies for the quality of their ratings and analytical reporting with regard to Japanese companies. It seems that the full services from Moody's and S&P have a lead over the other rating companies, but the other companies do offer competition in their specialised services.

The Asian currency crisis and rating performance

Nature of the crisis

The Asian currency crisis, triggered by the Thai baht crisis in July 1997, is regarded as a twenty-first century archetype that differs in character from conventional sovereign crises. Here are some of the reasons:

- It was brought about by massive and quick short-term movements of private funds during the globalisation of financial and capital transactions.
- The abrupt change in the perceptions of market participants led to plunges in exchange rates and stock prices in various countries, and these spilled over into the real economy.
- Contagion occurred among countries within the Asian region, and later in Latin America.

Accordingly, for many economists and policy-making officials, it was difficult to forecast completely the recent series of crises, and the same applies to rating companies. The successive revisions to ratings by rating companies during these Asian currency crises have possibly exacerbated the currency and economic crises in Asian countries. Ratings have been transplanted to emerging markets virtually unchanged from advanced markets that are sophisticated and highly transparent, and in which most market participants are well conversant with the mechanism and significance of ratings.

Content of rating reports

Looking back at the content of the ratings and analysis reports of the leading rating companies (Moody's, S&P, Fitch-IBCA, and TBW) before and after the outbreak of the Asian crises, all of them issued numerous warnings to investors about the fragility of Asian countries' financial institutions and financial systems well before the outbreak of the crises.

It cannot be said, however, that they foresaw adequately the speed and intensity with which this fragility of financial institutions and financial systems expanded into sovereign crises. More than one rating company started downgrading the sovereign rating of Thailand only after the Thai baht was devalued in July 1997. Some rating companies downgraded the sovereign rating of Korea rapidly and substantially from its very high rank, but after a short period they revised the rating upward. Meanwhile, there were subtle differences among rating companies with respect to such matters and the timing of their revisions of sovereign ratings based upon such problems.

Moody's

Moody's issued some degree of warning through its reporting to investors regarding the process by which the risks inherent in banks and banking systems in Asian countries spread to sovereign risk. However, as was seen very noticeably in Indonesia and South Korea, the manner in which it took steps to lower its sovereign ratings only at the stage when the contagion of the currency crises had become very clear, indicates that it did not adequately discern the speed and intensity of the process.

Standard & Poor's

From a review of the sovereign rating of Thailand, S&P does not appear to have seen that the problems concentrated in the private sector at the outset of the financial crisis would have such a major impact on the country's sovereign creditworthiness. However, in its December 1997 report, it stated that the course of countries with fragile financial sectors has showed how essential is the soundness of banking systems to the stability of the macro-economy and the maintenance of economic growth.

Fitch-IBCA

Fitch-IBCA did not issue sufficient advance warning to investors concerning the fact that even in countries with no particularly excessive outstanding debt, such as South Korea, an increase in short-term debt can give rise to sovereign risk, and the fact that it is necessary to scrutinise the overall balance of outstanding debt, including private sector debt as well as public sector debt. Based on this experience, however, Fitch-IBCA became the first rating company to issue a report in January 1998 reviewing its own rating performance during the Asian financial crises. This is worthy of note insofar as it indicates that the company has sincerely carried out its obligation to give explanations to investors.

Thomson Bank Watch

Thomson Bank Watch's ratings of Asian countries suggest that the company tries to attach importance to the stability of ratings, as sovereign and bank ratings have not been dictated to any great extent by short-term market movements. It is also of note that in January 1997, before the outbreak of the currency crisis, TBW was the only major rating company to rate Indonesia with a speculative grade (BB+). After having maintained a cautious view up to the beginning of 1997, however, TBW upgraded Indonesia in April 1997 to investment grade.

The correlations between ratings and default rates

In the USA, where the history of ratings goes back nearly one hundred years, there is a large accumulation of historical data concerning ratings and defaults. Every year Moody's and S&P release detailed data on the relationship between their ratings and defaults. These releases show the stable relationship between ratings and default rates. This can be interpreted as indicating that rating performance has been good. Caution must be paid, however, to the fact that the majority of firms rated by both rating companies have been US firms, and that the rating methods used by both were originally devised and reformed with the objective of measuring the credit risk of US firms.

In countries and regions in which the history of ratings is still short, neither of these rating companies has had its rating performance verified sufficiently. Of particular note is that in Japan, where there have been extremely few defaults on publicly offered bonds, it is not easy to conduct statistical verification in the same way as in the USA. Moreover, there are substantial divergences (split ratings) between the ratings of the identical firms by international rating companies and by Japanese rating companies.

Moody's rating coverage of Japanese firms provides an important clue. For example, with regard to the bonds of 25 Japanese firms whose long-term bonds were given speculative grade (Ba or lower) ratings by Moody's five years ago, no defaults have occurred to date. On the other hand, according to Moody's default study of firms worldwide (the majority of which are US firms), the probability of default within five years by companies receiving ratings of Ba is 11.4%. In the period around 1990, when the US economy was affected by recession and a credit crunch, this ratio rises to more than 20%.

Methodology of the questionnaire survey

	Companies requesting ratings	Companies subject to unsolicited ratings	Companies using ratings as investment information	Companies using analytical reports as investment information
JCR	55	4	87	53
R&I	97	7	107	84
Fitch-IBCA	11	7	26	22
Moody's	46	57	128	100
S&P	50	34	122	79
T&W	10	–	5	16

All figures show the number of applicable companies from among the survey respondents.

Survey method	Anonymous questionnaires
Sample	Major financial institutions (175) and major industrial companies (89), primarily members of JCIF
Responses	149 valid responses (response rate of 56.4%). The survey emphasised anonymity, so no questions were included that would identify the specific characteristics (industry, size, etc.) of responding companies
Survey period	Survey conducted between June and August 1998
Content	The survey attempted to gauge how participants in Japanese markets view the major issues confronting the rating industry as a whole (unsolicited ratings, relationship between ratings and regulators, etc.). The survey also represents the report card given by Japanese market participants to the major rating companies (the seven rating companies designated by MOF). Duff & Phelps is excluded from the tabulation even though it has been designated by MOF because it does not in fact rate Japanese companies and there were extremely few valid responses for it
Tabulation method	Simple response totals used. On some questions the respondents were asked to grade ratings companies on a four-step scale: A (agree), B (somewhat agree), C (somewhat disagree), D (disagree). Here JCIF has shown component percentages of A to D marks for each rating company
Supplementary interviews	To add more depth to the survey results, JCIF also conducted separate supplementary interviews with officers in the financial and planning departments of financial institutions and industrial companies, and others who had experience working for rating companies. The analysis touches on the findings from these interviews and the opinions expressed in the 'free comments' sections of the survey questionnaire

Issues concerning the rating industry as a whole

Which of the following do you consider currently to be the most important problems in the rating industry as a whole? Choose three

The influence of two major US rating companies is too strong, and the principle of healthy competition among rating companies is not functioning	93 companies
When ratings are announced, the explanations are inadequate or inappropriate, causing confusion to investors	84 companies
Investors place excessive reliance on information provided by rating companies, and tend to abandon their own investment judgements	82 companies
The organisations (quality and number of analysts, etc.) of rating companies have not been able to keep pace with the rapid expansion of the ratings market	64 companies
Rating companies themselves do not disclose sufficient information	49 companies
Rating companies are subject to inadequate regulation and monitoring	15 companies
The 'profit first' attitude at rating companies has distorted their ratings	4 companies
Political and administrative pressure on rating companies has distorted their ratings	3 companies

Valid responses from 144 companies.

When asked about the problems in the rating industry as a whole, two-thirds of the respondents said that 'the influence of the two major US rating companies is too strong, and the principle of healthy competition among rating companies is not functioning'. The predominant opinion was as follows:

- Issuers who raise funds internationally may be dissatisfied with the rating methods of the two US companies, but they have such a dominant position in the markets that issuers are forced to select one of them regardless.
- There is an oligopoly in the market as manifest by high ratings fees.

According to a study conducted by the Nomura Research Institute in 1996, Moody's and S&P between them have an estimated 80% share of revenues on the world market, which itself is an indication of a near oligopoly in the rating market. The US Department of Justice has also shown an interest in the oligopolistic conditions in the rating industry and has expressed its intention to review the nationally recognised statistical rating organisation (NRSRO) system to address these issues.

The next most commonly recognised problems in the rating industry were inadequate accountability and disclosure on the part of rating companies. To summarise the comments made during interviews with market participants, most thought that when publishing ratings, rating companies should at least provide the issuer with a detailed rationale for the rating, including the items covered in the evaluation and the allocation of points.

There was also a great deal of support for the idea that 'investors place excessive reliance on information provided by rating companies, and tend to abandon their own investment judgements'. This indicates that many of the issues related to rating companies must be viewed not only as problems for rating companies themselves but also as problems for all market participants, including the recipients of rating information.

Which of the following most closely matches your opinion of so-called unsolicited ratings? Choose all that apply

Unsolicited ratings are a fact of life, but rating companies should disclose in greater detail the grounds for their unsolicited ratings	90 companies
Unsolicited ratings are a fact of life, but when publishing ratings, rating companies should clearly distinguish between which are unsolicited ratings and which solicited ratings	87 companies
Unsolicited ratings are used by rating companies in their marketing strategy to solicit ratings, and this creates problems regarding reliability of ratings	43 companies
Rating companies should be free to issue unsolicited ratings if they are required by investors	19 companies

Valid responses from 144 companies.

Issuers have recently expressed a great deal of dissatisfaction with unsolicited ratings, and it is notable that more than 60% of respondents agreed with these two statements: (1) Rating companies should disclose in greater detail the grounds for their unsolicited ratings. (2) Rating companies should clearly distinguish between which are unsolicited ratings and which solicited ratings.

S&P does distinguish between the two, with the rationale that it does so in recognition of the fact that unsolicited ratings rely on more limited information than solicited ratings and are therefore of limited precision. Moody's, on the other hand, takes a more aggressive stance and asserts that it is possible to arrive at unsolicited ratings of the same quality as solicited ratings, even if the issuer has not solicited the rating, and therefore makes absolutely no comment on which of its ratings are solicited and which unsolicited. According to the JCIF survey, market participants consider the distinction between unsolicited ratings and solicited ratings to be a valuable piece of information and therefore tend to support the stance of S&P.

Some 30% of the survey respondents agreed that 'unsolicited ratings are used by rating companies in their marketing strategies to solicit ratings'. This indicates a deep-rooted suspicion of unsolicited ratings among Japanese market participants. A commonly expressed opinion in interviews with market participants was that 'there are sales activities that encourage companies subject to unsolicited ratings to switch to solicited ratings'.

It is of course entirely possible that much of the dissatisfaction with unsolicited ratings is merely an emotional reaction by companies given low ratings. Still, the influence of ratings has grown very strong very rapidly, and rating companies have established themselves in a superior position vis-à-vis issuers, which makes it easier for them to succumb to the pressures of sales staff to use unsolicited ratings as part of their hard sell strategies.

The term 'unsolicited ratings' refers to ratings that were not solicited by the issuer being rated (and therefore do not involve any payment of rating fees). But different agencies define the term in different ways:

- Moody's does not admit any difference in quality between unsolicited ratings and solicited ratings, and its unsolicited ratings reflect both non-public information obtained in interviews with companies and information about the industry and company learned from the markets. However, there are several companies that do not voluntarily agree to interviews when unsolicited ratings are made.
- Fitch-IBCA also takes the stance that whether it is an unsolicited rating or a solicited rating, there is no difference in the rating process except whether a fee is collected.
- S&P, in contrast, puts its unsolicited ratings (pi ratings) in a completely different framework from its solicited ratings. Even if it conducts

corporate interviews, it does not use anything other than publicly available information for its pi ratings.

- The unsolicited ratings of Japan Credit Rating Agency (p ratings) and the unsolicited ratings of Japan Rating and Investment Information (op ratings) rely primarily on publicly available information and are clearly distinguished from solicited ratings.

Which of the following proposals regarding the regulation of the rating industry in Japan (the relationship between the rating industry and regulatory authorities) would you agree with? Choose all that apply

Regulations should not be imposed directly on the activities of rating companies, but from the standpoint of investor and client protection, regulators should play a more activist role than at present, including requesting reports from rating companies, setting disclosure standards, and monitoring for inappropriate sales activities	92 companies
Regulators should not interfere in any way because the market will ultimately render judgement on the value of rating companies	48 companies
Rating companies should establish a certification testing systems for their analysts	44 companies
The designated rating company system should be abolished	16 companies
In light of the strong influence that rating companies have over the financial markets, regulators should strengthen their regulation	6 companies

Valid responses from 144 companies.

There was almost no support for the idea of strengthening the regulation of rating companies, an idea that attempts to curb in some way the vast influence that rating companies have over financial and capital markets. The general view is that the market itself should solve the problems involving rating companies rather than direct government interference.

However, there was broad support for the idea that 'regulation should not be imposed directly on the activities of rating companies, but from the standpoint of investor and client protection, regulators should play a more activist role than at present, including requesting reports from rating companies, setting disclosure standards, and monitoring for inappropriate sales activities'.

There is little active discussion of this system in Japan, though in the USA the Securities and Exchange Commission (SEC) has noted a broad range of issues surrounding the NRSRO system on which the Japanese system was modelled.

Major rating companies' influence on Japanese companies

Which rating companies' ratings do you find to be the most important in ensuring that your fund-raising proceeds smoothly? Select one rating company

Moody's Investors Service	54 companies
Japan Rating and Investment Information	37 companies
Standard & Poor's	33 companies
Japan Credit Rating Agency	9 companies
Fitch-IBCA	0 companies
Thomson Bank Watch	0 companies
Other	4 companies

Valid responses from 137 companies

Which rating company's ratings do you place the greatest emphasis on in investment decisions and risk management standards? Select one rating company

Moody's Investors Service	69 companies
Japan Rating and Investment Information	28 companies
Standard & Poor's	20 companies
Japan Credit Rating Agency	9 companies
Fitch-IBCA	1 company
Thomson Bank Watch	0 companies
Other	16 companies

Valid responses from 143 companies.

The survey asked respondents which rating companies' ratings they valued the most in their fund-raising and investment decisions, as a means of gauging the strength of the influence exerted by rating companies on Japanese firms. On both questions the respondents predominantly selected Moody's, confirming that Moody's ratings are very influential with Japanese firms. Broad coverage of domestic markets makes R&I the most emphasised rating company for financial institutions and industrial companies that primarily serve domestic clients.

Evaluation of major rating companies

The survey next asked how rating companies are evaluated by the Japanese market. This was in two parts: evaluation from the fund-raising side (issuers) and evaluation from the investment side (investors). Here is a summary of the trends seen for individual companies on individual evaluation items.

Evaluation from the standpoint of institutions raising funds (issuers)

Focusing on their evaluation of the ratings process, the questionnaire asked issuers if the rating company gives the issuer sufficient opportunity to explain before deciding or changing ratings

Focusing on their evaluation of the ratings process, the question-naire asked issuers if the rating company provides the issuer with convincing explanations of its reasons for deciding or changing ratings

Issuers gave high marks to two Japanese rating companies, including JCR, but low marks to the international rating companies, probably because they have high ratios of unsolicited ratings.

I think the analysts handling our rating have strong analytical skills

Less than half the sample said they agreed or somewhat agreed with this statement. Based on comments heard during interviews with major issuers, many expressed the following opinions as to why rating companies were short-staffed in their corporate bond departments:

- Staff turnover rates are high, so there are problems with the continuity of expertise
- Rating companies tend to put their best people into the relatively high-profit area of structured finance ratings
- The number of analysts has not risen to keep pace with the sharp expansion in the number of ratings being performed

I think there is sufficient disclosure of ratings standards and the specific method employed

Issuers gave low overall marks in their evaluation of disclosure, particularly in their evaluation of the disclosure to international rating companies. Issuers appear to be expressing their dissatisfaction with not knowing which items and point allocations decided their ratings.

I think rating standards appropriately reflect specifically Japanese factors in areas like corporate governance

Issuers gave high marks to the two Japanese rating companies and low marks to the international rating companies. These results indicate how the perception among Japanese issuers is that international rating companies emphasise uniform, global ratings standards to the point where they place relatively little weight on uniquely Japanese systems. There is a unique corporate governance system in Japan that works against default.

I think profit-oriented business policies have the potential to impair the fairness of ratings

A comparatively high percentage of respondents agreed or somewhat agreed that this statement is applicable for Moody's and S&P. This appears to reflect the suspicion of unsolicited ratings felt by Japanese issuers.

I think that overall this is an excellent rating company

In the overall evaluation there was little variation among the four rating companies that perform many ratings of Japanese companies (JCR, R&I, Moody's, S&P). Although Fitch-IBCA and TBW were graded a bit lower, these low grades were probably due to two factors: (1) both rating companies only rate a small number of Japanese firms and (2) both rating companies perform their ratings of Japanese firms basically at their headquarters or their Hong Kong offices, so their operations in Tokyo are very small.

Evaluation from the standpoint of investors

Information from this rating company is an indispensable reference when making investment decisions because of the broadness of the company's ratings coverage

Information from this rating company is an indispensable reference when making investment decisions because of the influence the company has in the markets

There is a strong correlation between the rating company's ratings coverage and its perceived influence in the markets. For investors investing on a global scale, the broadness of its coverage carries decisive weight when selecting a rating company.

Information from this rating company is an indispensable reference when making investment decisions because of the excellent objectivity and foresight of its ratings

S&P, followed by TBW, scored highest in the objectivity criteria. The two Japanese rating companies were graded as less objective than the international companies.

Ratings from this rating company can be trusted because it publishes detailed and clear explanations of the rationale behind the rating

Marks were low overall, indicating that investors want a more detailed rationale to be published. Interviews with market participants suggest that where there are split ratings, it is hard to know what differences in opinion among rating companies led to the differing conclusions.

Ratings from this rating company can be trusted because it publishes studies of correlations between past ratings and default rates

In evaluating the relationship between past ratings and default rates, Moody's was given the highest marks, followed by S&P. Both rating companies have conducted long-term verifications of the relationships between their historical ratings and default rates. Fitch-IBCA and TBW have not performed these verifications because their ratings primarily cover financial institutions and it is rare for defaults to occur.

This rating company tends to follow market trends

A relatively high percentage of investors agreed or somewhat agreed this to be the case for the two Japanese companies. Many were of the opinion that 'the Japanese rating companies in the early 1990s took a far laxer view of the bad debt problem of Japanese banks than did the international rating companies'. TBW got high marks on this question, indicating that it is not following the markets. Market participants say of TBW that 'compared to the Big Two, it sees its core customer service as providing information on the financial institutions rather than just ratings results, and it emphasises stability in its ratings'.

This rating company produces high-quality sovereign ratings and analytical reports

This rating company produces high-quality industrial company ratings and analytical reports

This rating company produces high-quality financial institution ratings and analytical reports

This rating company produces high-quality structured finance ratings and analytical reports

This rating company produces high-quality Japanese corporate ratings and analytical reports

This rating company produces overall high-quality ratings and analytical reports

Turning to investor evaluations of ratings and analytical reports for specific areas, S&P had the highest overall score, followed by Moody's. The duopoly are given consistently high marks on the quality of their ratings and analytical reports in all areas: sovereigns, industrial companies, financial institutions, and structured finance. Among the other international rating companies, Fitch-IBCA is given significantly higher marks than the duopoly in structured finance, while TBW is highly regarded in financial institution ratings. To sum up, Moody's and S&P lead the other four in overall service, but each of the others appears fully able to compete within its areas of expertise.

Summary

As compared to the Cantwell survey, the JCIF survey offers a Japanese viewpoint on the ratings business. This is interesting insofar as the ratings business is primarily a US-generated phenomenon exporting its methodologies and Weltanschauungen to the world. There are of course other developed economic powerhouses such as Japan, and it is interesting to note how other non-US players view the business.

The survey has some limitations, however: it reflects only the opinions of participants in Japanese markets; global evaluations could be quite different. It is particularly hard to include the evaluations of Fitch-IBCA and TBW alongside the other evaluations because their operations in Tokyo are extremely small-scale.

> The ostensible function of rating companies is to collect and analyse information about firms issuing bonds on behalf of investors and to clarify for investors the investment risks involved. Ratings companies are to some extent dependent on ratings fees from issuers. These fees are levied to cover the rating company activities of correctly analysing and transmitting its information to the markets so that it is able to raise funds at a fair price. Therefore, as long as rating companies continue with their current style of business, which is dependent on revenues from both investors and issuers, they will need to balance the demands of [conflicts of interest existing between] issuers and investors by explaining results, avoiding pressure tactics such as issuing unsolicited ratings, and disclosing ratings methods.

Assessing agencies in the Asian crisis

Introduction

The Asian currency crisis triggered by the collapse of the Thai baht in July 1997 has been described as a a twenty-first century currency crisis, differing in nature from sovereign crises that have occurred in the past. This conclusion is based on three facts:

- The crisis was caused by massive and quick private short-term capital flows made possible by the globalisation of financial and capital transactions.

- Rapid changes in the perceptions of market participants caused the collapse of exchange rates and stock prices, which in turn impacted on real economies in the region.
- The crisis was contagious, spreading among countries in the Asian region and later in Latin America.

These features made it difficult for many economists and policy-makers to foresee in its entirety the chain of crises that occurred, and the same applies to rating companies. The ratings assigned to Asian countries by such companies have subsequently come under increasing scrutiny, and analysts have in the main been critical of their performance.

Uncertainty in the markets makes them sensitive to negative information, with the result that negative forecasts become self-fulfilling prophecies. The financial institutions whose existence critically depends on credit are even more likely to succumb to this tendency. In a sense, therefore, it is quite conceivable that the changing ratings assigned during the Asian currency crisis resonated with the market's response, thus magnifying the currency and economic crises in countries in the region. The Asian currency crisis has thus served to reveal problems surrounding the assignment and use of ratings in emerging markets.

Examining the ratings assigned to Asian countries, it can be seen that the leading rating companies were critical in their assessments and comments concerning financial institutions and systems in the region considerably prior to the outbreak of the crisis. However, they failed to properly foresee the scale and speed of contagion of the sovereign crises that their weakness would engender. For instance, the downgrading of Thailand's sovereign rating by several rating companies occurred only after the devaluation of the baht in July 1997, while countries such as South Korea with extremely high sovereign ratings were sharply downgraded only to be upgraded again within a short space of time.

The Asian currency crisis has uncovered serious weaknesses in the analyses made by rating companies. A study by the JCIF traced the changing assessments made during the currency crisis by rating companies of Thailand, Indonesia, and South Korea, three countries so badly affected by the currency turmoil that they had to seek international aid from sources such as the IMF.

JCIF East Asia study parameters

JCIF's study first summarises the main features of the currency crisis in each of these countries, and then traces the changes over time in the rating companies' analyses, sovereign ratings, and bank ratings before, during, and after the crisis. It compares the different traits displayed by each rating company during the Asian currency crisis. The period chosen for analysis is the 18-month period before and after the devaluation of the Thai baht that marked the onset of the Asian currency crisis. However, reference is also made to prior reports and other appropriate data.

Due to their wide coverage of financial institutions and sovereign ratings for Asian countries, Moody's, Standard & Poor's (S&P), Fitch-IBCA and Thomson Bank Watch (TBW) were selected for the study. A total of 18 banks—9 Thai, 3 Indonesian, and 6 South Korean—were selected to compare the average bank ratings assigned by each company except S&P. S&P was excluded from the comparison as, unlike the other companies, it has no ratings that do not take into account sovereign risk or the possibility of support being provided by the authorities.

An examination of the banks surveyed for the present study shows that, in the immediate past, 11 Thai banks have been rated by Moody's, 10 by Fitch-IBCA, and 15 by TBW; 12 Indonesian banks have been assigned ratings by Moody's, 3 by Fitch-IBCA, and 38 by TBW; and 16 South Korean banks have been rated by Moody's, 8 by Fitch-IBCA, and 38 by TBW. Although the number of banks rated by the three companies varies from country to country, it is obvious that TBW, with its strong reputation for bank ratings, provides noticeably higher coverage. Table 4.1 shows the sovereign rating scales, Table 4.2 shows the bank rating scales, and Table 4.3 shows the rated banks.

Table 4.1   Sovereign rating scales

	Moody's	S&P	Fitch-lBCA	TBW
1	Aaa	AAA	AAA	AAA
2	Aa1	AA+	AA+	AA+
3	Aa2	AA	AA	AA
4	Aa3	AA−	AA−	AA
5	A1	A+	A+	A+
6	A2	A	A	A
7	A3	A−	A−	A−
8	Baa1	BBB+	BBB+	BBB+
9	Baa2	BBB	BBB	BBB
10	Baa3	BBB−	BBB−	BBB−
11	Ba1	BB+	BB+	BB+
12	Ba2	BB	BB	BB
13	Ba3	BB−	BB−	BB−
14	B1	B+	B+	B+
15	B2	B	B	B
16	B3	B−	B−	B
17	Caa1	CCC+	CCC	C
18	Caa2	CCC	CC	D
19	Caa3	CCC−	C	
20	Ca	CC	D	

Source: JCIF

Table 4.2   Bank rating scales

	Moody's[a]	Fitch-IBCA[b]	TBW[c]
1	A	A	IC-A or CE-1.0
2	B+	A/B	IC-A/B or CE-1.5
3	B	B	IC-B or CE-2.0
4	C+	B/C	IC-B/C or CE-2.5
5	C	C	IC-C or CE-3.0
6	D+	C/D	IC-C/D or CE-3.5
7	D	D	IC-D or CE-4.0
8	E+	D/E	IC-D/E or CE-4.5
9	E	E	IC-E or CE-5.0

Source: JCIF
[a] Financial strength rating
[b] Individual rating
[c] Intra-country rating or credit evaluation

Table 4.3   Banks assigned ratings by Moody's, Fitch-IBCA, and TBW

Thailand	Indonesia	South Korea
Bangkok Bank	Bank Dagang	Bank Negara Indonesia
Bank of Asia	Nasional Indonesia	Commercial Bank of Korea
Bank of Ayndhya	Bank Ekspor Impor Indonesia	Hanil Bank
First Bangkok City Bank		Kookmin Bank
Krung Thai Bank		Korea First Bank
Siam City Bank		Seoul Bank
Siam Commercial Bank		Shinhan Bank
Thai Farmers Bank		
Thai Military Bank		

Source: JCIF

JCIF summary for individual rating companies

Moody's

Moody's rated Asian banks critically from before the outbreak of the currency crisis. This applied even more so in the case of Indonesian banks than Thai and South Korean banks. The reasons given for its critical assessment of banks in all three countries included banks' deteriorating asset portfolios and liquidity shortages, and the fragility of the banking systems in these countries.

Moody's gave some warning in its reports for investors of the possibility that the risks borne by banking systems and individual banks in the Asian region could spread to affect sovereign risk. Nevertheless, the fact that it only decided to downgrade sovereign ratings when it was obvious that the currency crisis was spreading indicates that Moody's was unable to predict the speed and seriousness of the contagion of the currency crisis, especially in Indonesia and South Korea. But note that Moody's did start to lower Thailand's sovereign rating before the collapse of the baht.

Standard & Poor's

S&P warned frequently of the fragility of the banking systems in Thailand, Indonesia, and South Korea prior to the currency crisis. In the case of Thailand, S&P warned of the sharp growth in short-term debt and Thai banks' declining creditworthiness, while in South Korea it warned that the weakness of the financial sector could place a serious financial burden on the government. The changing ability and willingness of governments to protect their banking systems during the crisis meant that the lack of a means of rating banks' financial strength independently made the warning less clear.

S&P's rating of Thailand's sovereign risk suggests that it did not believe at the start of the currency crisis that the problems concentrated in the private sector would have such a serious impact on sovereign creditworthiness. The fact that the S&P ratings followed the trend set by other rating companies during the crisis is a reflection of S&P's view of the impact of private sector problems on sovereign creditworthiness.

S&P's rating of South Korea's sovereign risk appears to have been closely correlated with fluctuations in the market. Its ratings wobbled sharply over a short period of time, as when South Korea's rating was upgraded by three notches just two months after twice being downgraded by a total of seven notches in December 1997.

Fitch-IBCA

Around the end of 1997, Fitch-IBCA downgraded its bank ratings for Thailand, South Korea, and Indonesia in particular to a lower level than the other rating companies, and the critical ratings it assigned served to warn of the problems inherent in the banking sectors in these countries.

While Moody's was quick to warn of the impact of the growth in short-term debt on South Korea's sovereign risk, Fitch-IBCA appeared relatively unconcerned by the surge in external debt. The lessons learned from the recent crisis—even in countries such as South Korea that do not have particularly excessive gross balances of debt, growth in short-term debt can increase sovereign risk, and the overall balance of debt (including the debts of the private sector and the public sector) requires close monitoring—suggest that Fitch-IBCA's analysis was incomplete. It learned from its experience, however, and became the first to analyse its own ratings record during the currency crisis when it issued a report in January 1998, a move demonstrating its commitment to investor accountability.

Fitch-IBCA's sovereign ratings for South Korea were closely correlated with market fluctuations and varied widely over short periods, as when the country's sovereign rating was raised by five notches two months after twice being downgraded by a total of ten notches in December 1997.

Thomson Bank Watch

TBW's sovereign and bank ratings for Asian countries were largely un-affected by short-term market trends, a reflection of the company's emphasis on providing stable ratings. It also provided investors with timely reports on the problems facing banking sectors in countries in the region. In the case of South Korea, for example, it consistently warned of problems with the coun-try's banks and banking system, such as the problem of bad loans, low profitability, and poor equity capital levels, during the previous few years when the country enjoyed sustained economic growth. With respect to Thai-land, TBW was quick to recognise the need to revise ratings to allow for problems such as bank liquidity. All these problems have grown more ob-vious or worsened in the course of the currency crisis in Asia. In January 1997 only TBW rated Indonesia's sovereign risk as speculative (BB+). Despite its cautious assessment until the start of the year, TBW then upgraded Indo-nesia's sovereign rating to investment grade in April 1997.

Rating records by country

Thailand (Table 4.4)

Moody's

- Moody's was quick to warn and downgrade on the basis that sudden inflows of short-term capital lead to the risk of liquidity shortages.
- Critical assessment of the banking system due to deteriorating asset port-folios and liquidity shortages.
- Downgrading of sovereign rating to speculative grade due to poor mar-ket confidence caused by factors such as problems in the banking sector.

Standard & Poor's

- From before the currency crisis, S&P warned of the sudden growth in external short-term debt and declining bank creditworthiness, but com-mented this would have no impact on sovereign creditworthiness.

● Downward trend in sovereign rating appears to follow path set by other rating companies.

Fitch-IBCA

● Strong scale of revision of bank ratings

Thomson Bank Watch

● From before the outbreak of the currency crisis, TBW tended to emphasise the soundness of economic fundamentals in its analyses while keeping ratings somewhat lower than other rating companies.
● Recognised from an early stage the need to reassess ratings due to factors such as the liquidity shortage faced by Thai banks.
● Smaller revision of sovereign rating in comparison with other rating companies.

Table 4.4 Comparison of main rating actions in Thailand

	Moody's	S&P	TBW	Comments
Rating as of end 1996	A2	A	A–	1 notch
investment grade or speculative grade	invest	invest	invest	difference
Start of downgrading (in or after 1997)	4/97	9/97	9/97	Moody's first to downgrade
Rating as of end June 1997	A3	A	AA	1 notch
investment grade or speculative grade	invest	invest	invest	difference
Number of rating changes since July 1997	3	3	2	Ratings almost
upgrades since July 1997	–	–	–	coincide
Maximum difference in ratings since July 1997 (notches)	3	4	3	Ratings almost coincide
Minimum rating since July 1998	Ba1	BBB–	BBB–	Only Moody's
investment grade or speculative grade	spec	invest	invest	rates as spec
month of downgrade	12/97	01/98	12/97	
Month downgraded to speculative grade	12/97			
Rating in June 1998	Ba1	BBB–	BBB–	Only Moody's
investment grade or speculative grade	spec	invest	invest	rates as spec
notches difference on end June 1997	–4	–4	–3	

Source: JCIF

Indonesia (Table 4.5)

Moody's

● Much more critical than other rating companies in its assessment of banks from prior to the currency crisis.
● Rapid downgrading of sovereign rating from end of 1997.

Standard & Poor's

- Warned investors of the features of the currency crisis in Indonesia, such as the lack of confidence in the government and the debt problems of the corporate sector.
- Biggest downgrading of sovereign rating.

Fitch-IBCA

- Warned repeatedly of the political uncertainty and the external debt problem since it started rating.
- Drastic revision of bank ratings.

Thomson Bank Watch

- Early to note the possibility of political and economic factors increasing sovereign risk and affecting the banking system.
- Despite being the only rating company to upgrade Indonesia's sovereign rating in April 1997, it quickly downgraded from December 1997.

Table 4.5 Comparison of main rating actions in Indonesia

	Moody's	S&P	Fitch-IBCA	TBW	Comments
Rating as of end 1996 invest or spec	Baa3 invest	BBB invest	–	BB+ spec	Only TBW grades as speculative
Start of downgrading	12/97	10/97	12/97	12/97	S&P first to downgrade
Rating as of end June 1997 invest or spec	Baa3 invest	BBB invest	BBB– invest	BBB– invest	TBW upgrades in April
Rating changes since July 1997 upgrades since July 1997	3 –	6 –	4 –	4 –	Wide variation
Maximum difference in ratings since July 1997 (notches)	6	8	6	7	Variation
Minimum rating since July 1998 invest or spec month of downgrade	B3 spec 04/98	CCC+ spec 05/98	B– spec 03/98	C spec 05/98	1 notch difference
Month downgraded to speculative grade	12/97	12/97	12/97	12/97	Coincide
Rating in June 1998 invest or spec notches difference on end June 1997	B3 spec –6	CCC+ spec –8	B– spec –6	C spec –7	1 notch difference

Source: JICF

South Korea (Table 4.6)

Moody's

- Quick to note the impact of the large growth in short-term debt on sovereign risk.
- Rapidly downgraded South Korea's sovereign rating toward the end of 1997.
- More critical of banks than other rating companies from before the currency crisis.

Standard & Poor's

- Identified the problem of deteriorating assets in South Korea caused by the growth in credit and the asset-price bubble.
- Seriously concerned by the impact on sovereign risk of the heavy burden placed on government finances by the weakening financial sector.
- Frequent and large rating revisions.

Fitch-IBCA

- Commented that public debt was extremely low and the surging level of external debt was little cause for concern.
- Frequent and large rating revisions.

Thomson Bank Watch

- Provided timely reports for investors.
- Extremely minor rating revisions in comparison with other companies.

Summary of the Asian financial crisis

The JCIF study, the severity and rapidity of the downgrades in Asia, and the 'catch-up' nature of the rating agencies' reaction have dented their credibility. In an unusual departure from industry tradition, Fitch-IBCA (a new challenger to the US duopoly and possibly hoping to gain favourable media coverage) has openly admitted this. In retrospect, it is obvious that the very rapid growth seen in emerging markets would inevitably be followed by some form of major correction, which in turn would probably be followed by a more normal growth pattern. Pinpointing where the bubble would burst,

Table 4.6 Comparison of main rating actions in South Korea

	Moody's	S&P	Fitch-IBCA	TBW	Comments
Rating as of end 1996 invest or spec	A1 invest	AA– invest	AA– invest	AA– invest	1 notch difference
Start of downgrading	11/97	10/97	11/97	11/97	Ratings almost coincide
Rating as of end June 1997 invest or spec	A1 invest	AA– invest	AA– invest	A+ invest	1 notch difference
Rating changes since July 1997 upgrades since July 1997	3 –	5 1	5 1	3 –	Variation
Maximum difference in ratings since July 1997 (notches)	6	10	12	4	Wide variation
Minimum rating since July 1998 invest or spec month of downgrade	Ba1 spec 12/97	B+ spec 12/97	B– spec 12/97	BBB invest 12/97	Wide variation Only TBW rates as invest
Month downgraded to speculative grade	12/97	12/97	12/97	–	Coincide
Rating in June 1998 invest or spec notches difference on end June 1997	Ba1 spec –6	BB+ spec –7	B– spec –7	BBB invest –4	Only TBW rates as invest
Month of upgrade number of notches		02/98 3	02/98 3		

Source: JCIF

however, was less obvious; it happened to be in Asia but the same developments could just as well have emerged in Central and Eastern Europe.

In any case, how does this impact a rating agency's credibility and modus operandi in the international credit markets? Two inevitable consequences of these developments have already occurred:

- Spreads have dramatically increased for all borrowers from emerging markets.
- The identity of investors in these securities has shifted as previously 'conservative' investors depart and investors that are openly more 'yield oriented' begin to look at such securities.

Here are three more consequences, perhaps not so obvious but still important to issuers:

- Even if not publicly stated as policy, the practice of the credit rating agencies will be to automatically take a 'go slow' approach to any new issuers in emerging countries as well as emerging industries.
- In similar fashion, rating upgrades in these countries and industries will be virtually impossible to obtain in the near future. This trend will override even the most recent comments about upgrades that the agencies may have made to specific issuers.
- In any future rating meetings, all issuers will be expected to quantify their exposure to Asian markets and this should be specifically included in the rating presentation materials.

Japanese ratings and default rates

Analytical approach

The importance of ratings as a source of investor information lies in the fact that they provide an estimate of the possibility of a loss of credit arising from factors such as late payment or inability to service debt. One method of measuring the performance of ratings is to study the relationship between past ratings and default rates. If ratings are to serve as a useful source of information for making investment decisions, it is important that the relationship between ratings and defaults should be stable. Should there be wide variation in the relationship over time or between regions, this presents problems for investors. For example, if the probability of default on a bond issued by a US company rated BBB and the probability of default on a bond issued by a Japanese company rated BBB are significantly different, this poses a problem to investors.

The USA, with almost a century of experience in ratings, has accumulated abundant historical data on rating trends and defaults. Consequently, the relationships between rating companies' ratings and default rates are on the whole good. This is hardly surprising considering the duopoly are US companies, the majority of firms rated by the duopoly are from the USA, and the rating methods used by the duopoly were developed to measure the credit risk of US firms. Exporting these US methods to international markets such as Europe or Japan, however, poses challenges due to their different economic systems, their different historical patterns of corporate development, their links between industry and finance, and their structural modes of financing as affected by culture (e.g. debt versus equity).

As a consequence, the rating performances in these developed and emerging markets, where ratings were introduced more recently, have yet to be fully analysed. For Japan, in particular, the exceedingly low default rates on publicly offered bonds make it difficult to undertake statistical studies of rating performances like the studies performed in the USA. It is with these questions in mind that we compare the results of default studies made by Moody's, S&P, and Japan Rating and Investment Information (R&I) of ratings and default rates. Over the past few years, observers of the Japanese market have increasingly criticised US rating companies' ratings of Japanese firms for being too low, and the aim therefore is to determine the statistical evidence for such criticism.

Comparing the results of default studies

Every year in the USA, rating companies publish detailed data on trends in ratings and default rates. These serve not only as a means of verifying, ex post facto, the performance of ratings, but have recently also come to be used for a variety of other purposes, such as calculating credit enhancements for structured finance, and forecasting asset pool cash flow. The JCIF study only considers the contents of the US duopoly since Fitch-IBCA and TBW until recently were only concerned with financial institutions, which offer a paucity of historical default data to work with.

Moody's and S&P: default studies

Defaults on rated bonds usually occur when the issuing company goes bankrupt. However, bankruptcy and default do not always go hand in hand. Defaults as defined by US rating companies include not only formal defaults but also de facto defaults; exchanges of bonds designed to reduce the financial burden, for instance, are treated as defaults. In this respect, there is little difference between the definitions used by Moody's and S&P.

Moody's defines default as any missed or delayed disbursement of interest and/or principal, bankruptcy, receivership, or distressed exchange where (i) the issuer offered bondholders a new security or package of securities that amount to a diminished financial obligation (such as preferred or common stock, or debt with lower coupon or par amount), or (ii) the exchange had the apparent purpose of helping the borrower avoid default.

The default rate is determined by dividing the number of issuers that defaulted in a given period by the number of issuers issuing bonds during that period. The annual default rates thus obtained can then be used to determine default rates extending over a number of years, and these cumulative default rates are the most important index for evaluating, post facto, the performance of rating companies. Knowing the cumulative default rate, it is possible to determine the probability that a group of issuers rated BBB in a certain year will default each year. Moody's publishes data on cumulative default rates beginning in 1970, and S&P publishes data beginning in 1981. The following observations may be made about the results of both companies' default studies:

- A close correlation was observed between ratings and cumulative default rates. The higher the rating, the lower the default rate, and vice versa.
- This stable correlation is observable over several decades. However, the absolute level of the cumulative default rates for each group is itself influenced by the business cycle, and varies depending on which year the group of issuers was rated.
- The gap between the default rates of different rating levels increases for bonds rated Baa (BBB) or under, and the default rate rises sharply for bonds rated Ba (BB) or under. This is why investors generally consider bonds rated Baa (BBB) or above as investment grade, and those rated Ba (BB) or under as speculative grade.

The presence of these similarities is due to the fact that there are no major differences between the rating scales used by Moody's and S&P. One more valuable indicator of the performance of rating companies is the rating transition of issuers that defaulted in the period leading up to their default. Moody's publishes data tracing ratings prior to default for senior unsecured debentures. These data show quite clearly that, on average, the median rating declines to Bat (speculative grade) five years prior to default, Ba2 twenty-two months before default, and Ba3 eight months before default. It is therefore apparent that Moody's generally warns investors of the risk of default on bonds a considerable time before actual default occurs.

R&I's credit risk ratio

In the case of Japan, however, only top-rated firms have been allowed to issue bonds under traditional issue standards, and as a consequence, defaults by rated issuers have been practically non-existent. Little information on default rates, rating transition probabilities, and debt recovery rates has therefore accumulated in Japan, and default studies have made little headway.

It is because of this that R&I calculates 'credit risk ratios' (a type of simulated default rate) as a substitute for default rates. (R&I is the first rating company to publish simulated default rates by rating level for Japanese firms.) The credit risk ratio is defined as the proportion of firms awarded a given rating that will run into business difficulties within a certain period of time. Business difficulties include not only a company's collapse or bankruptcy but also corporate insolvency, three consecutive quarters of net pre-tax loss, and three consecutive quarters of current deficits.

The firms surveyed included all the other 3000 or so over-the-counter and listed firms as well as those actually assigned ratings by the former Japan Bond Research Institute (JBRI) and Japan Investors Service (NIS). The period studied was the 20-year period from 1977 to 1996, which was subdivided into groups of 10-year periods. The credit risk ratios of a total of 11 groups from the 1977–86 period and the 1987–96 period were then traced. Companies were classed by rating within each group on the basis of their rating in the base fiscal year, and the credit risk ratio (estimated default rate) for each group and rating class determined by dividing the number of companies that are assumed to have countered business difficulties by the number of firms in the rating group.

The 10-year cumulative credit risk ratio was derived from the simple averages for the 11 groups. In addition, the probabilities that a given firm would go bankrupt or collapse or would become insolvent were determined statistically (assuming a normal distribution) from the standard deviation and equity ratio levels. In Japan it is not infrequent for support from a firm's main bank to prevent its de facto collapse from leading to default on bonds. The use of credit risk ratios and the statistical probability of bankruptcy or insolvency enables a comparison of real default rates that excludes such special factors. The following conclusions are evident from R&I's default studies:

- There is a strong correlation between ratings and simulated default rates (credit risk ratios and statistical probabilities of bankruptcy and insolvency). The higher the rating, the lower the simulated default rate, and vice versa.
- There is a greater gap between simulated default rates for different rating levels rated Baa (BBB) or lower. This gap is even more pronounced in the case of ratings Ba (BB) or lower.
- The difference between the individual rating default rates (or the simulated default rates in the case of R&I) of Japanese and US rating companies is not particularly great. In other words, a comparison of Moody's and S&P's 10-year average cumulative default rates and R&I's 10-year cumulative credit risk ratios and probabilities of bankruptcy and insolvency shows them to be relatively similar.

Ratings and default rates of Japanese firms

The above comparison of default studies suggests there is a close correlation between ratings and default rates in the case of the Japanese and US rating companies. And it suggests there is a comparatively small difference between Japanese and US companies' estimates of the real default rates for the same rating level if the effects of special factors are excluded, such as the traditional Japanese practice of having banks underwrite bonds (which tended to prevent de facto business collapses from resulting in defaults).

If the Japanese and US rating companies estimated that default rates for each rating level are relatively similar, then one would expect there to be little difference in the ratings assigned to the same Japanese firm by Japanese and US rating companies. However, the ratings assigned to Japanese A's by US rating companies are on average three to four notches lower than those assigned by Japanese rating companies.

Recently there has been criticism that US ratings of Japanese firms are too low, or that Japanese rating companies' ratings are too high. This difference in ratings appears to be the result of the differing assessment by Japanese and US rating companies of Japanese firms, i.e. their different views on the probability of default in the future by Japanese firms.

Defaults by Japanese firms rated at speculative grade

Moody's data were used for the following analysis due to Moody's coverage of Japanese firms. Twenty-nine Japanese companies (excluding subsidiaries) were rated as speculative (Bat or lower) by Moody's five years ago in January 1994, some 25 of which were continuously rated for five years until January 1999 without having their ratings withdrawn.

As none of these defaulted on bonds, the default rate was zero. What does this mean statistically? Put simply, the calculations show that if it is assumed the results of Moody's default studies of mostly US firms apply equally to Japanese firms, then it is statistically fairly unlikely that not one of the 25 Japanese firms rated as speculative five years previously will default. From the investor's viewpoint, it is difficult to accept that Moody's rates Japanese firms and US firms by the same standard unless two or three of the 25 companies default. JCIF statistical studies suggest that there exist certain structural factors that keep defaults low in Japan, and the evidence of the past five years suggests that Moody's may be paying insufficient attention to these factors.

The record of past defaults suggests there is a possibility that US companies' ratings of Japanese firms are a little on the low side. However, this does not mean the same will hold true for the next five years. Under the traditional Japanese-style corporate and financial systems, when a company's business operations deteriorated, its 'main bank' and group firms have been deeply committed to restoring its health by such means as assigning personnel and forgiving or reducing interest payments. But such systems are changing amid the tides of deregulation and globalisation. It has become difficult for banks to increase loans if there is a risk they will become bad debts.

In addition, the practice of cross-shareholding among companies is also gradually decreasing. However, it is still unclear whether Japanese-style management that gives importance to the company as a going concern will change rapidly, and whether structural change will proceed to the extent that the rate of bankruptcies of Japanese firms will rise to the same level as in the USA. The relatively low ratings of Japanese firms by international rating companies can be explained as they have factored in this structural change more quickly than Japanese rating companies. There have been signs that the disparity between the ratings of Japanese and international rating companies is narrowing. Henceforth we should focus our attention on how Japan's corporate and financial systems will be brought into line with global standards, and how these rating disparities will change in accordance with such developments.

Moody's in Japan

Gohei Nishina, president of the Rating Issue Research Committee, posed the following questions regarding Moody's activities in Japan:

> Moody's is said to possess power over the fate of companies. While Moody's ratings claim to be based on 'independent, neutral and impartial' analysis, there has recently been an outcry from corporate managers who feel their company has received unfair ratings. Moody's itself does not disclose their rating process, leaving companies perplexed. What is Moody's rating process and who are their analysts?

There has recently been an outburst of criticism in Japan towards Moody's, the American rating agency. This uproar has been caused both by the downgrading of the Japanese government, various practices such as unsolicited ratings, and by various industries who have openly questioned Moody's rating procedure and methodologies. The attack is not limited to Japan, as evidenced by numerous lawsuits in the USA, certain comments in the European press by renowned publications such as *Euromoney* and *The Economist*, various ratings industry spokesmen in Europe, and the controversies regarding the granting of NRSRO franchises by the SEC and subsequent inquiry into the matter.

This has led various parties in Japan to look into the true nature of Moody's, who earned the name 'market killer' in 1997 when their analysis put an end to Yamaichi Securities. Moody's, as the prime exponent of the aggressive and controversial practice of unsolicited ratings, has made several headlines in Japan. *President* magazine analysed at length Moody's behaviour in the Japanese markets. Some of the developments and anecdotes they covered make interesting reading.

Taking on Toyota

During Toyota's midterm statement of accounts, Vice President Iwao Ohkijima responded to stockowners' questions regarding their recent downgrading by Moody's as follows:

> We feel that the recent lowering from triple A is completely undeserved. Moody's has criticised our policy of lifetime employment but Toyota has maintained a flexible employment structure. There is no way lifetime employment would be a burden to our management.

In response to further questioning, Ohkijima estimated that this recent downgrade by Moody's will cost the Toyota group, which runs several financial companies abroad, an annual one billion yen. 'This downgrade is unpleasant,' he added. Moody's cited the intensifying competitive environment in the global auto markets and the decrease in domestic consumption as the primary reasons behind their action. Moody's also noted that Toyota's policy to preserve lifetime employment weakens the company's competitive edge without necessarily providing conclusive cause and effect evidence to support this view. Hiroshi Okuda, Toyota's president said:

> The nature of these ratings is to provide analysis on a company's capacity to refund corporate bonds. Given this fact, Toyota has the capacity to refund all our bonds tomorrow, so there is no doubt we should receive a triple A. Moody's is rather unfair or biased in our eyes. I feel it is necessary to grasp the hidden side of these ratings.

Idemitsu suffers an arbitrary hit

Idemitsu company is also perplexed about Moody's ratings. Tetsuo Izeki, director and accounting manager said, 'Our stocks are not publicly listed, and we have no plans for direct financing. *There is no reason why we should be rated in the first place.* The recent rating is completely arbitrary, and although Moody's claims the rating is in response to investor requests, we have a hard time understanding why they rated us'. The process leading to Idemitsu's unsolicited rating was reported by the magazine as follows.

Idemitsu received a letter from Moody's in May which read, 'Due to requests from foreign financial institutions, Moody's will announce your rating in the near future. This rating will be based on information we have gathered domestically and internationally'.

Idemitsu sent a response which explained the company had no plans of issuing corporate bonds or commercial paper. Although there was no response from Moody's regarding the letter, Idemitsu received a telephone call from them in August, reiterating their intention to announce the ratings. In mid August Idemitsu held a meeting with Moody's and explained that they do not conduct business with general investors and hence have no need for ratings; Moody's did not accept this explanation. In September Moody's released the arbitrary rating. Idemitsu's investment rating was B2, the fifth class from the top. According to Moody's definition, B is 'a rating given to bonds which fail to qualify as a good investment instrument'. B2 is positioned in the middle of the B ratings.

Moody's cited that Idemitsu's financial basis was relatively weak compared with industry norms and that their business environment was becoming harsher due to the drop in gasoline prices. Moody's, moreover, referred to its US experience as justifying the rating. Moody's noted that petroleum industry deregulation resulted in a weeding out of gasoline stations. When the gasoline stations were redeveloped, gasoline spilled out of the tanks causing land contamination, which forced gasoline companies to pay enormous compensation expenses. Moody's point was that Japanese petroleum companies were likely to repeat the same mistake.

'But such accidents are unlikely here since Japanese petroleum companies are managed under strict legislature such as the fire fighting law. We explained that we managed to avoid those kinds of accidents even during the Kobe earthquake, but *Moody's just wouldn't listen*,' said Izeki. Had Idemitsu listed their stocks or issued bonds, there would have been a panic in the market. Idemitsu, upset by the unexpectedly bad ratings, issued a counterstatement to the media on the day the ratings were announced and provided an explanation to their clients. Fortunately for Idemitsu, 'The financial institutions understood our situation and promised to support us as usual. There has been no irregular response coming from oil-producing nations or our suppliers,' said Izeki.

Is Moody's CAMEL missing management?

Moody's recently reported that they were examining a possible downgrading for Sekisui House. President Isamu Wada of Sekisui House argued against this: 'It's appalling to know that we're being downgraded based on the idea that it's bad to possess land. The real estate we possess is mostly acquired for sales purposes. It's not right to regard it as bad debt'. Mikio Yamada, managing director of Sekisui House, has also questioned the fairness of Moody's ratings:

> They don't take into consideration the *specific financial and legal conditions that are unique to Japan*. American housing manufacturers mainly sell ready-built houses. By contrast, the development aspect occupies a predominant part of the business here in Japan. Although we insisted that possessing real estate was necessary for that purpose, Moody's refused to listen. If one were to read the figures listed in our securities report in a strictly American fashion, perhaps the rating would turn out as such, but I very much doubt that it reflects the true state of our company.

The accounting manager of a construction machinery company that was given an unsolicited rating shared the following story on the condition that he remained anonymous: 'About five years ago Moody's suddenly reported our ratings. We were not contacted beforehand—it was a *pre-emptive attack*. Five years later, Moody's called us requesting an interview. That time we actually said, "will you stop—it's an unwelcome favour" '. A board member of a major electric manufacturer argued, 'Is it possible to analyse a company without attempting to understand the manager's strategy?' The chairman of a major trading company also commented, 'It would be desirable if they truly understood the full picture of the company but sometimes that doesn't seem to be the case'. What has happened to the M in Moody's CAMEL?

Moody's criticises the JCIF investigation

As criticisms towards Moody's escalate, the Japan Center for International Finance (JCIF), a research foundation headed by former Ministry of Finance commissioner Tomomitsu Ohba, started investigating rating agencies. The detailed 150-page report produced by the JCIF has already been discussed at length. As with its uncompromising dismissal of concerns from the US Department of Justice, Moody's counter-attacked JCIF by saying, 'Although we sent an inquiry to the JCIF regarding its objective behind evaluating rating agencies, we received no response from them'. Does Moody's practise the same reciprocity in communications with other parties? 'Whether or not they are completely independent from the government remains unclear and their objectivity is questionable,' adds Moody's.

The rating agencies' attitude towards government may be the key to this whole situation. And the head of Moody's main competitor, S&P, gave a pretty clear hint of this attitude during an interview for *Euromoney*: ' "I don't want to be a government employee," says O'Neill, pointing to a photograph on a shelf behind his desk. "Those three kids up there can't afford it. They've got a definition of a lifestyle which doesn't match with that salary level" '. It's heartening to see what rating agencies' senior managers think about governments and their employees. Instead of addressing and countering the arguments in the report, Moody's attempts to move the goalposts by *demanding* JCIF to release information on its sponsors plus its relationship with government and related institutions.

The JCIF report is a particularly detailed work relying on questionnaires and statistical methodology, excerpts of which featured earlier in this chapter. A financial authority who read the report stated his opinion as follows:

> I was surprised after seeing the questionnaire results. Asked whether they feel the ratings are trustworthy, less than 10% of the respondents replied 'yes' for Moody's or Standard & Poor's. Asked whether they feel the analytical skills of the analysts are high, less than 20% replied 'yes' for either company. It's shocking to know that Moody's has so little trust.

JCIF's criticisms expressed in the report were as follows:

- In Japan, Moody's and S&P are a virtual duopoly.
- Rating agencies, usually occupying a dominant position over the Japanese companies they rate, tend to neglect providing the reasons underlying their ratings.
- The ratings given out to Japanese companies are comparatively harsh.
- In Japan, arbitrary ratings seem to be used as a sales strategy in order to gain rating requests.
- The selection criteria and grounds for arbitrary ratings should be made public in further detail.
- Arbitrary ratings and ratings based on requests should be distinguished. (While S&P adds 'pi' to arbitrary ratings, Moody's does not make any distinction in its reports.)

'I completely agree with the criticism,' says an executive of a financial institution. These conclusions in Japan corroborate the results of other surveys such as Cantwell's as well as industry lobbying groups such as the USA's Investment Company Institute; the ICI is the national association of the American investment company industry.

> In addition to the fact that there are many mistakes made by their analysts, they absolutely refuse to clarify the basis for their ratings. Our position is similar to that of a defendant making a court statement. They demand a detailed disclosure from other companies, while they themselves refuse to show their cards. Their whole process is too problematic.

And with regards to the arbitrary ratings:

> Depending on whether a rating is arbitrary or based on a request, there is great difference in the amount of information Moody's has access to, so that should clearly be distinguished.

An insurance company executive expresses a similar thought:

> In the beginning, it was almost like the old protection racket—*it was hinted that we would receive a low rating if we didn't request a rating.* So we ended up requesting but felt ambiguous when paying the fee. If Moody's truly makes no distinction between arbitrary ratings and ratings based on requests, they should just go ahead and rate all companies on their own. It's almost as if we're losing by making a request. I think this is another reason why rating agencies are failing to earn market trust.

The International Financial Information Centre's report even says it is likely that arbitrary ratings are given to companies which Moody's feels will later become requests—'easy pickings' so to speak. In the case of S&P, the ratings for Taiyo Life Insurance and Mitsui Life Insurance rose one notch after switching from an arbitrary rating to a request rating. The fact that Moody's increased arbitrary ratings in the 1990s is also viewed by some as a sales strategy to increase requests. A financial insider points out:

> Moody's business consists of report sales and revenue from rating requests. *But report sales can't be that lucrative. The only real way to earn a profit is to increase rating fees.* After all, Moody's is a profit-making organisation. Although I don't think Moody's expected so many Japanese companies to come back with a 'so what' attitude, refusing to request.

Incongruous default ratios

JCIF notes that the classifications American rating agencies have given to Japanese companies are, on average, three to four notches lower than those given by Japanese rating agencies. It is easy to check whether ratings for Japanese companies are low or not by looking at the relationship between the former ratings and the default ratio. If the relationship between the former ratings and the default ratio greatly differs according to the region, it can lead to various problems. For example, if the default ratio of a bond given the same rating of Baa differs significantly in the USA and Japan, it means the investor faces a different risk for the same rating depending on the country.

The International Financial Information Centre's report touches upon this problem. According to its investigation, 25 Japanese companies received a

Ba1 or lower rating, which signifies speculative or so-called junk bonds, at the beginning of 1994 and retained the same rating for five years until December 1998. However, none of these companies went into default, which makes the five-year cumulative default ratio 0%. On the other hand, the five-year cumulative default ratio for all companies Moody's has rated, mostly American companies, is an average 11.4% for Ba and 28.59% for B.

In addition, Japan entered a recession during 1994 to 1998, which increased the total number of bankruptcies. Therefore, it is more appropriate to compare it with the five-year cumulative default ratio during America's recession, which increases to 24.01% for 1988 and 24.22% for 1989. The accuracy of the ratings becomes questionable when a quarter of the American companies are defaulting but there are no defaults among the Japanese companies given the exact same ratings. While it is true that business customs in Japan make default less likely, the above comparison demonstrates how low the ratings of Japanese companies have been in the past five years. The criticism of Moody's rating practice is not limited to Japan. *Euromoney* published the following observation by an executive of a major financial institution: 'I don't find it surprising that Japanese companies are upset at Moody's'.

Rating analysts' pay is peanuts

So who assigns the ratings, and how? Hirokazu Moriyama, president of Moriyama Office, a consulting firm for rating agencies, explains their method like this:

> Analysts are, after all, employees. By giving a lenient rating to a certain company, they run the risk of receiving an official reprimand in case the company later goes bankrupt. It's natural for them to lower the rating of Japan or Japanese companies, a nation and its companies which essentially appears inscrutable to them. That's safer for the analyst himself. Moody's rating analysts are American in terms of mentality. They can't quite understand the way Japanese companies operate. That's why it's probable for Japanese companies to become the target of a downgrade.

Another researcher who specialises in rating agencies says:

> There have been some odd ratings. It could be that the analyst in charge is relatively inexperienced, or the specific conditions of the Japanese market are not reflected. In addition, the pay for rating analysts is not at all good compared to stock analysts.
>
>   I know certain analysts who say their annual income doubled or tripled when they switched over to think tanks, etc. Out of 20 analysts who work at

rating agencies, there are probably only about two or three who can be described as truly excellent. Analysts who rate financial institutions are the ones who bring in more than 50% of the total profit, and the quality of everyone aside that is considerably lower. Ratings are by no means the absolute truth. The future assignment of rating agencies is to raise the quality of their analysts.

A former rating agency analyst looks back and says:

> Rating agencies know everything, if not, it wouldn't be possible to make ratings. *Analysts are trained to hide their ignorance based on that creed.* As a result, one ends up creating rating material data without certain knowledge.

Perhaps these conditions are what make rating agencies such as Moody's insist that 'it's after all, just an opinion'.

A rating is an opinion

A foreign strategist, who knows Moody's well, explains its recent transfiguration like this:

> Frequent downgrading is all too common, at times causing serious confusion in the market. While the company has to react to market developments, downgradings pose the rating agency a problem.

In the words of one rating specialist:

> It is not preferable to have frequent rating adjustments, because ratings are based on the next five years. In other words, the recent rating adjustments mean that the original ratings were mistaken.

Another rating specialist says:

> Rating is not simply a figure. It's the artwork of the independent analyst. To a certain extent, it's a personal judgement that could be biased despite the focus on committee deliberations. In order to give a rating, the analyst first creates a roadmap. If the analyst can create a long roadmap extending into the future, that company will receive good ratings. . . . Factors such as company prospects, profit and disclosures are important, but the biggest problem for Japanese companies lies in their messed up accounting. This makes it difficult for the analyst to create a roadmap, naturally leading to a downgrade.

The fact that Moody's tries to excuse its ratings by insisting that 'it's just an opinion' is a source of criticism for Japanese companies. Many support the idea that 'from the perspective of investor and client protection, administrative authorities should create a standard of disclosure for rating agencies as well as supervise any inappropriate sales activity'. The JCIF report points out the necessity of sufficient monitoring to make sure that rating agencies are not conducting inappropriate sales activity by taking advantage of the oligopolistic market.

Professor Kurosawa of Nihon University says:

> Superior companies such as Toyota should take Moody's to court, and *debate the right and wrong of downgrading based on lifetime employment.* An argument which is clearly ethnocentric if not ideological in nature. Only this will prevent them from downgrading Japanese companies so easily in the future. In America, there are numerous instances where rating agencies have been sued.

No tea talk in Tokyo

Moody's Representative Director Yu Kakuya moved to America when he was in high school. After graduating from Cornell, Kakuya received an MBA. He first entered Bank of America (BofA) but moved to Moody's in the mid 1980s. He is thus a pure product of the US educational and business mill—a suitable candidate to head up an office for the export market. At Moody's there is a network of former BofA employees. In that circle in Japan, Kakuya is at the top.

According to one rating specialist, Moody's is viewing Japan's future in an unnecessarily negative light. It can't see the decision-making process of the Japanese government and thus it perceives the government as not having the ability to solve the problem. How does Kakuya respond? With regards to arbitrary ratings and ratings based on requests:

> There is no difference in terms of the rating process and the decision-making procedure.

In other words, Moody's, the originator of the CAMEL matrix (capital, assets, management, earnings, liquidity), is asserting that CAMEL = CAEL, so to speak, an interesting proposition. With regards to his wife joining the Bank of Japan:

> I think it's completely irrelevant to discuss personal issues.

This seems at odds with statements levelled by Moody's at the JCIF, for example. A. Yoshinami, public relations manager of Moody's smoothly adds:

> The issue should not be a problem because any activity that may lead to personal interests are strictly prohibited through an internal ethics code.

In other words, it's perfectly normal for the wife of a senior Moody's manager to work for the financial market bureau of Bank of Japan, and there is no possible chance of any confidential information being disclosed over a cup of tea.

Having tried unsuccessfully to obtain an interview, a Japanese journalist from *President* magazine wrote to Yu Kakuya with two questions relating to market trust:

- What is the content of the internal ethics code?
- Doesn't the company find the conflict problematic from the perspective of neutrality to the financial market?

The journalist later received the following response from Matsuo Sogo Law Office, Moody's representative:

> As individuals who engage in a highly specialised occupation, the employees of Moody's take full responsibility to fulfil a high ethical and social standard with regards to his/her relationship with a third party, including his/her spouses. We are convinced that both Yu Kakuya and Yuko Sato act according to a high ethical standard at all times, in order to meet the duty of confidentiality which is demanded from the organisations they belong to.

Moody's seems to be using the same stonewalling techniques as it criticised in JCIF. The fact that Moody's resorted to a lawyer to answer a simple question regarding the company's ethics code provides food for thought.

In the Big Apple: heard on the street

On a more down-to-earth level, since we have raised the subject of 'high social and ethical standards in specialised occupations with regards to relationships with third parties including spouses', this section concludes with excerpts, names omitted, compiled from AP press releases dated 23 December 1999, 21 January 2000 and 24 April 2000 on 'Marylin Does Miami'. The insider dealing scenario could come straight out of a Brett Easton Ellis novel.

In late 1999 a former chief executive officer of the investment bank of Keefe, Bruyette & Woods pleaded innocent to allegations he engaged in insider trading and shared news of pending deals with 'Marylin Star', the porn star of a videotape entitled 'Marylin Does Miami'. An indictment was returned against the ex-CEO and Marilyn Star. A third codefendant also was charged. All three were charged with conspiracy and securities fraud. *US News and World Report* states that the ex-CEO 'earned USD 4 million last year as the head of Keefe, Bruyette & Woods' before resigning in June 1999.

The New York investment bank chief was accused of tipping Marylin Star about companies on the verge of mergers that would dramatically affect their stock prices. The actress then allegedly bought the stocks and shared the information with the third codefendant, a friend.

The actress was intimately involved for more than a year with the ex-CEO according to a federal criminal complaint. The ex-CEO and the third co-defendant had both admitted having extramarital affairs with the actress but had denied engaging in insider trading. The third codefendant was a busi-nessman who had not met the ex-CEO, but he allegedly traded on informa-tion he received from the actress. The ex-CEO, who is married, was released on USD 1 million bail after appearing before US magistrates. Associated Press (AP) noted that the third codefendant and actress

> became the targets of an investigation by the SEC after each opened a bro-kerage account at Charles Schwab in mid-1997 and began purchasing the stocks of obscure, small, regional banks. The trading activity was deemed suspicious because the bank stocks being purchased had just been placed on a watch list of potential acquisition targets by Keefe, Bruyette & Woods, which specialises in bank mergers.
>
> 'As a top Wall Street executive, the ex-CEO had access to confidential, non-public information about potential corporate mergers and acquisition transac-tions and provided the actress with such information about at least six mergers,' authorities said.
>
> Prosecutors and the SEC alleged that the ex-CEO tipped the actress about companies that were about to be involved in mergers dramatically affecting their stock prices. The actress then allegedly shared the information with the third co-defendant, a friend.
>
> In its complaint, the SEC said the third co-defendant told investigators that the actress also worked as a prostitute and boasted that her clients included 'well-connected Wall Street types' such as lawyers and stockbrokers.

The ex-CEO and third codefendant were charged with conspiracy and se-curities fraud. On 27 April 2000 AP announced that the ex-CEO was found guilty by a federal jury along with the third codefendant. The press release noted that the jury in US District Court in Manhattan returned its verdict after deliberating for parts of three days. The ex-CEO was convicted on seven of eight counts in the indictment, as was the third codefendant. The ex-CEO took a deep breath before the verdict was read but showed no emotion once it was delivered, holding his head high as the jury forewoman spoke. They could receive up to ten years in prison; sic transit gloria mundi.

Various debates on unsolicited ratings

The duopoly have for the past several years aggressively published un-solicited ratings (ratings that were not solicited by the issuer being rated), and there is an active debate on the pros and cons of this practice in the USA, but also in Japan and Europe. The arguments offered by the rating agencies to justify the practice of unsolicited ratings can be summarised as follows:

- The customers of rating companies are not issuers but investors. Therefore, if investors need the information, rating companies have an obligation to make ratings based on publicly available information regardless of whether the rating has been solicited by the issuer.
- Whether solicited or unsolicited, there should be no basic differences in the quality of ratings information. If there are differences, they are the responsibility of the issuer because it did not make sufficient information available to the public.
- Unsolicited ratings should be performed fairly and objectively. Were the rating company to intentionally give lower ratings than warranted as an attempt to capture ratings business, it would impair the credibility of its ratings and ultimately drive the rating company from the markets.

These arguments are, however, not so simple or straightforward as they might seem, and they ignore some basic facts which we discuss below in further detail.

Premise 1: Unsolicited ratings provide investor service

> The customers of rating companies are not issuers but investors. Therefore, if investors need the information, rating companies have an obligation to make ratings based on publicly available information regardless of whether the rating has been solicited by the issuer.

This is the tail wagging the dog. The validity of this premise falls flat upon examination of the revenue stream breakdown of most (not all) rating companies. That is, the agencies may claim to provide 'investor service' since investors buy their information services, but this is neatly contradicted by the fact that the vast majority of their revenues, which can be seen in any 10-K filing available at the SEC's web site, come from lucrative ratings fees charged to firms requesting ratings. Moreover, not only is the argument fallacious, the situation suggests a conflict of interest between generating fee income and providing public service.

Another fact contradicting the 'investor service' argument is the current system of three kinds of ratings:

- Unsolicited ratings
- For-publication solicited ratings
- Not-for-publication solicited ratings

The mere existence of not-for-publication solicited ratings poses a problem. For if the agencies maintain their claim to provide investor service, this service is being compromised by the existence of not-for-publication solicited ratings. Looking at the obverse of the problem (follow the money—look at the fees, not the issuers), a cynic might suggest that these not-for-publication solicited ratings exist simply as a tool for agencies to avoid potential issuers that have paid rating fees from being embarrassed, thereby protecting their fee relationship, or they exist as a tool to encourage issuers with unsolicited ratings to pay a rating fee (generating new business).

As regards unsolicited ratings, the 'investor service' argument would suggest that such unsolicited ratings be performed in order of investor needs. Indeed, it is unclear what selection criteria are used to target companies for unsolicited ratings. It would be interesting to see industry surveys analysing this point, to see if there is any truth to allegations by some Japanese market participants that 'the companies and industries given unsolicited ratings are selected not because of investor needs so much as because they are considered easy targets for soliciting ratings'.

As long as rating companies depend on ratings fees for the majority of their revenues, they are undeniably susceptible to sales policy governing their selection of companies and industries for unsolicited ratings, as a tool to generate ever more rating fees. The only way the 'investor service' argument can ever become convincing is if information fees from investors come to account for the majority of rating company revenues, which is certainly not the case, as evidenced by a breakdown of the rating agencies' revenue streams in their financial statements or by the results of impartial market studies such as the Cantwell survey.

Premise 2: Unsolicited ratings are the same quality as solicited ratings

> There is no difference in quality between solicited and unsolicited ratings; if there are differences, this is because the issuer did not make sufficient information available to the public.

This argument is convincing if one accepts that corporate information disclosure is complete. But in reality, most market participants believe that the information available for unsolicited ratings is limited, certainly more limited than the information available in a solicited ratings process (e.g. future strategies, full assessment of loan portfolio characteristics). Since this is the case, rating companies should distinguish between unsolicited ratings and solicited ratings in their publications, because to do otherwise is to provide less than a full 'investor service'.

Unsolicited ratings, for example, will not typically be privy to the information held by the top managers and executives of the firm being rated. Assuming quality and vision of management are important factors in ratings (as noted in the various checklists produced by the agencies), unsolicited ratings will be of lower quality than solicited ratings by the very definition from the rating agencies themselves. Conversely, during a solicited rating, a company may provide internal information to the rating company. However, acting in its own interests, the company will only provide information that is to its own advantage. One therefore cannot conclude that solicited ratings are necessarily based on higher-quality information than unsolicited ratings.

Considerable ambiguity could therefore be avoided if, as a matter of standard operating procedure, unsolicited ratings and solicited ratings were clearly identified as such, thereby enabling investors to make their own decisions.

Premise 3: Unsolicited ratings are as objective as solicited ratings

> Unsolicited ratings should be performed fairly and objectively. Were the rating company to intentionally give low unsolicited ratings as a hard sell technique to capture rating fees, it would impair the credibility of its ratings and ultimately drive the rating company from the markets.

S&P acknowledges the differences in precision between solicited ratings and unsolicited ratings, and therefore identifies its unsolicited ratings with 'pi'. Some market participants have alleged that rating companies have been known to invoice companies for fees when they perform unsolicited ratings, a pushy sales practice that invites further misunderstanding.

To assess this matter, the JCIF compared Japanese companies with solicited and unsolicited ratings. The JCIF analysis divided Japanese firms rated by S&P into group A (companies that solicited ratings) and group B (companies given unsolicited ratings), and then studied how many notches lower companies in both groups were compared to the solicited ratings given by R&I. The JCIF results yielded a 2.0 notch gap for group A (68 companies) compared to a 4.0 notch gap for group B (46 companies). In other words, if the ratings of R&I are taken as the standard, then the unsolicited ratings performed by S&P are about two notches lower than solicited ratings.

This rough calculation suggests a tendency for unsolicited ratings (performed with limited access to information) to be ultimately more conservative (assume negatives for unknown factors). This corroborates with the general view of unsolicited ratings as being harsh among market participants. The argument is also incorrect in that the 'driven out of the markets' assertion assumes a perfectly competitive market with multiple service providers, a description in contradiction to the reality of the duopoly. The duopoly, moreover, ensure that neither player will be driven out of business over such ephemeral problems since their market presence is so massive and large as to diversify any such risk.

The fact of the matter is the duopoly dominate the world ratings market (or triumvirate if the Fimalac-Euronotation-IBCA-Fitch-Duff & Phelps quilt is considered a bona fide member of the club). Moreover, their ratings have such a large impact on the financial and capital markets that ratings, which are essentially measures of corporate fundamentals, do themselves have the potential to impact corporate fundamentals. It is because of this situation that there has been concern in the financial press in Europe and Japan opining how the duopoly exerts vast if not excessive influence over issuers. Even if one concedes that competition exists, the degree of concentration in this competition underscores the need for sufficient monitoring given the potential that rating companies have of using their influence to engage in unfair sales activities—a theme we will come to later.

Indeed, the USA has also been engaged in a debate on unsolicited ratings. A suit brought against Moody's for unsolicited ratings caused the Department of Justice to begin studying the latent dangers in unsolicited ratings and considering the formulation of appropriate regulatory responses by meeting with raters, investors, and issuers. In its comments on the SEC's proposal to restructure the NRSRO system, the Department of Justice said that 'current rules (which do not require distinctions) should be amended to obligate rating companies publishing unsolicited ratings to simultaneously publish statements that the rating was not made at the request of the issuer (and therefore based on limited information)'. Moody's has responded by maintaining its position that it 'cannot accept the view that ratings not solicited by the issuer are incorrect or untrustworthy'.

As another example of the objections to unsolicited ratings in the USA (and dilemma in terms of the US Constitution's provisions for free speech), the Public School System of Denver, Colorado, in October 1995 sued Moody's for USD 769 000 in compensation, alleging that a Moody's unsolicited rating caused the yield on bonds issued by the school system to rise 15 basis points, which made it difficult to sell the bonds. The amount sought was equivalent to what the system could have raised had the rating not been published. The Colorado state courts rejected the suit, upholding the Moody's argument that publication of a rating was a right guaranteed under the Constitution's freedom of speech provisions.

This poses a thorny dilemma. Had the Public School System of Denver paid Moody's a rating fee, it could have availed itself of the not-for-publication solicited rating. The fact it chose not to do so and could not prevent the issuance of an unsolicited rating (as upheld by the Colorado state courts) appears to mean that school funds available for education can be hijacked by a rating agency.

Rating agencies as predictors of risk

Much criticism has been levelled at credit rating agencies for failing to spot impending crises, such as the Asian financial crisis. Various trade publications, e.g. *Euromoney*, have reported how some traders and investors also think the rating agencies are too slow to react. For example, the rating agencies en masse downgraded Asian banks only after the meltdown had been covered in the press. Sophisticated investors increasingly supplement external ratings with their own internal research. Publications like *The Economist* take a less in-house look at the ratings business than trade publications like *Euromoney*, and along with specialised entities such as Cantwell, JCIF, and Everling Advisory Services, they also note that credit rating agencies have come in for a bit of a bashing from various players in the financial community.

Investment banks, who are active in the capital markets and who undertake their own analyses, don't have a high opinion for the wares of credit rating agencies, dismissing them as 'nonsense' and 'irrelevant'. This contempt is also perhaps exacerbated by the relatively low salaries paid by the rating agencies to their analysts, when compared to those paid by the major investment banks. Much has been written about the agencies' reputation being grievously harmed by their failure to warn of the crisis in Asia. That is why although they still occupy an oligopolistic position in the markets for levying rating fees as an obligatory rite of passage, markets now pay their various pronouncements relatively little attention.

As noted by *The Economist* in 1999, Mexico's debt is rated as junk, yet compared with Colombia's debt, it trades at a spread over American Treasury bonds of some 165 basis points lower, and Colombia's debt is rated investment grade. Clearly the markets and the rating agencies have different perceptions on the risks of default. Yet the agencies are thriving. And this begs the question, If the agencies' methodologies are so deficient and their record in Asia so bad, why is business booming? And why such a boom in Euroland, with its hitherto fragmented bond markets? Demands for ratings from companies that want to issue bonds have soared. At Fitch-IBCA, which claims to be the leading rating agency in Europe, revenue from European companies rose by 162% in the first quarter of 1999 compared with last year. Standard & Poor's more mature business similarly expects to post a strong growth of 25% this year; and it plans to increase European staff by 30%.

The answer can be summed up in a single phrase: it may be a lousy game but it's the only game in town. While there are concerns as to how rating agencies go about assessing issuers, the heaviest criticisms concern their reliability in assessing sovereigns (countries). As the Asian crisis demonstrated, rating countries is a lot harder than rating companies. Some reasons for this include the relatively small population size and relative newness of the activity; this means the agencies have a paucity of data to work with compared to more vast data pools on corporates or commercial paper.

Moreover, although there are ratios to look at (e.g. debt to exports, debt to GDP), countries are far more complex than companies. A country's rating indicates not just its ability to pay but also its willingness. And willingness to pay is a largely subjective assessment. Obtaining reliable information from a government can be more difficult than from a corporate entity, since the agency is desperate for the prestige of the business and its negotiating strength is relatively weaker. Gossip in the world's financial centres suggests that analysts in the rating agencies are not up to the job because they are relatively younger, inexperienced, and cheaper than their counterparts in investment banks, who typically command telephone number salaries.

The end result is that rather than rely on rating agencies as a source of information, investors are now more interested in studying a country's prospects for themselves—a trend borne out in various market studies such as the Cantwell surveys or the JCIF market survey on rating agencies—suggesting that issuers pay to get rated but do not pay to consume the 'research' produced by the agencies. This would suggest that the sovereigns obtain ratings in order to be able to access the markets, and that the 'opinions' put out by the agencies as 'investor service' meet largely with indifference.

Indeed, some countries are sharpening up their street cred. Brazil, with its diversified albeit volatile economy, has taken this process to its logical conclusion. The government has hired a bunch of investment bankers in senior posts, and its central bank governor is a former hedge fund manager; the country has consequently become expert at mouthing the jargon so dear to investors and fund managers (whether they have the more down-to-earth ability to communicate these policies to the electorate is another question).

Corporate ratings are another story. Whatever criticisms one may have against rating agencies, it must be said that their track record vis-à-vis corporates is better established than in sovereign ratings, simply due to the population size and number of years of data to work with. This enables cross-border comparisons and oils the workings of the market. But it also leads to an abdication of independent credit assessment capability, as cost-conscious banks lay-off cost centres such as credit department analysts and practically abdicate independent credit assessment capability by a de facto delegation of credit policy to the duopoly. Rating agencies have certainly established their presence in the USA. The activity has had time to implant itself since 1909, when John Moody issued his first ratings of railway bonds. Credit ratings have become second nature in the formulaic and demanding landscape of the US economy.

In pursuit of diversification and increased revenue streams, rating agencies have expanded into rating other areas such as complex securities and collateralised bonds, they are looking at different classes of debt, and they are providing 'educational' services (naturally fitting well within the US economic Weltanschauungen). Moreover, a boutique industry has sprung up to advise potential issuers how and under what circumstances rating agencies might change their opinions of a firm's debt for undertaking a course of action (or not). This is crucial since a change in a credit score can shift the market capitalisation of a company as well as its ability to access the financial markets.

The duopoly like to boast that over time there has been a close historical correlation between their ratings and the likelihood of companies defaulting. Those to which they originally granted a good rating rarely default although Confederation Life, a Canadian life insurer which had an A+ rating on a Friday and managed to default the following week, makes old market hands wince.

There is no doubt, however, that one of the main reasons why ratings are so prevalent is simply because they are there, and besides making life easier for other users, they enable them to pass the buck and shift or cloud the burden of responsibility.

For example, many trust funds use ratings and rating scales to give guidelines to fund managers and traders. Similarly, some banks with small credit departments and inexperienced analysts pass the buck by basing credit decisions on ratings, thereby abdicating credit policy (but not responsibility) to the agencies. Other harebrained risk assessment models such as country risk assessment schemes will factor in all sorts of variables, including GDP, income levels, and rating levels into 'weighted risk assessment matrices', making sure the omission of some arcane, albeit potentially important variable is not overlooked in the event of future problems or sovereign defaults.

5 Quis custodiet ipsos custodes?

SEC, DOJ, ICI, NRSROs, and rating agencies

One of the reasons why rating agencies have become so powerful and militant in the protection of their oligopoly is due to the status they have been accorded by the regulatory agency of the country with the largest economy in the world. For they have been granted the franchise to exploit a lucrative gold mine with tremendous barriers to future entrants. In other words, the rating agencies by default occupy the role of a quasi-official arbiter and gatekeeper to entry of the US and international financial system as sanctioned by the Securities and Exchange Commission.

The agencies have been granted a de facto monopoly which has helped them fill their coffers, endowing them with the power to make or break companies or indeed governments, to issue pronouncements which they are ultimately unaccountable for, and to levy fees on a captive market. The rating agencies hide behind the US Constitution's provisions for free speech but the issues are wider than a mere free speech argument. We enter the realm of predatory pricing, monopoly situations, fostering market inefficiencies, obstructing free flows of information, the propagation of corporate ideology as an instrument of regulation by the government, and defining professional qualifications. Various parties are in the NRSRO debate, including the Securities and Exchange Commission (SEC), the Department of Justice (DOJ), the Investment Company Institute (ICI), and the rating agencies.

That the ratings industry is indeed ripe for overhaul and reform is a certainty. The question which needs to be asked is whether this monstrous oligopoly with its arrogance, concentration of power, and lack of regulation and accountability should be permitted to continue or be replaced with a regulatory regime that is normally in place for any other practice that has public ramifications such as doctors, lawyers, accountants, foods, drugs, and the manufacture and piloting of motor vehicles, ships, or aircraft. For the moment an entity's acts impact the environment and community, prudence suggests that these activities be regulated. Since the government is not clouded by the profit motive, this suggests it is the natural candidate for the regulatory role. The government, however, is an instrument subjected to the pressures of the prevailing ideologies which pretend that the liberal economic model is a universal panacea and that government is an impediment, a problem, rather than the guarantor of civil liberties and a level playing field. Here is where we find some of the background to the ratings game.

The crux of the matter

In cases such as the 1996 case of *Orange County v. McGraw-Hill Companies (S&P)*, or the 1993 case of *Creditors of Pan American v. S&P*, both parties attempted to sue rating agencies for the repercussions arising from their various pronouncements, or subpoena witnesses bound by confidentiality agreements to provide evidence. Both cases were lost; Orange County withdrew its case and the Pan American creditors had theirs overturned. The key point was the First Amendment 'free speech' provisions under the US Constitution.

In the case involving the now defunct airline, Pan American, Presiding Judge Loretta Preska ruled that the defendant, rating agency Standard & Poor's, was protected by the same constitutional right to free speech as news organisations. O'Neill of Standard & Poor's adds, 'Ultimately, we always come back to the First Amendment and the right to deliver an independent opinion on the issues we analyse'. Whilst Judge Preska upheld that right; this 'free speech' argument tends to enormously simplify the issues surrounding the role and performance of the rating agencies. The reality is they are living on borrowed time for various reasons wholly separate to the 'free speech' argument. These areas will be the primary focus of this chapter.

In the *Orange County* and *Pan American* cases, the defendants only had a limited box of tools with which to attack the rating agencies and seek redress. For the real issue at hand is not freedom of speech but rather abuse of power and the heavy-handed ways in which rating agencies behave, as we saw in Chapter 4. It is in this domain (where the concerned parties opposing the rating agencies can muster coordinated lobbying power and financial clout as they are part of the system rather than marginalised entities seeking redress in isolation) where we will most likely see developments affecting the industry.

As to regulation, paradoxically the SEC seems reluctant as well as powerless to prevent it. 'There has been some regulatory creep into the rating agency business over the past couple of decades,' admits the SEC's Commissioner Richard Roberts, 'We are concerned that regulation may affect the industry, but I suspect that process will continue.' This situation has been in gestation for some 30 years and is the result of drift and failing to address various issues until, due the to the confluence of numerous factors no one could have foreseen 30 years ago, they have all have come to a head.

Origins of the NRSRO debate

The appointment of ratings agencies as NRSROs goes back to 1970. In 1970 the Penn Central Railway Co. filed for bankruptcy. Wall Street broker-dealers were holding a lot of Penn Central commercial paper and were caught by surprise. This is because the National Credit Office, a subsidiary of Moody's parent Dun and Bradstreet, had more than 600 commercial paper ratings outstanding. All of them were rated prime, the highest rating available to the short-term debt issue. The resulting panic got the SEC thinking. Rival agencies, including Standard & Poor's and Moody's, had introduced a credit ranking system into their work in the commercial paper market but the system had not caught on. Who would want to run the risk of a lower credit rating when the National Credit Office was certain to award a prime rating?

In 1975 the SEC made its first and biggest mistake. In that year, under the Securities and Exchange Act of 1934, the commission adopted Rule 15c3–1 in the net capital rules. Under the rules, broker-dealers, when computing net capital, were required to deduct a certain percentage, or 'haircut', of the market value of their proprietary security positions. But the commission also adopted certain qualifications to the rule. Among others, broker-dealers' proprietary positions in commercial paper, non-invertible debt securities, and non-invertible preferred stock would be accorded preferential treatment if the instruments had been rated investment grade by at least two nationally recognised statistical rating organisations (NRSROs). In other words, they would get a shorter haircut. The commission did not attempt to define what an NRSRO was, but three rating agencies were given the honour—Moody's, Standard & Poor's, and Fitch. From such modest beginnings, the use of credit ratings for regulatory and self-regulatory purposes has proliferated rapidly, both within and without the SEC.

What is an NRSRO?

NRSRO is the acronym used in rule 2a-7 to stand for a nationally recognised statistical rating organisation, as per paragraph (a)(17) of rule 2a-7, as amended. NRSROs are designated as such by the commission's Division of Market Regulation through the no-action letter process for purposes of the commission's net capital rule (17 CFR 240.15c3–1). In more mundane terms, NRSRO status confers upon the agency a quasi-official role as one of the 'official rite of passage' players for any entity accessing the capital markets in the USA. The fact there are a mere handful of NRSROs means they are all practically guaranteed a slice of the economic pie (as there will always be a need for more than merely two players) and they are in a virtually unassailable oligopoly.

They are in effect market regulators but not agencies of the US government nor subject to any particular regulatory control of aspects, such as the qualifications and knowledge of their analysts, either by educational qualifications or some sort of examination like the bar examination a lawyer is required to pass. The clear inadequacies of the NRSRO nomination and control process lead one to pose the thorny question, Quis custodiet ipsos custodes? (Who guards the guardians themselves?) Because of this, NRSRO status has taken on more and more the aspect of a basic condition to be met by rating companies for entry into the US market, as illustrated by IBCA's complicated machinations to enter the market, first on its own and later via expensive acquisitions of second-tier US rating agencies, in order to avail itself of the NRSRO status.

Getting hooked on NRSRO

By modifying the Investment Company Act of 1940, the commission had incorporated NRSRO terminology to distinguish the types of security that may be issued using simplified registration procedures. In 1991, worried about the stability of money market funds, the commission put strict credit limits on securities eligible for investment by such firms. Only securities rated in one of the two highest categories for short-term debt by the requisite number of NRSROs would be eligible. In other words, obtaining a rating became a virtual prerequisite for issuers seeking to access the financial markets.

This dependence has also spread to Congress. Struggling with a rapid growth in the mortgage-backed securities market, Congress sought in 1984 to define a mortgage-related security. Among other things, it concluded that mortgage-related securities must be rated by at least one NRSRO. Again, there was no attempt to define the term. In the meantime, state authorities, self-regulatory organisations, and great swathes of the US mutual fund industry have adopted ratings to define, control, and advertise risk appetites and investor behaviour. All this has occurred without actually defining what an NRSRO is or what the admission criteria are. In other words, the entire edifice is founded on ambiguous elements.

The SEC's actions have had two main consequences. For issuers, particularly in the US public markets, obtaining a rating is now practically mandatory. Moreover, because from the very outset the SEC has limited and controlled the number of agencies qualifying for NRSRO status, the agencies' business is closely protected. One could describe it as an oligopoly or closed shop with exceedingly high entry barriers, hence not a competitive market. Under the wings of the SEC, the rating agencies have grown in status and influence. 'In 1968 we had maybe half a dozen analysts,' recalls O'Neill, who joined Standard & Poor's in April of that year, 'Today we've got 1200 employees and 15 offices around the world.' The transformation of the global financial markets, growth in cross-border capital flows, privatisation, and shift from debt financing to equity financing have all fuelled this growth in demand for ratings.

With the decline of the traditional bank credit officer, the rating agencies have stepped in to fill the gap in credit analysis. Moreover, many banks are using ratings as a way of delegating (or outsourcing) responsibility and shedding credit department staff. Together these two secular trends have served to stimulate the growth witnessed in the rating industry. Nevertheless, in 1975 the SEC gave its chosen agencies an authority, a purpose and, best of all, a captive market: 'We used to joke that SEC recognition was a licence to print money,' recalls one former Moody's analyst, 'This is a government-sanctioned oligopoly, and the barriers to entry are becoming higher and higher every year'. It is also an oligopoly that is imposing its ideological model and modus operandi in Europe and Asia. But the underlying ambiguity of the NRSRO status continues to remain unresolved, like the riddle of the chicken and the egg.

The SEC: what have we wrought?

In August 1994 the SEC awoke from deep slumber and took a long look at what it had wrought. The SEC's 'concept release' solicited public comment on the commission's role regarding the rating agencies by addressing three key areas:

- The commission's role in using the ratings of designated NRSROs
- The process by which agencies become NRSROs
- The commission's regulatory role, if any, with regard to NRSROs

The mere composition of this inquiry is indicative of a deep-seated unease at the SEC. Predictably the agencies were up in arms. While their arguments are couched in terms of concern about 'the regulation of opinions' and 'free speech', it appears more likely that the rating agencies are not acting as sentimental guarantors of individual freedom but rather as guarantors of the lucrative oligopoly they have been granted, as suggested by their various pronouncements, some of which appear in this book.

One can only conclude that the SEC's previous behaviour was illogical and this is an effort to close the barn door although the horse has bolted. The SEC regulated investor behaviour and practices by depending on a group of risk analysts it did not know how to define. Moreover, in using the term subsequently in other regulatory contexts, the commission generally propagated the original ambiguity. Since 1975 the SEC has presided over an oligopoly with these three characteristics:

- There are no clear standards for entry
- There are no formal application procedures for obtaining NRSRO status
- There is no process for systematically monitoring rating agencies

The NRSROs do have a quasi-official role as regulators but there is nothing else to impose industry standards and to outlaw abusive practices.

The SEC, moreover, did not seem enthusiastic to regulate rating agencies. The SEC's Roberts offers the following tautological argument to justify the SEC's position: 'We relied increasingly on the rating agencies and judgements. It is logical, therefore, that we should pay more attention to how the agency's decisions are reached. But if we were in a position to judge their opinions, we would not need them in the first place. Their judgement is better than of ours, and that is why we rely on them'. The SEC obviously has no initiative to address the issue. Or perhaps there were other issues to consider. Former SEC chairman Richard Breeden had no time for the problem it seems. When Arthur Levitt was appointed to the post, he asked his staff in the first week of his tenure what was on their minds. Their response was unanimous—the rating agencies.

The SEC's position has been further compromised by a number of foreign agencies that have applied for NRSRO status. The list is believed to include both Canadian and Japanese rating agencies as well as a major Franco-British player, and the process has become a Kafkaesque nightmare of rules that mean nothing and lead nowhere. The final objective is to persuade the SEC to provide a letter stating that it will take no enforcement action against an agency, if 'the rating agency is used as an NRSRO for purposes of applying the relevant subdivisions of the net capital rules'—the famous no-action letter.

Proposed reforms to the NRSRO system

In August 1994 the SEC began seeking the opinions of market participants on whether NRSRO should continue, and based on these opinions it submitted at the end of 1997 a proposal to change the criteria for public recognition. There are five points emphasised in the proposed new selection criteria:

- *National recognition* so the rating organisation is recognised as an issuer of credible and reliable ratings by predominant users of securities ratings in the USA.
- *Adequate resources* in terms of staff, finance, and organisational structure to ensure it can issue credible and reliable ratings of the debt of issuers,

including the ability to operate independently of economic pressures or control by firms it rates, and a sufficient number of staff members qualified in terms of education and experience to thoroughly and completely evaluate an issuer's credit.

- *Systematic rating procedures* should be designed to ensure credible and accurate ratings.
- *Extent of contacts* with the management of issuers, including access to senior-level management of issuers.
- *Internal procedures* to prevent misuse of non-public information and compliance with these procedures.

The SEC is currently seeking comments on this proposal, but a cynic might be tempted to dismiss these measures as a Band-Aid solution, failing to address the underlying practices of power and the abusive manifestations thereof.

Another issue the SEC is interested in is whether, from the perspective of rating company neutrality, there should be some sort of standard governing arrangement as to how ratings fees are charged. We have already noted the obvious potential conflict of interest just from the fact that the rating company is taking ratings fees from the companies it rates, and there are many who also express misgivings about the widespread current practice of setting fees proportional to the size of the bond issue. In other words, if rating companies are dependent on large fund-raisers for their revenues, there is an incentive to give their large customers laxer ratings.

In early 1998 the DOJ expressed its support for the SEC proposal, noting that bringing greater objectivity to criteria would encourage new participation and improve the trustworthiness of ratings. However, the DOJ did oppose the SEC's first criterion (that the rating organisation be broadly recognised in the USA) because it would serve as a barrier against domestic financial institutions, consultants, and others that have the potential to enter the ratings industry, and also discriminate against non-US rating companies with strong track records in other countries.

ICI's comments on SEC's proposal

The Investment Company Institute (ICI) is the national association of the American investment company industry. Its membership includes 6742 open-end investment companies (mutual funds), 442 closed-end investment companies, and 10 sponsors of unit investment trusts. Its mutual fund members have assets of about USD 4.359 trillion, accounting for approximately 95% of total industry assets, and have over 59 million individual shareholders.

Some market participants were asked to comment to the SEC on the process of conferring NRSRO status on rating agencies. In 1988 the ICI filed with the SEC a comment letter on the SEC's proposed amendments to its 'broker-dealer net capital rule (Rule 15c3–1) under the Securities Exchange Act of 1934'. These amendments would define the nationally recognised statistical rating organisation (NRSRO) for the purposes of that rule. The letter is interesting in that it represents the viewpoint of the investor community, that is, the entities that need information to base their investment decisions on. Hence it only selectively addresses the abusive practices of the agencies.

The ICI letter generally supports the proposal to the extent that it formalises the NRSRO designation process for the purpose of issuing credit ratings relied upon by the commission in certain instances. The letter also stresses that the SEC should more actively oversee NRSROs to ensure continued compliance with the criteria included in the rule, including, most importantly, periodically soliciting public comment on the performance of NRSROs, as at present they have no accountability to anyone on their underlying methods, conduct, or effects of their various pronouncements.

The letter further recommends that the NRSRO designation process not be expanded to cover other types of ratings issued by rating agencies where such agencies' expertise is not a meaningful qualification to issue such other ratings. The letter also urges that the rule be modified to authorise the SEC staff to make limited-purpose NRSRO designations for rating agencies whose expertise and experience are limited to certain types of securities. Finally, the letter recommends that the SEC consider rescinding NRSROs' Rule 436(g) exemption from expert liability under Section 11 of the Securities Act of 1933.

The ICI letter

Re: Proposed Definition of Nationally Recognised Statistical Rating Organisation (File No. S7–33-97)

March 2, 1998
Mr. Jonathan G. Katz
Secretary
Securities and Exchange Commission
450 Fifth Street, NW
Washington, D.C. 20549

Dear Mr. Katz:

The Investment Company Institute appreciates the opportunity to comment on proposed amendments to the Securities and Exchange Commission's net capital rule (Rule 15c3–1) under the Securities Exchange Act of 1934.[1] The proposed amendments would define the term "nationally recognised statistical rating organisation" ("NRSRO").[2]

While the scope of this proposal is fairly narrow—to provide a definition of the term "NRSRO" that sets forth the criteria that a rating entity must satisfy to be an NRSRO—it must be evaluated in the context of broader policy issues regarding the role and status of NRSROs under the federal securities laws. In this regard, mere codification of the designation process should not be viewed as effective regulation of NRSROs, particularly since NRSROs are shielded from so-called "expert liability" under Section 11 of the Securities Act of 1933 if their ratings appear in a security's prospectus. Moreover, absent more comprehensive regulation of NRSROs, the Commission should exercise caution in relying too heavily on NRSRO ratings in regulating the securities industry.

The ICI generally supports the proposal to the extent that it formalises the NRSRO designation process for the purpose of issuing credit ratings relied upon by the Commission in certain limited instances, such as distinguishing different grades of debt securities under Rule 15c3–1.

Nevertheless, the Commission should more actively oversee NRSROs to ensure continued compliance with the criteria included in the rule, including, most importantly, periodically soliciting public comment on the performance of NRSROs. In addition, as discussed below, it is extremely important that the NRSRO designation process not be expanded to cover other types of ratings issued by rating agencies where such agencies' credit ratings expertise is not a meaningful qualification to issue such other ratings.

The rule should also be modified to authorise the Commission staff to make limited purpose NRSRO designations for rating agencies whose experience and expertise are limited to certain types of securities. Finally, the Commission should consider rescinding NRSROs' exemption from expert liability under Section 11 of the Securities Act. The Institute's specific comments on the proposed amendments to Rule 15c3–1 and on the broader issues regarding NRSROs generally are set forth below.

Commission Reliance on NRSROs

Rating agencies have been rating securities in the United States since the early part of this century. However, the concept of regulatory reliance on ratings issued by NRSROs did not arise until 1975, when the Commission adopted amendments to Rule 15c3–1 to require broker-dealers, when computing net capital, to deduct from their net worth certain percentages of the market value ("haircuts") of their proprietary securities positions.[3]

These deductions are intended to serve as a buffer against the risks associated with price fluctuations of a broker-dealer's proprietary securities. Rule 15c3–1 allows broker-dealers to take reduced haircuts for certain commercial paper, nonconvertible debt securities and nonconvertible preferred stock that are rated investment grade by at least two NRSROs.[4]

At the time Rule 15c3–1 was amended to provide for such reduced haircuts, however, it did not define the term NRSRO, nor did the rule specify what criteria would be used in designating NRSROs. Instead, NRSROs are designated through the Commission staff's no-action process.[5]

Since 1975, the Commission has expanded the use of the term NRSRO into other regulatory areas. The Commission's reliance upon NRSRO credit ratings may be appropriate where credit quality, or factors highly dependent upon credit quality, are important considerations (although, as discussed below, reliance on rating agencies in Commission regulations requires that the rating agencies themselves should be subject to greater oversight). For example, Rule 2a-7 under the Investment Company Act of 1940 uses NRSRO ratings to determine which securities are eligible for investment by a money market fund in order for the fund to use the amortised cost or penny-rounding methods of pricing portfolio securities.[6]

However, such reliance upon NRSRO credit ratings is not appropriate where credit quality is not among the most important considerations, such as in Rule 3a-7 under the Investment Company Act, and the important protections provided by the federal securities laws should not be further eroded by such inappropriate reliance in the future.[7]

Indeed, the ratings agencies themselves have acknowledged that NRSRO ratings should not be used as a substitute for actual financial market regulation and market discipline. As one Moody's official stated in a 1995 speech before the Commission, "[b]y using securities ratings as a tool of regulation governments fundamentally change the nature of the product agencies sell. Issuers pay rating fees to purchase, not credibility with the investor community, but a license from a government. . . . And if the present trends of regulatory use of ratings are not arrested, the credibility and integrity of the rating system itself will inevitably be eroded."[8]

NRSROs Should Be Subject to Greater Oversight

Credit ratings play a significant role in the investment decisions of both retail and institutional investors. In many instances, investors lack the expertise and resources necessary to adequately evaluate an issuer's creditworthiness, and thus credit ratings can provide useful information to such investors in making investment decisions. However, NRSROs' importance in the marketplace also raises issues concerning the extent to which they require regulatory oversight and monitoring.

Although NRSROs are required to register as investment advisers under the Investment Advisers Act of 1940, as two former SEC Commissioners aptly observed, "the investment adviser registration system applies awkwardly at best" to NRSROs.[9]

Moreover, the no-action letters allowing ratings agencies to serve as NRSROs leave it to the NRSROs to self-police their own activities. The letters simply require NRSROs to advise the Commission of any material change in facts that serve as the basis for granting the no-action relief. Because of the substantial financial impact that withdrawal of NRSRO designation could have on a rating agency, NRSROs have a strong disincentive to report any such change in circumstances.

Given the prominent role that NRSROs play—and apparently will continue to play—in the regulation of the securities markets, it is important that the Commission subject NRSROs to meaningful oversight and not merely codify their past no-action letters. Thus, the Commission should be required to more actively oversee NRSROs to ensure continued compliance with the criteria included in the rule, including periodically soliciting public comment on the performance of NRSROs.

In addition, the Commission should emphasise that the NRSRO designation applies only with respect to credit ratings. Finally, the Commission should authorise the Commission staff to grant limited-purpose NRSRO designations for rating agencies whose expertise and experience in rating securities is limited to certain types of securities. Each of these recommendations is discussed below.

Ongoing Monitoring of NRSROs

The proposal provides that, once it had been designated an NRSRO, a rating agency would be required to notify the Commission when it experiences material changes that may affect its ability to continue to meet any of the requisite criteria. Thus, the Commission is assuming that rating agencies will readily divulge any shortcomings within their organisations that could jeopardise their NRSRO status without the need for ongoing Commission oversight.

Given the enormous financial impact that a loss of NRSRO designation could have on a rating agency, ratings agencies will have strong incentives not to report such deficiencies. Although this condition is consistent with representations in prior Commission no-action letters granting NRSRO status, we are not aware of any rating agency reporting such information and subsequently losing its status as an NRSRO. It seems doubtful that this self-policing structure will ensure that NRSROs will maintain the necessary attributes to continue to function as an NRSRO.

Accordingly, the proposal should be revised to require greater Commission oversight of NRSROs as a condition to maintaining that status. The Commission should conduct periodic reviews of NRSROs to ensure that they have necessary national recognition, staffing, resources, structure, internal procedures, and issuer contacts to serve as an NRSRO.

In particular, given that some NRSROs are now also recommending securities to clients (including the same securities which are rated by the NRSRO), it is critical that NRSROs have internal procedures designed to prevent the misuse of confidential information obtained through the rating process.

For example, NRSROs should have in place ethical walls and other internal control procedures to prevent information divulged by a rated issuer from being used in recommending that issuer's securities. The Commission may wish to provide more specific requirements with respect to such procedures.

The Commission also should inspect NRSRO records relating to past ratings to ensure that the ratings were based on sound reasoning, and that the ratings were issued free from economic pressures and controls by the issuer being rated. To ensure the economic independence of NRSROs, as required by the proposal, such examinations should include review of fee arrangements between issuers and NRSROs.

As part of its ongoing monitoring of NRSROs, the Commission should solicit public comment on the reliability and quality of the ratings issued by a particular NRSRO. In the Proposing Release, the Commission notes that the most critical attribute for an NRSRO is that it is a nationally recognised issuer of credible and reliable credit ratings by the users of securities ratings in the US. It would seem that the best way to ensure that an NRSRO continues to meet this attribute would be to periodically solicit public comment on that particular rating agency.

To the extent that its national reputation is slipping, the Commission would have first-hand evidence which would assist it in determining whether the NRSRO's designation should be revoked.

Additionally, NRSROs are playing an increasingly important role in setting industry-wide standards for structured obligations. For many types of structured obligations, issues of structure and credit quality are inexorably intertwined. If a mutual fund disagrees with an NRSRO's credit analysis, it can simply avoid a particular security or issuer. However, if a fund disagrees with an NRSRO's evaluation of structural risk, frequently the only way to avoid the risk may be to exclude whole categories of investments.[10]

Because the negotiations over these requirements involve NRSROs and issuers, but not investors, the Commission should be more proactive in ensuring that investors can influence NRSRO structural standards. The periodic review and public comment process we propose could help make NRSROs more sensitive to investors' structural concerns.

This solicitation of public comment is not without precedent for private organisations that serve a quasi-public function, such as NRSROs. For example, television and radio stations that receive broadcast licenses from the Federal Communications Commission must periodically reapply for their license renewals, at which time the station must publish notice of its renewal application and solicit public comment to the FCC on the station's performance.[11]

Given the very important role that NRSROs serve in the regulation of the US securities markets (and the enormous benefit attached to NRSRO designation), it seems appropriate to impose a public comment and review process on a periodic basis (such as every two years) to ensure that rating agencies that have received the special designation of NRSRO should be entitled to continue receiving such a designation.

Application to Credit Ratings: Only the proposing release states that the designation of an agency as an NRSRO would apply only to a rating organisation's opinion concerning the creditworthiness of debt instruments, and that other opinions and views of the rating organisation would be outside the scope of the NRSRO designation.[12]

The ICI strongly supports limiting the scope of the proposed amendments in this manner. Allowing NRSRO ratings to be used for other purposes would be highly inappropriate. For instance, NASD Regulation, Inc. recently filed a proposal with the Commission to allow volatility ratings in mutual fund supplemental sales literature, so long as the volatility rating is issued by an NRSRO. Nevertheless, the expertise that NRSROs have in issuing credit ratings of debt securities is not at all indicative of their ability to predict the expected volatility of a bond mutual fund.

This expansion of the use of NRSROs in securities regulation underscores the importance of limiting the NRSRO designation to ratings expressing an opinion of the creditworthiness of debt instruments.

Limited Purpose NRSRO Designations

Finally, it may be appropriate to modify the proposal to authorise the Commission staff to issue limited NRSRO designations permitting a rating agency to issue credit ratings with respect to only certain securities with which the rating organisation has the necessary experience and expertise. By issuing limited purpose NRSRO designations, the Commission ensures that an NRSRO will not issue ratings on securities that are outside of its knowledge and experience. For example, some ratings agencies may have expertise in rating the credit of US issuers, but do not have experience in rating securities issued by foreign corporations. Similarly, some rating agencies may be familiar with rating ordinary debt offerings but do not have significant experience in rating asset-backed securities. A limited purpose NRSRO designation would prevent such an NRSRO from issuing ratings for which it is not qualified.[13]

NRSROs Should Be Accountable for Their Ratings

In addition to being free from all but minimal government regulation, the rating agencies are also relieved of any legal accountability for their ratings. NRSROs are shielded from expert liability under Section 11 of the Securities Act if their ratings appear in a securities prospectus. In 1982, Rule 436 under the Securities Act was amended to provide that ratings assigned to debt securities, convertible debt securities or preferred stock by an NRSRO would not be deemed part of a registration statement under Sections 7 and 11 of the Securities Act. As a result, issuers do not have to obtain the consents from NRSROs before publishing their ratings and NRSROs are exempt from Section 11 liability if their ratings are included in a registration statement. The broad exemption of NRSROs from the normal liability provisions of Section 11 of the Securities Act means that NRSROs are not held to a negligence standard of care. The rating agencies also maintain that they are members of the "media" that are providing their "opinions," and thus claim that they can only be liable if their conduct can be said to have been "reckless."[14]

As a result, the exemption from expert liability pursuant to Rule 436(g) lessens the incentives of NRSROs to issue credible and reliable securities ratings.

The NRSROs' exemption from Section 11 liability represents a significant departure from the normal requirement that an expert's opinion may be published in a registration statement only with the expert's consent and if the expert is liable to investors for negligently misleading opinions. Quite frankly, it is difficult to conceive of the rationale for providing this exemption when NRSRO credit ratings are relied upon so heavily by the Commission and the investing public, while at the same subjecting NRSROs to only minimal government regulation.[15]

Accordingly, the Institute believes that, at the very least, the Commission should seriously consider, and invite public comment on, rescinding the NRSROs' exemption from expert liability under Rule 436. If this is not done, the need for greater oversight of NRSROs is even more compelling.

We appreciate the opportunity to comment on this proposal.

If you have any questions, please do not hesitate to telephone me.

Sincerely,
Craig S. Tyle
General Counsel

Notes

1. SEC Release No. 34–39457 (Dec. 17, 1997), 62 Fed. Reg. 68018 (Dec. 30, 1997) (the 'Proposing Release').
2. In particular, the proposed amendments would for the first time include within Rule 15c3–1 a formal list of attributes to be considered by the commission in designating rating organisations as NRSROs. NRSROs that have already received no-action assurances regarding NRSRO status would retain this status without having to reapply with the commission, although the commission has stated that it would conduct reviews of current NRSROs to ensure that they meet the requirements of the proposed definition.
3. SEC Release No. 34–11497 (June 26, 1975), 40 Fed. Reg. 29795 (July 16, 1975).
4. See 17 C.F.R. §§ 240.15c3–1(c)(2)(vi)(E), (F) and (H).
5. Currently, there are five rating agencies that have this designation: Moody's Investors Service, Inc. (Moody's), Standard & Poor's Corporation (Standard & Poor's), Fitch-IBCA, Inc., Duff & Phelps Credit Rating Co., and Thomson Bank Watch, Inc. Proposing Release at 6–7.
6. See id. §§ 270.2a-7. Specifically, Rule 2a-7 restricts the securities eligible for purchase by a money market fund to those that have received certain high NRSRO ratings or which, if unrated, are of comparable quality to such highly rated securities. Other examples of commission rules that rely on NRSRO ratings that are cited in the Proposing Release include Regulation S-K (17 C.F.R. § 229.10) and

Forms S-3, F-2 and F-3 (17 C.F.R. §§ 239.13, 239.32 and 239.33) under the Securities Act; Rule 101 (17 C.F.R. § 242.101) and Form 17-H (17 C.F.R. § 249.328T) under the Exchange Act; and Rules 10f-3 (17 C.F.R. § 270.10f-3) and 3a-7 (17 C.F.R. § 270.3a-7) under the Investment Company Act. These rules are premised on the availability of reliable ratings from multiple sources. If events occur that limit the availability of such ratings (e.g. a decrease in the number of NRSROs), these requirements would need to be promptly revisited.

7. In this regard, Rule 3a-7 under the Investment Company Act, which provides an exemption from the act for certain issuers of asset-backed securities that have received an investment grade rating from an NRSRO, extends NRSROs beyond their traditional role of evaluating debt securities' risk of default to determining what level of disclosure and other protections investors are entitled to receive.

8. 'Ratings in Regulation: A Petition to the Gorillas', speech by Thomas J. McGuire, executive vice president and director of Moody's Corporate Department, before the US Securities and Exchange Commission (April 28, 1995).

9. Letter from Mary L. Schapiro and Richard Roberts to Congressman John D. Dingell, dated August 12, 1992.

10. This result would significantly impact the supply of high-quality money market instruments. The majority of municipal money market obligations involve some structural elements to achieve the liquidity, maturity, or credit quality required by Rule 2a-7 under the Investment Company Act. For municipal money market mutual funds, therefore, structural issues are particularly important.

11. See 47 C.F.R. § 73.3584.

12. Proposing Release at 10.

13. The commission has already made such a limited-purpose NRSRO designation with respect to Thomson Bank Watch, which is recognised as an NRSRO only for the purposes of rating debt issued by banks, bank holding companies, non-bank banks, thrifts, broker-dealers, and broker-dealers' parent companies. See Proposing Release at 7 note 10.

14. See, for example, *First Equity Corporation of Florida v. Standard & Poor's Corporation*, 869 F.2d 175 (2d Cir. 1989).

15. These concerns are exacerbated by the fact that in more than several instances, reliance on NRSRO credit ratings has been questionable at best and injurious at worst. For example, over the years, both Standard & Poor's and Moody's have been heavily criticised for failing to downgrade the ratings of various bonds, such as those issued by the City of New York that defaulted in April 1975, bonds issued by Washington Public Power Supply System that defaulted in 1983, and bonds issued by First Executive Life Insurance Company that defaulted in 1991. See Francis A. Bottini Jr, 'An Examination of the Current Status of Rating Agencies and Proposals for Limited Oversight of Such Agencies', 30 San Diego L. Rev. 579, 583–594 (1993). More recently, NRSROs have been strongly criticised for failing to respond in a timely manner to the Asian crisis. See Steven Irvine, Caught with their pants down? *Euromoney*, Jan. 1998, pp. 51–53.

Salient points

- As noted in the JCIF and Cantwell studies and by the ICI, the data suggests that the entities buying ratings often do this because they are not

buying credibility with the investor-creditor community but rather a licence from the government, effectively a monopoly levying 'tolls' to
accede to the 'economic highway'.

- The proposals requiring NRSROs to notify the commission when they
  experience material changes which may affect their ability to continue to
  meet any of the requisite criteria are assuming that the agencies will
  idealistically offer information detrimental to their interests or even
  jeopardising their existence, of their own free will, to the commission.
  This assumption could most charitably be described as naive.

- The ICI believes that the commission should ensure that the underlying
  rationales behind ratings are issued according to sound and logical reasoning commensurate with the rigorous methods of academic or scientific research and not subject to profit-driven motives. This control
  function should also extend to the nature of the fee structures used by the
  agencies as well as the selection criteria underlying the selection of 'targets' being 'hit' with unsolicited ratings.

- The granting of NRSRO status should not be an open-ended commitment
  free from all subsequent control, but rather one renewed regularly according to control mechanisms such as those in place by the FCC for
  renewal of television or radio broadcasting licences. After all, 80 year old
  retirees are required to renew their driving licences.

- The fact that rating agencies are relieved from any legal accountability for
  their ratings, due to their being shielded from expert liability pursuant to
  Section 11, Rule 436(g) lessens the incentive for NRSRO to issue credible
  and reliable ratings. Since these NRSROs have been granted an effective
  monopoly, the least one would expect is that they be held accountable
  for their quasi-official actions.

DOJ urges SEC to increase competition

The US Department of Justice (DOJ) has also entered the fray in the argument on rating agencies from the viewpoint that the oligopoly inhibits free
competition. In March 1998 the DOJ urged the SEC to modify its proposed
rules for securities rating agencies so that new rating agencies could more
easily enter the market, thereby increasing competition. In addition, the DOJ
recommended that the SEC require rating agencies to disclose when they rate
a security offering that was not requested by the issuer of the security (in
other words, disclose when they are going to issue an unsolicited rating).
These two recommendations were among comments filed with the SEC by
DOJ's Antitrust Division. These comments supported proposals for

regulating the agencies that rate the creditworthiness of securities offerings. These proposals would help ensure that securities ratings were credible and accurate.

One provision in the proposed rules which generated criticism was a proposal that would require a ratings agency to be recognised as an issuer of credible and reliable ratings *by the predominant users of ratings in the USA* before being recognised as an NRSRO. Joel I. Klein, assistant attorney general for DOJ's Antitrust Division, noted that 'the SEC's proposal would erect a nearly insurmountable barrier to entry by new and well-qualified firms into the market for securities ratings services. This could have chilling effects on competition and could raise prices for securities ratings'. The provision could protect the duopoly and other incumbents from additional competition and could prevent well-capitalised firms with reputations for quality financial analysis from entering the market.

The DOJ's Antitrust Division also urged the SEC to require rating agencies to disclose when they assign ratings not solicited by the securities issuer since 'unsolicited' ratings are not as accurate as ratings by retained agencies, because they usually do not have access to the same type and amount of information as in a solicited rating. Klein noted: 'When unsolicited ratings are not based on the same type of information as solicited ones, the ratings agency runs the risk that its rating is not accurate. When the fact that a rating is unsolicited is withheld from investors and the capital markets, they cannot assess the credibility of the rating. Disclosure benefits the markets and improves competition, which benefits consumers'.

One of the proposed SEC criteria requires rating agencies to use systematic rating procedures to ensure credible and accurate ratings. Another requires the rating agencies to have access to senior management because such access enables them to better evaluate the securities. Agencies giving unsolicited ratings may not have had access to senior management. Requiring agencies to disclose that a rating was not solicited will help ensure the SEC's criteria are met. What is interesting is that each lobbying faction—the rating agencies, the SEC, the investor community, the issuer community, and the DOJ—is seeking reform but only from the limited confines of its sphere of interest. Whether it will lead to reform in the rating industry, that is anyone's guess.

A new generation of indicators

With hindsight, the SEC's use of credit ratings for regulatory purposes looks both inadequate and counterproductive. Against this backdrop, some agencies have begun developing and aggressively marketing a new generation of risk indicators. Fitch has led the charge. In June 1993 the agency launched volatility ratings for bond funds which purport to describe 'the relative impact of changing interest rates and general market conditions on a fund's total return'. Among the risk components analysed are interest rate, prepayment, credit, spread, liquidity, and currency risks. Not to be outdone, in January S&P also unveiled a single-scale volatility rating for bond funds. S&P added an extra 'r' to a number of existing credit ratings to alert investors to the additional market risks associated with certain hybrid and derivative-linked securities.

So far, however, the SEC has blocked the use of such ratings in the primary markets. Under the prevailing rules, any information included in the sales literature accompanying a fund's launch must also appear in the fund's prospectus. This would require the rating agencies to agree to be treated as experts under the terms of the Securities Act. Such consent would expose the agencies to an unacceptable level of legal liability. The SEC has proposed amending the rules, but as yet no action has been taken. Its hesitation is understandable since 'market risk ratings' have no track record. There are also deep divisions within the industry itself as to whether the agencies should be involved in quantifying and rating market risk in the first place.

Powerful lobby groups are now arguing that such ratings, far from clarifying and differentiating market and credit risks for retail mutual-fund investors, will only serve to mislead them further. Paul Stevens, on the ICI's general counsel, wrote to the SEC saying, 'The use of these ratings is likely to prove highly misleading to the investing public'. More worryingly, argues Stevens, 'there is a significant danger that investors will place too great a reliance on the rating as the only or the most relevant presentation of the fund's risk. The rating could discourage investors from reading any narrative discussion of the fund's investment risks, which might include more relevant information'.

To compound matters, the SEC is dearly interested in accommodating market risk ratings into its regulatory agenda to patch up the holes that have appeared. But this will merely get it deeper into the hole it has dug for itself. As the agencies struggle to adjust to a closer regulatory relationship with the SEC, it is difficult to find any sympathy for them. 'Over this whole period of time,' says O'Neill, 'S&P has been adamant—vociferous—in its opposition to ratings being used as an investment minimum.' But protected and encouraged by the SEC's actions, the agencies have grown into strong, healthy, and remarkably profitable organisations. As for the SEC, it is at a complete loss over what to do. 'The concept release is a stalling tactic,' says one source familiar with the SEC's strategy. But it cannot stall forever.

Some legal challenges to rating agencies

DOJ antitrust probes re Moody's ratings activities

In 1996 CNNfn reported that Moody's Investors Service, Inc. said the US Department of Justice had asked it for information on its ratings practices, but would not confirm it was the target of an investigation of antitrust law violations. Sources have said the DOJ is investigating whether Moody's pressured bond issuers to use its services to evaluate their debt or face negative comments and lower ratings that could affect the marketability of their bonds. An investigation could result in criminal charges against Moody's and its representatives. Officials at Standard & Poor's and Fitch Investors Service said the department had asked their firms for information about their business practices and those of competitors.

A DOJ spokeswoman declined to comment on whether Moody's is the target of an investigation, but did confirm that 'the antitrust division is looking into anticompetitive practices in the bond-rating industry'. The probe comes at a time when Moody's, the most powerful and expensive of the three leading credit rating agencies, faces criticism and increased competition from some bond issuers, such as Standard & Poor's and the much smaller Fitch. Moody's has been criticised frequently in recent years by bond issuers who say the company's ratings are too harsh. Colorado's largest school system is suing Moody's in a federal court in Jefferson County, alleging that after the district refused to hire Moody's services the company issued a negative outlook on a 1993 bond sale.

Moody's denied its rating policies are anticompetitive and defended its right to freely express opinions about bond sales even against the wishes of the issuer. According to the *Wall Street Journal*, the DOJ is focusing on Moody's mortgage-backed market and its municipal bond market. The department seems particularly interested in how Moody's decides what fees to charge on bond deals and whether it has pressured bond issuers to hire its rating services. The investigation follows an announcement that Moody's President John A. Bohn Jr will step down from his position on April 1. The *Journal* said Bohn strongly denied his departure is in any way connected to the investigation.

County of Orange v. McGraw-Hill Companies, Inc. (S&P)

A complaint was filed on 11 June 1996 in the United States Bankruptcy Court, Central District of California, in an action captioned *County of Orange v. McGraw-Hill Companies, Inc., d/b/a Standard & Poor's* (case no. SA 94–222-72-JR; adversary no. SA 96–01624-JR). The complaint alleged that

Standard & Poor's breached its contracts with Orange County, was professionally negligent, and aided and abetted the county's officers in breaching their fiduciary duty by, among other things, assigning unduly high ratings to debt instruments issued by the county and by failing to advise the county's Board of Supervisors of the illegal acts being committed by the county's officers. The trial, previously scheduled to commence on 2 March 1999, was adjourned by the court pending a decision by the California Supreme Court in the *City of Atascadero v. Merrill Lynch* litigation concerning the issue of aiding and abetting a breach of fiduciary duty. The county has claimed compensatory damages of approximately USD 2.1 billion, subject to certain offsets. The county has also claimed unspecified punitive damages.

On 15 June 1999 Standard & Poor's announced that Orange County had dropped its lawsuit. In return for the dismissal of the case, Standard & Poor's agreed to partially refund the county's rating fees in the amount of USD 140 000. Orange County sought more than USD 2 billion in damages in the three-year-old lawsuit. On 1 June 1999 the Ninth Circuit Court of Appeals refused to hear Orange County's appeal of an earlier Federal District Court ruling which upheld the constitutional principle that debt ratings are protected by the First Amendment. According to Kenneth Vittor, executive vice president and general counsel for the McGraw-Hill Companies, Standard & Poor's parent company, 'the ruling affirms that constitutional protections of free expression apply to rating agencies that issue opinions concerning the creditworthiness of debt issues. Both free markets and free speech are clear winners today'.

Orange County had sued Standard & Poor's in 1996, claiming that high ratings of its debt in 1993 and 1994 had been inaccurate and had contributed to a pattern of county financial and investment blunders culminating in the county's voluntary bankruptcy in late 1994. Standard & Poor's replied that its ratings were based on information supplied by Orange County itself, that the creditworthiness of the county was proven by the fact that the county repaid its debts, and that its ratings are also fully protected by the First Amendment. In a ruling earlier that year, Judge Taylor of the US District Court affirmed the applicability of the First Amendment to the county's claims against Standard & Poor's. The District Court's decision applying the First Amendment to the county's claims will require the county to satisfy a very stringent standard of proof at trial. Orange County will have to prove that Standard & Poor's acted with 'actual malice' under the First Amendment in issuing its high ratings of the county's bonds.

In a related case, the Tenth Circuit Court of Appeals recently ruled that rating agencies are fully protected by the First Amendment against liability arising from their credit reports and other publications because such reports are opinions. Kenneth Vittor said, 'Significantly, a Federal District Court and the United States Court of Appeals for the Ninth Circuit strongly supported our view that ratings are fully protected by the First Amendment'. He continued: 'The Constitution clearly grants Standard & Poor's the right to freely give independent opinions on whether an issuer has the capacity and willingness to repay its debts. To Orange County, the lawsuit against Standard & Poor's is only about money and attempts to shift the blame for its financial misdeeds. We believe the case is about protecting Standard & Poor's from the kind of legal intimidation that could lead to a chilling effect on protected expression under the First Amendment'. Mr O'Neill of Standard & Poor's commented, 'Standard & Poor's agreed to a partial refund of ratings fees because Orange County claimed that Standard & Poor's was the county's financial advisor and the county did not understand Standard & Poor's independent role in the debt rating process'.

6 The future

All who recall the condition of the country in 1890 will remember that there was everywhere among the people generally, a deep feeling of unrest. The nation had been rid of human slavery—fortunately, as all now feel—but the conviction was universal that the country was in real danger from another kind of slavery sought to be fastened on the American people: namely, the slavery that would result from aggregations of capital in the hands of a few individuals and corporations controlling, for their own profit and advantage exclusively, the entire business of the country, including the production and sale of the necessities of life.

Excerpt from the decision of the court in *Standard Oil of New Jersey v. United States*, 221 US 83 (1911)

This book has accumulated many examples of the goings-on and practices in the ratings industry, as seen from the perspectives of the rating agencies, the issuers, and the investors. It does not espouse the cause of any particular lobbying group. Evidence suggests the entire ratings industry is an abusive oligopy ripe for firm-handed government regulation instead of the rudderless passing-the-buck accumulations of policy based on an initial inconsistent foundation which has characterised the SEC approach up to now. The ratings industry depicts itself as providing a public service, but the market feedback from various sources suggests that is not the view of the entities being rated or the organisations consuming the offerings which rating agencies describe as research.

The ratings industry cloaks itself as the guarantor of free speech under provision of the First Amendment of the US Constitution without drawing the distinction between the responsible use of free speech and the erosion of equally important civil rights such as oligopolistic abuse, predatory pricing, invasion of privacy, repercussive damage arising from various pronouncements, and the ability to run a company or business free from the threats of extortion and protection rackets. Extortion may be a strong word to use but the practices fit the definition. A cynic might suggest that the rating agencies are not the protectors of any freedoms whatsoever but rather the beneficiaries of a system which has enabled them to prosper by engaging in abusive practices.

Moreover, the rating agencies represent the propagation of 'corporate ideology' above all others since they are being used as a de facto instrument of regulation by the government, which should be above ideology. For which is less clouded by the profit motive, academic research or corporate research? The corporate world naturally prefers being assessed by minds of a similar ideological bent in the world of business, subject to the profit motive, rather than subversive economists in academia who are ideologically suspect. Moreover, the agencies will obviously justify the status quo since they are its beneficiaries. They look at risk, especially sovereign risk, from a limited intellectual framework that only serves to justify their corporate ideology and not engage in true scientific research. Their abysmal track record in assessing sovereign risk, as we have seen, is a damning indictment.

The rating agencies' arguments defending the accuracy of their ratings, based on accumulated historical data of ratings and default rates, are not as quantitative as one might believe. The argument is based on the premise that there is continuity in their research. For this argument to be scientifically consistent and applicable over the entire time frame in question, this would mean that the analytical tools used to analyse economic risks today are exactly the same as those used 30, 40, or 50 years ago, and that today's economy is not more complex or volatile or technologically more sophisticated than it was in the past. Since this is obviously not the case, it means there is no substance to the rating agencies' argument that the strength and accuracy of their ratings are based on the consistency of historical correlation data between ratings and default rates over the time frame of ratings activity, because you cannot compare today with the 1950s or 1960s. Each fundamentally different period was analysed using essentially different yardsticks.

In other words, the entire argument behind ratings can be summarised as a subjective exercise based on pseudoscientific methods, inconsistent criteria, and ethnocentric viewpoints practised by analysts who have no recognised qualifications and whose sole criterion for their credibility is the blind faith of the entities consuming their wares. Up to this point, fair enough, one might say, 'Take it or leave it; switch off the TV if you don't like the show'. Yet this subjective exercise in 'opinionising' has been endowed with a legal and regulatory function that can impose its will on others and export its economic, political, and social Weltanschauungen on other countries and economies and get paid for it to boot. There's the rub.

The predatory pricing policies practised by the agencies and the ambiguities surrounding unsolicited ratings suggest abuse of power arising from the oligopolistic state of the industry. They are a negation of the very system they purport to serve. They are anticompetitive with insurmountable entry barriers to new competitors. There is also a case to be made that the NRSRO system is ethnocentric in nature. The preceding chapters have treated these matters in detail, and the following points are offered as a summary.

As the *Pan American* case so amply demonstrated, rating agencies are privileged insiders. As the *Orange County* case and the *Denver School System* case demonstrated, governmental agencies (and hence the taxpayer) can be held ransom by rating agencies. There is a serious need to clarify and review the entire selection process underlying the granting of NRSRO status as well as a need to supervise the rating agencies' information provision and market practices. There is a serious need to understand the methodologies used by rating agencies to pronounce their judgements on swathes of industry, commerce, finance, and government, expecially since they are de facto sanctioned by the SEC. For under examination, these methodologies hardly seem rigorous as in the method of rigorous scientific inquiry. They exhibit the characteristics of pseudoscience hijacked by marketing gurus.

There is a serious need to regulate rating agencies with systematic mechanisms used to regulate all professions whose activities have public ramifications such as doctors, lawyers, accountants, foods, drugs, and the manufacture and piloting of motor vehicles, ships, or aircraft. Since governments are abdicating their role of providing pensions, they should at least ensure the methods used to monitor privatised pension schemes remain in governmental control in order to avoid a capitalist free-for-all stranding pensioners in poverty. Why should rating agencies be exempt from normal regulatory processes? Many rating agencies suffer from a serious conflict of interest between chasing fees and providing investor service. For the largest agencies, the vast majority of their revenues are derived from issuers. This fee issue, moreover, translates into two other market competition concerns:

- Pricing of the fees
- Unsolicited ratings as a sales tool

Unsolicited ratings are another area of concern already considered in this book. Because of the high standards of disclosure associated with the US public debt markets, the rating agencies can make a convincing case for unsolicited ratings on their home turf of the USA. But in the structured market, international markets, or developing markets, this argument breaks down, as demonstrated by the JCIF study. The result is a heavy-handed sales tool of no use to anyone. The SEC accordingly finds itself in an uncomfortable position since it makes no distinction between solicited and unsolicited ratings. The ratings that are used for regulatory purposes should be solicited ratings; they should be done under contract. If a rating is unsolicited, it should be indicated that it is unsolicited, and it should not qualify for regulatory purposes. The move towards multiple ratings confirms the fact that competition in the market does not exist, because all players are guaranteed a slice of the business. The sector is therefore an anticompetitive oligopoly which negates the very principles of the free enterprise system it purports to serve.

Whilst many of the ambiguities, inconsistencies, and lack of credibility in international markets we have noted remain unanswered, the rating agencies' marketing efforts in new geographic areas continue unabated, not surprising when viewed against the marketing strategies clearly enunciated in their 10-K filings. Standard & Poor's hosted a marketing roadshow in Moscow in early 2000, treating local politicians and financiers to the standard PowerPoint presentations. S&P's aim was to convince the Muscovites of the utility and advantages in paying for its rating services and consuming its research (opinions).

Likewise, as noted in the *St Petersburg Times* of 25 August 2000, Moody's is taking steps to reassess Russia's credit rating in the light of recent developments. The article notes that Moody's plans to review Russia's ratings as well as those of Russian eurobonds, OFZ bonds, and MinFin bonds. The local consensus, however, is not much impressed with these missionary initiatives as the article notes that once again, as in the Asian crisis, 'the agencies are behind the curve in reacting to events instead of anticipating them'. The article quotes a market strategist at Lehman Brothers as saying that 'the agencies have been behind the curve in Russia for about half a year' and that 'if we look at the market, we can see that foreign investors' interest in Russia was already picking up in the third or fourth quarter of 1999'.

Despite the rating agencies' failure to provide a satisfactory explanation of their lack of performance in the Asian meltdown, and provide convincing arguments on their rating methodologies, their efforts to drum up new business in areas where they have little expertise or credibility remains unabated. Whilst the rating agencies stress that their credibility rests on their track record of ratings and historical default rates, they offer no convincing explanation of why investors should believe their pronouncements on a market in which they have virtually no track record and which exhibits substantial and profound differences from Western economic models.

In other words, they are entering a new market offering US-crafted wares whose credibility in new markets relies on blind faith (or perhaps ideological enthusiasm). For it is certain that their pronouncements on the viability of a country with a transitional economy will be loaded with ideological imperatives. And in effect, this ideological agenda means that Russian government policy will have to kowtow to the agencies' Weltanschauungen. But one thing is certain, given the agencies' lack of a track record and historical data on the Russian economy, their efforts to issue pronouncements on the Russian economy can most charitably be categorised as guesswork, albeit elaborate and expensive guesswork. And as we have seen in the Asian meltdown, this guesswork can also backfire. The local Russian press seems to be on to this.

In short, these elements all suggest the need to rein in the power and market dominance of the agencies. The SEC's regulatory function is too important for it to be clouded by the agencies' agenda. If entities wish to consume the rating agencies' corporate research, they should obviously be free to do so. Likewise, the rating agencies should be free to undertake and sell this corporate research. However, the obligatory 'rite of passage' via rating agencies that entities accessing the capital markets are subject to, as well as the monopoly position rating agencies occupy by levying 'tolls' for access to the 'economic highway' should not be an imposition sanctioned by government. A regulatory role is a role for government, not a role to be abdicated to corporate entities with their own narrow ideological imperatives, subject to the profit motive. After all, academic or scientific research is concerned with finding out the truth, not yielding up a profitable product.

The quasi-official regulatory role should therefore be removed from the rating agencies since they are clearly subordinated to the proft motive. The goverment should assume its responsibilities by assuming the regulatory function, insulated from the vulgar pressures of the marketplace. Truth, after all, is not the sole preserve of the market economy and its practitioners and aficionados. Governments have and can play a positive role in economic matters, provided the public will exists for governments to exercise this prerogitive. For this public will to exist, however, there must be a debate and airing of the issue. At the same time, it is obvious that it is not a debate which will transform the industry, it is horse-trading and the shifting and jockeying for power among the power groups and their various lobbying groups and lawyers.

Any forthcoming reform will inevitably be the result of some behind-the-scenes power struggle and horse-trading which will of course not incorporate items from the agenda of weaker players. But they will at least grasp the significance of the developments. The succinct and revelatory words of a former Moody's analyst once again come back to haunt us: 'We used to joke that SEC recognition was a licence to print money'.

Glossary

Acceleration   Occurs after an event of default (*q.v.*) where the whole loan is declared immediately due and payable even though the agreed repayment date has not been reached.

Acceptance   A type of bill of exchange. By accepting (or adding acceptance to) a bill of exchange, the drawee undertakes to pay it on the maturity date. Accepted bills are often called acceptances. Acceptance can also be by endorsement. Bankers' acceptances are those where a bank has endorsed the bill and thus guarantees payment.

Accepting house   In the UK a bank or financial organisation whose speciality is adding its acceptance to its customer's bills of exchange so that they can be discounted in the discount market at favourable rates. They are members of the Accepting Houses Committee.

Accounting period   Period of time from one balance sheet to the next. Period of the income statement, usually one year.

Accounts receivable   Also receivables, trade credit. Money owed to you by customers. UK variant: debtors.

Accounts receivable financing   Procedure whereby a specialised financial institution or bank makes loans against the pledge of accounts receivable.

Accrual liability   Creditor, accounts payable, current liability. Accounting concept: income and expense for the accounting period must be included whether for cash or credit.

Accrued interest   The interest earned since the latest interest payment due but not yet paid.

Accumulated depreciation   Extent to which the fixed-asset cost has been allocated to depreciate expense, since the asset was originally acquired. 'Reserve' for depreciation. 'Provision' for depreciation. Deducted from fixed assets.

Acquisition   The purchase of assets or a controlling interest in a company by another company. It is generally used to describe cash transactions as opposed to equity transactions.

Advance   A generic term for the ways in which a bank lends money, whether loan, overdraft, or discount.

Advance payment guarantee   A guarantee issued by a bank on behalf of, say, a contractor to protect the buyer and which provides for repayment of the advance payments in the event of the contractor's failure to carry out the contract terms.

AIBD   Association of International Bond Dealers.

American option   Option that can be exercised any time before the final exercise date (cf. European option).

AMEX   American Stock Exchange.

Amortisation (1)   The expending of an intangible asset in a company's income statement over a period of time judged to be the economic life of the asset. Like depreciation, amortisation is a non-cash expense.

Amortisation (2)   The paying off of a loan in staged payments (repayment instalments).

Arbitrage   Simultaneous purchase and sale of the same or equivalent items, to take advantage of a price discrepancy. The purchase of a security traded on two or more markets at the same time; also, occurs in the foreign exchange, commodity and money markets. The two deals can be in the same market (e.g. FX) or different markets. Arbitrage relies on the continuous movement of sections of markets at different speeds to create 'opportunities'.

Arrangement fees   For their efforts in arranging a deal, banks collect arrangement fees. These fees are attractive for the bank because they represent revenues that do not have to be generated by the balance sheet, which is subject to capital adequacy (Cooke) ratios.

Arranging banks   The banks which arrange the financing on behalf of a corporate borrower. Usually, the banks commit to underwrite the whole amount only if they are unable to place the deal fully. Typically, however, they place the bulk of the facility and retain a portion on their books for themselves.

Average life   The total of the amounts outstanding at the end of each year of the loan for its entire life, divided by the total principal sum borrowed to give the average life of the loan in years.

Back-to-back loan   Companies with surplus liquidity in one currency may wish to obtain funds in another, for investment or expansion, by employing their own surplus resources without conversion or incurring exchange exposure, or without incurring increased interest costs by borrowing unmatched funds; this may be arranged by means of a parallel, or back-to-back loan.

Balloon payment   Large final payment (e.g. when a loan is repaid in instalments).

Banker's acceptance (BA)   A written demand that has been accepted by a bank to pay a given sum at a future date (cf. trade acceptance). US equivalent of UK sterling bills of exchange, i.e. a draft or bill of exchange accepted by a bank. The accepting institution guarantees payment on the bill.

Basis (or reference) rate   The benchmark cost of funds to which the margin will be added or deducted to determine the total rate payable by the borrower (e.g. LIBOR, LIBID, and prime are basis rates).

Basis point   1/100 of 1%. It is the smallest unit for price quotations. Thus, 10 basis points = 0.10%.

Bear market   Widespread decline in security prices (cf. bull market).

Bearer negotiable security   Security for which primary evidence of ownership is possession of the certificate (cf. registered security).

Bid rate   The lower side of interest rate quotations. It is the rate of interest a bank is prepared to pay for deposits or to acquire securities.

Bond   Long-term debt.

Book debts   The item in the balance sheet of a company representing the amount owing for goods sold as shown by the books.

Borrower risk   Risks pertaining to the company, including management, profitability, non-performance, and bankruptcy: all factors relating to the borrower.

Break-even analysis   Analysis of the level of sales at which a project would just break even (e.g. project revenues cover project costs).

Bretton Woods   A conference held in 1944 where fixed exchange rates were agreed upon as the basis for FX trading.

Bull market   Widespread rise in security prices (cf. bear market).

Bull-bear bonds   Bonds whose principal repayment is linked to the price of another security. The bonds are issued in two tranches. In the first tranche the repayment increases with the price of the other security; in the second tranche the repayment decreases with the price of the other security.

Bullet loans   A loan whose interest is payable at intervals agreed in the loan agreement, and whose principal is repayable in a lump sum (bullet repayment) at final maturity. There are no principal repayments along the way. The source of repayment is usually a new facility which is put into place.

Bullet repayment   A facility under which the whole of the loan is repaid in one lump sum at maturity (rather than in instalments).

Call deposits   Deposits which are repayable on the demand either of the bank or of the depositor.

Call money   Interest-bearing bank deposits that can be withdrawn on 24 hours notice. Thus, money can be placed on deposit 'on call'.

Capital markets   The market for debt and equity instruments.

Capitalisation   Long-term debt, preferred stock, plus net worth.

Capitalised interest   Accrued interest (and margin) which is not paid but added (rolled up) at the end of each interest period to the principal amount lent (e.g. in relation to balloon repayment).

Cash   Money assets of a business. Includes both cash in hand and cash at bank. Balance sheet current assets.

CEDEL   A clearing system for notes based in Luxembourg with representative depositories in all major financial centres, where notes are physically exchanged and stored in safe custody.

Certificate of deposit (CD)   Interest-bearing negotiable bearer certificate which evidences a time deposit with the bank.

Cheque   An unconditional order in writing, drawn on a bank, signed by the drawer, requiring the bank to pay on demand a sum certain in money to or to the order of a specified person or the bearer, also a bill of exchange.

CHIPS   The New York Clearing House's computerised Clearing House Interbank Payments System through which most large US dollar transactions are settled.

COB   Commission des Opérations de Bourse. The French stock exchange supervisory and regulatory agency.

Collateral   *See* security.

Commercial paper   Short-term promissory notes which are secondly listed or in which certain dealers make markets. For high-quality borrowers, this can be a source of low-cost albeit uncommitted funding.

Common stock   Ordinary shares.

Contingent liabilities   Items which do not represent a liability on the balance sheet at the time of statement date but which could do so in the future. Such items include guarantees issued in favour of third parties, and lawsuits currently in progress whose outcome is uncertain.

Convertible bonds   Bonds issued by a corporation which may be converted by the holder into stock of the corporation within a specified time period and a specified price.

Convertible security   Bond or preferred stock that may be converted into another security at the holder's option.

Cooke ratio   The capital adequacy or risk-weighted asset ratios prescribed by the Basle Committee on Banking Supervision.

Correspondent banks   Banks which have an agency relationship with each other and act for each other in their respective parts of the world. Very important for the financing of world trade.

Cost of funds   A term sometimes used as the basis for a loan pricing, particularly when the source of funding is uncertain or includes reserve asset costs. A precise definition of what is meant by this term should be established if it is to be of any practical value; note that the normal funding cost of a commercial loan is the offered rate, being the rate which the bank has to pay to another bank in the market for the funds obtained for the purpose.

Country exposure   Country exposure is the amount of an institution's total investment and/or claims on borrowers in a specific country, direct as well as indirect.

Country limit   Country limits are the numerical amounts up to which an institution such as a bank or company is willing to take an exposure in a particular country.

Country rating   Country ratings are the result of the individual appraisal of a particular country in view of its standing to honour its foreign debts in relation to other countries or groups of countries.

Credit limit/credit lines   The limits up to which a bank is prepared to lend money or grant credit to a customer. Credit limits or credit lines are usually used for internal management purposes and guidelines are not normally a legal commitment, only a willingness to do business.

Credit scoring   Technique used to evaluate a potential borrower according to a predefined matrix procedure (e.g. a matrix such as the Altman Bankruptcy Predictor using multiple discriminant analysis to generate a Z-score). Usually used in retail banking and credit card processing, also used in evaluating corporates.

Creditor Payable, account payable, liability. Money owed to other parties. Current or long-term liability.

Cross default One of the events of default which leads to the loan becoming immediately repayable. Triggered if the borrower defaults under any other indebtedness to other lenders (under a separate facility).

Currency swap A contract between two parties to convert currencies from one currency to another, and then to convert back again into the original currencies at an agreed forward exchange rate.

Debenture A formal acknowledgement of a debt, usually incorporating a charge over the unencumbered assets of the company issuing it; the rights of debenture holders rank before those of shareholders and unsecured creditors in the event of the issuer's liquidation. Often also used to refer to a document creating a charge, mortgage, or other security interest.

Debt equity ratio The ratio of a company's ordinary share capital to its fixed-interest capital, including debentures, loan stock, and preference shares; calculations are often simply based on the ratio of ordinary shares plus retained reserves to prior charge capital.

Debt ratings The classification of a company's financial (credit) standing by specialist agencies such as Moody's and Standard & Poor's (e.g. A+, A, A–, B+, B, B–, C).

Debt service The payment of interest, fees, and principal in accordance with the loan agreement.

Deed poll A deed to which there is only one party or one set of parties and that party makes 'unilateral promise' to members of any identifiable class which, although they have no privity of contract, can enforce against the promisor.

Default The debtor notifies the creditor that he or she will definitely cease making any further service payments because he or she cannot, or does not want to pay.

Deposits Current liabilities of the bank in the form of current account funds or monies at call, notice, or fixed term, in sterling or foreign currency.

Direct country risk Direct country risk in cross-border lending and/or investment is the country risk of the country where the borrower takes up his or her liabilities and/or the investment is made.

Discount basis In relation to notes, this means the way in which the interest over the life of the note is calculated when the note is issued and deducted from the amount paid by the purchaser to the issuer so that the interest is paid 'up front'.

Disintermediation Withdrawal of funds from a financial institution in order to invest them directly (cf. intermediation).

Dividend Payment by a company to its stockholders.

Documentary credit   A method of financing overseas trade where a bank pays for goods by issuing a letter of credit. Usually coupled with a pledge of documents of title and sometimes a trust receipt.

Documentation risk   The risk of non-repayment due to defect in the loan agreement or security arrangements. This can arise due to faulty drafting, mitigating circumstances, juridically non-enforceable and faulty collateral, or guarantees which have expired and not been renewed. Analysts are not expected to assess legal issues, but are expected to obtain legal opinions when necessary and note them accordingly.

Domestic issue   Loans, notes, or equity raised in the indigenous capital market and currency of the country of issue. USD raised in the United States, FRF raised in France, etc.

DTI   Department of Trade and Industry (UK). The DTI is a valuable source of information on companies and many business matters in the UK and abroad.

EBRD   European Bank for Reconstruction and Development.

Efficient market   Market in which security prices reflect information instantaneously.

Efficient portfolio   Portfolio that offers the lowest risk (standard deviation) for its expected return and the highest expected return for its level of risk.

EIB   European Investment Bank.

Eurobond   Bond denominated in a currency and issued outside the currency's issuing country.

Euroclear   A computerised clearing house for eurobonds located in Brussels.

Eurocurrency   Currency held and traded outside its country of origin.

Eurodollar deposit   Dollar deposit with a bank outside the USA.

European option   Option that can be exercised only on final exercise date (cf. American option).

Events of default   The events set out in the facility agreement upon the happening of which the loans can be declared immediately due and payable.

Exchange rate   The price of one currency in terms of another.

Exposure   The extent to which a bank or institution is reliant on one or more counterparties as a result of trading transactions.

Facility   The grant of availability of money at some future date in return for a fee.

Facility agent   The agent of the banks in the syndicate who provides the committed facility, who fixes LIBOR, LIBID, and other reference rates and who coordinates the banks.

FASB   Financial Accounting Standards Board.

Fed   Federal Reserve System. US central regulatory banking authority.

Fee letter A very important document, it sets out the fees to be paid to the arranging bank and/or agent. This is very confidential, as often not all fees paid are shared with the syndicate members.

Final maturity date The date for payment of the last repayment instalment.

Fixed charge A charge usually contained in a debenture over a company's assets which prevents the company from dealing in any way with the property covered by the fixed charge without the consent of the chargee.

Fixed-rate loan A term loan for which the interest rate for the whole period is determined at the outset.

Floating charge A charge usually contained in a debenture as well as fixed charge over stock, book debts, and the general undertaking of a company. The company can deal with the charged assets in any way in the ordinary course of business. They become crystallised when security documents' terms are breached. Automatic ability of the chargee to appoint a receiver upon crystallisation.

Floating-rate note Notes bearing interest that will be determined at regular intervals by a formula based upon prevailing short-term money market rates.

Forex Foreign exchange market from spot or forward exchange dealings.

Forward contracts You may buy or sell a currency for future delivery, fixing the future exchange rate today. This is a forward contract. Forward rates reflect the cost of interest on the money to be used.

Forward market A market where a rate is agreed for a transaction due to occur at a defined future time.

FRA Forward rate agreement. A transaction designed to lock in a future fixed interest rate.

FRN Floating-rate note. Note whose interest payment varies with the short-term interest rate.

Front-end costs Commission, fees, or other payments that are taken at the outset of a loan, such as discounting; the front-end charges for capital issues are very considerable and in calculating the total cost, a borrower should be aware of the additional cost of being short of such disbursements at the outset when compared with the cost of interest payments that are payable after the loan period and not before.

Funding Acquisition of liabilities to match, cover, or balance the particular asset or assets for which they are required.

Futures These are formal agreements to purchase a given item in the future at a price agreed today. The purpose is to hedge against price changes. The practice began in Chicago in the nineteenth century and centred on the agricultural market, but records show that it was common in Holland and Japan in the sixteenth century.

Futures market Centrally organised market where contracts for future commodity deliveries are transacted in a formalised way.

FX   Forex, foreign exchange.

Glass Steagall   A 1933 act in the USA which forbids banks to deal in securities.

Grace period   A period of days within which the borrower is allowed to remedy a breach or failure of payment before that breach or failure becomes an event of default; it can also mean the period before the first repayment instalment is due (e.g. repayment by 5 semiannual instalments, 2 years' grace, which means that the loan is repaid at six-monthly intervals starting after 2 years).

Grossing up   The provision in the facility agreements whereby the borrower agrees that in the event of any withholding tax or similar taxes being imposed in its country of incorporation, it will pay such additional amount as will ensure that the banks are effectively free of such taxes.

Guarantee   An undertaking in writing by one person (the guarantor) given to another, usually a bank (the creditor) to be answerable for the debt of a third person (the debtor) to the creditor, upon default of the debtor. Different from, but usually coupled with, an indemnity.

Hedge   An action taken to reduce liability to market price fluctuations of an asset including money.

Horizontal integration   A diversification strategy that calls for the acquisition of similar businesses or businesses that could benefit directly from existing operational capacity.

Horizontal merger   Merger between two companies that manufacture similar products (cf. vertical merger, conglomerate merger).

IBRD   International Bank for Reconstruction and Development (the World Bank), based in Washington DC.

IMM   International Monetary Market. The financial futures market within the Chicago Mercantile Exchange; cf. LIFFE (London), MATIF (France).

Indemnity   An undertaking to hold harmless by one person to another, distinguished from a guarantee as it need not be in writing and is a primary liability rather than a collateral liability.

Indirect country risk   Indirect country risk in cross-border lending and/or investment is the country risk of the guarantor or of the main security if guarantor or security is in a different country than the one where the borrower has taken up his or her primary liabilities or where the investment has been made. The lender qualifies this risk as his or her ultimate country risk.

Interest   The cost of money; money paid for the use of money.

Interest period   The period by reference to which interest is paid, typically 1, 3, or 6 months as this tracks the interbank funding market. Interest is paid at a fixed rate during each period but is refixed at the start of the next period, thus reflecting the change in market conditions.

L/C   Letter of credit. Letter from a bank stating that it has established a credit in the company's favour.

Lead manager   A lead bank which syndicates or subparticipates a loan to various 'takers' (subparticipants) in the market.

Letter of credit   A document issued by a bank authorising the bank to whom it is addressed to honour the cheques of the person named to the extent of a fixed amount. A non-negotiable instrument.

Letter of pledge   A document setting out the terms of a pledge, but an effective pledge can only be created when the documents are delivered to the possession of the bank taking the pledge.

LIBOR   London Interbank Offered Rate; the rates upon which loans are frequently determined. LIBOR will vary according to market conditions and will of course depend upon the loan period as well as the currency in question. It my be found that for the same time, for the same currency, and for the same period, the quotation of a LIBOR figure by one bank in London and another bank in London will differ slightly; this would be expected if one bank is already long on the currency for that period, having just taken a matched deposit, while the other bank has a different position. LIBID is the bid rate and LIMEAN is the rate which is the mean of the bid and offered rates.

Lien   The right to retain chattels belonging to another until a debt due from the latter is paid. A banker's lien is a special form of lien which, as well as being the right to retain, can include a right to sell property after reasonable notice, and is more in the nature of an implied pledge.

LIFFE   London International Financial Futures Exchange.

Limit   Maximum exposure allowed in a currency, or to a counterparty, as set down internally by management.

Liquidity   The ability to service debt and redeem or reschedule liabilities when they mature, and the ability to exchange other assets for cash.

Listing   Obtaining a quotation on a stock market for bonds or equity instruments which may then be traded on the stock exchanges.

Management buyout (MBO)   The purchase of a business by its managers, usually part financed by a syndicate of banks; may be several layers of debt, including mezzanine finance.

Margin   The rate taken by the lender over the cost of funds, which effectively represents his or her profit and remuneration for taking the risk of the loan; also known as spread.

Marketability   The degree of investment demand for a particular asset offered at a given price.

MATIF   Marché à Terme d'Instruments Financiers. French equivalent of the London International Financial Futures Exchange (LIFFE).

Maturity   The date on which a loan, bill, or other debt instrument falls due for repayment.

Memorandum of deposit/letter of deposit   A document with the terms under which a deposit of security is made. It can be the written evidence of a pledge.

Mezzanine finance/debt A second level of debt, below the senior debt, it is generally secured by second-ranking charges and governed by a priorities deed.

Mismatched maturity When the maturities of the funding cover and the loan or other asset do not coincide.

MLA (reserve asset costs) Mandatory liquid assets. A cost imposed by the Bank of England in relation to sterling advances made by entities which lend through offices or branches in the UK, it is determined by a complex although pretty standard formula. Abolition of MLA is being discussed by the Bank of England; a replacement is likely to be a capital adequacy ratio levy.

MOF Multiple option facility. Usually consisting of two or more options for the borrower to take loans (committed or through a tender panel procedure), swing line advances, bills of exchange, or notes.

Moratorium A moratorium is the unilateral declaration of the borrower that he or she is unable and/or unwilling to honour all or part of his or her obligations and thereby stops the servicing of his or her debts.

Mortgage A security a borrower gives to a lender, usually over a specific property.

NASD National Association of Security Dealers (USA).

NASDAQ National Association of Securities Dealers Automatic Quotation System.

Negative pledge A covenant in a facility agreement by the borrower not to grant security over its assets to other creditors (since this would put those other creditors in a preferential position).

NIF Note issuance facility.

Nostro account Account held at a foreign bank, used for the receipt and delivery of funds in settlement of trades.

Note The promise or obligation to pay; promissory notes, bank notes, and floating rate notes all contain the issuer's primary responsibility for payment. In the context of euro notes, it generally means a maturity of less than one year of bonds which is generally used to describe instruments of more than seven years.

Novation The transfer of rights and obligations from one entity to another, for example, following the substitution of a new debtor for an old debtor or of one bank for another under a loan facility by way of substitution (transfer) certificate.

NYSE New York Stock Exchange.

Offshore Outside the jurisdiction of a particular country.

Option The opportunity to purchase a commodity at a given price at some time in the future. The option is paid even if never exercised.

OTC Over the counter. Securities traded direct between traders, not on a central exchange floor.

Paper Usually means a documented obligation such as bills of exchange or promissory notes, but may refer to any securities.

Pari passu Literally 'at the same rate'. Usually with reference to a borrower's or guarantor's obligations ranking equally with each other in an insolvency.

Pledge A delivery of chattels or a chose in action by a debtor to a creditor as security for his or her debt, the legal ownership remaining with the pledgor.

Political risk The exposure to a loss in cross-border lending, caused by political factors in a certain country, political factors which are, at least to some extent, under the control of the government but not under the control of a private enterprise or individual.

Portfolio A bank's or investor's loan and investment assets.

Position The relative status of a trader's dealings in various currencies or commodities.

Power of attorney An instrument by which one person is empowered to act for another. Banks often sign loan documentation by giving power of attorney to the facility agent.

Priorities deed A document governing enforcement of security when there is more than one secured lender. Often found in management buyouts.

Redemption The cancellation of a security by payment; redemption may be mandatory on a certain date, optional by the borrower after a certain date, or conditional upon certain described and defined events having taken place (such as a change in tax laws which might jeopardise the borrower's position).

Reference banks A group of banks (usually three) selected by the agent to quote their LIBOR (or other basis rate) on each rollover, the average of which is taken as the rate applicable to the transaction.

Regulatory actions Legal requirements on a company. If the government passes a law obliging chemical companies to process carcinogenic waste instead of dumping it in our drinking water or the air we breathe, this is known as a regulatory action. Regulatory actions can adversely impact a company's profitability although positively impact the taxpayer's environment and quality of life.

Repudiation The debtor notifies the creditor that he or she will definitely cease making any further service payment because he or she does not recognise the debt.

Rescheduling Rescheduling is a process by which the lender and the borrower agree to arrange new conditions for an existing loan agreement.

Revolver/evergreen facility A bank line of credit on which the customer (normally) pays a commitment fee and can draw down and repay funds according to his or her needs. Normally, the line involves a firm commitment from the bank for a period of several years.

Rollover The time when the interest rate of a floating-rate loan is periodically reviewed at an agreed spread over, at, or under the currently prevailing LIBOR rate. In 'true/classic' revolving facilities, the loans are repaid and redrawn on each rollover so that each loan is a separate and discrete borrowing.

SEC Securities and Exchange Commission. The regulatory agency which oversees the US securities markets and stock exchange.

Secondary market A market in which securities, bonds, or debts are traded after issue, with profits accruing to the trader rather than to the original issuer.

Securities   Notes, equity, loan stocks, bonds, or other debt instruments.

Security   An asset which has been charged, whether formally or informally, to secure the repayment of a debt.

Set-off   The total or partial merging of a claim of one person against another in a counterclaim by the latter against the former.

SIB   Securities Investment Board (UK).

Sovereign risk   The risk of lending to the government or a government-controlled agency of a sovereign nation.

Special-purpose vehicle   A legal entity created for the completion of a specific project such as a hotel, airport, or fund. SPVs are used to isolate the entity, legally and financially, from other participants such as the shareholders.

Spot   Price for immediate delivery (in foreign exchange two days from the date of trade).

Spot rate of exchange   This is the rate obtained in the spot market for immediate as opposed to future delivery. In the spot market for FX, settlement (i.e. delivery/ value) is normally two business days ahead of the day on which the 'deal' is struck.

Spread   Difference between the buying and selling prices quoted by a trader.

SSAP   Statement of Standard Accounting Practices (UK). A set of standardised guidelines and procedures which have become mandatory upon auditors in the UK for all company accounts.

Standby credit   The arrangement to lend money in case of need, usually at market rates and sometimes with a commitment fee. Overdraft facilities are sometimes used as stand-bys by corporate borrowers.

Subordination   A clause sometimes inserted in facilities whereby the rights of the lenders rank after the rights of some or all unsecured creditors of the borrower in the event of his or her liquidation.

Subrogation   The acquiring of another person's rights, usually as a result of assuming or discharging that person's liabilities, particularly in connection with guarantees.

Surety   Similar to a guarantor but with a wider connotation; there need not be a contract of guarantee for there to be a surety.

Swap   A general term used to describe an interest exchange agreement or a currency and interest rate exchange agreement.

SWIFT   Society for Worldwide Interbank Financial Telecommunications. An organisation owned by several banks based in Brussels.

Swing line   A facility enabling the borrower to draw substantial funds at very short, usually same-day notice. Used to provide emergency funds if the borrower is unable to issue or roll over commercial paper for some reason.

Syndication   The process of putting together the group of banks who will participate in the facility.

Tacking The advancement of further sums by a mortgagee on the same security which are added to the first advance in priority to any second mortgage prevented by Section 94 LPA unless, by the terms of the mortgage, the mortgagee is bound to make further advances.

Tap Security such as a certificate of deposit issued on an 'as required' basis by the borrower; it is not a 'managed issue' (*see* tranche).

Tombstone An advertisement which lists the managers and underwriters and sometimes the providers of a recently completed facility or issue.

Transfer risk The impossibility of transferring payments abroad (in foreign currency) because the government imposed exchange restrictions.

Trust receipt Also trust letter. Used only in conjunction with a letter of pledge of documents or title to goods whereby the documents are released to the pledgor to enable the pledgor to sell the goods while they are still pledged to the bank.

Ultra vires Literally 'beyond the powers', relating to the capacity of a company to enter into a transaction as authorised by its articles of association. Ultra vires transactions are void from the outset.

Units of account Composite currency units designed to reduce exchange rate exposures of both borrower and investor.

Vertical integration A diversification strategy that calls for the acquisition of businesses related to the production or distribution of the acquirer's product. A classic example is the oil refiner which acquires oil wells and gas stations.

Vertical merger Merger between a supplier and its customer (cf. horizontal merger, conglomerate merger).

Zero coupon bond Discount bond making no coupon payments.

Sources

- Old dogs, slightly new tricks. *Institutional Investor*, June 1998
- Caught with their pants down. *Euromoney*, January 1998
- Rating good and bad banks. *Euromoney*, September 1997

- R. Cantor and F. Packer (1994) Credit rating industry. *FRB Quarterly Review*
- R. Cantor and F. Packer (1996) Determinants and impact of sovereign credit ratings. *FRB NY Economic Policy Review*
- R. Cantor and F. Packer (1997) Differences of opinion and selection bias in the credit rating industry. *Journal of Banking and Finance*, 21 February
- A. Fight (1999) *Practical Introduction to Syndicated Lending*, Euromoney
- A. Fight and K. I'Anson (1999) *Analysing Bank and Country Risk*, Euromoney
- Financial Times (1998) *Credit Rating International*, Financial Times Publishing

- *Cantwell & Company*: annual international survey of cridit ratings
- *JCIF*: survey on rating agencies in East Asia
- *EAS*: information on rating agencies in Germany
- *CFPB*: information on French rating agencies and Elf-Gabon
- *CIB*: information of UK rating agencies, library and reference directories
- *Moody's*: web site information on rating scales and methodologies
- *Standard & Poor's*: web site information on rating scales and methodologies
- *Fitch*: web site information on rating scales and methodologies
- *Capital Intelligence*: web site information on rating scales and methodologies
- *Duff & Phelps*: web site information on rating scales and methodologies
- *Thomson Bank Watch*: web site information on rating scales and methodologies
- *Skate*: web site information on rating scales and methodologies
- *Euromoney*: various press cuttings

- *The Economist* various press cuttings
- *Financial Times*: various press cuttings
- *CADES*: web site references to ratings
- *President Magazine*: various press cuttings
- *SEC*: EDGAR database search, 10-K forms for various rating agencies
- *Federal Reserve Bank of New York*: various articles

Index